Praise for *Islamophobia and the Po*

"This is a timely and crucial book. ~~ ~~ ises, Islamophobia is studied in a holistic ~~ ~~ will understand why we need to stop be ~~ ~~ will be no peaceful and just future in our democratic societies if we do not fight this new type of dangerous racism."

—Tariq Ramadan, Professor of Contemporary Islamic Studies, Oxford University

"Deepa Kumar's *Islamophobia and the Politics of Empire* could not be more timely. In this deftly argued book, Kumar unearthes a genealogy of colonial construction that goes back to the earliest contacts between Muslims and Europeans. But the real power of her argument is when she grabs the politics of ideological domination by the throat and, with an astonishing moral and intellectual force, sets the record straight as to who and what the players are in turning a pathological fear of Muslims into a cornerstone of imperial hegemony. This is a must-read on both sides of the Atlantic, where mass murderers in Europe and military professors at the US military academies are in the business of manufacturing fictive enemies out of their fanciful delusions. Deepa Kumar has performed a vital public service."

—Hamid Dabashi, Professor of Iranian Studies and Comparative Literature, Columbia University

"This important book sets out to debunk Orientalist myths: in particular, that historical encounters between Islam and the West can be understood through a "clash of civilizations" framework. The author explores the specific historical and political contexts of this relationship from the Crusades to Obama, providing a nuanced and extensive analysis. Kumar presents these arguments with a force and passion that is supported by a wealth of evidence. A must for scholars of Islam, social and political science, and international relations."

—Elizabeth Poole, author of *Reporting Islam: Media Representations of British Muslims*

"In this remarkable primer Deepa Kumar expertly shows how racism is central to contemporary US imperial politics in ways similar to previous imperial wars, including the one that constituted the United States over the dead bodies of indigenous 'redskins.' An antiracist and antiwar activist as well as a model scholar-teacher, Kumar has written a comprehensive and most readable guide to exposing and opposing hatred of Islam."

—Gilbert Achcar, Professor of Development Studies & International Relations, School of Oriental and African Studies (SOAS), University of London

"In this compact but incredibly comprehensive book, Deepa Kumar success-fully debunks all of the major myths about Islam that continue to distort regular life, too often dangerously so, for Muslims in the United States and abroad. More important, she reveals how today's 'Green Scare' forges intimate con-nections between quashing dissent at home and exporting a disastrous foreign policy abroad, while reminding us that the future belongs not to the racists and imperialists but to ordinary people everywhere struggling heroically for their human rights."

—Moustafa Bayoumi, author of *How Does It Feel to Be a Problem: Being Young and Arab in America*

"*Islamophobia and the Politics of Empire* will be indispensable to anyone wanting to understand one of the most persistent forms of racism in the US and Eu-rope. Kumar demonstrates that Islamophobic myths did not arise spontaneously after the end of the Cold War but are rooted in centuries of conquest and co-lonialism, from the Crusades to the 'War on Terror.' Arguing with precision and clarity, she shows how these myths have been systematically circulated by liberals as much as conservatives and usefully lays bare the complex ways in which the US foreign policy establishment has, in different contexts, instru-mentalized Islamic political movements and exploited anti-Muslim racism. Ku-mar's text will be a crucial corrective to those who fail to see that the origins of the 'Islam problem' lie in empire, not Sharia."

—Arun Kundnani, author of *The End of Tolerance: Racism in 21st Century Britain*

"Against the historical backdrop of the rise of *pax Americana* in a unipolar world, Deepa Kumar's *Islamophobia and the Politics of Empire* stands out as a powerful and comprehensive overview of Islamophobia, forcefully underscor-ing its role as a keystone to maintaining US political and economic power abroad while simultaneously managing American politics and critical dissent at home. Prof. Kumar meticulously maps historical developments within the formation of American Islamophobia and names the players, institutions, and strategies central to the phenomenon, insightfully marking its permutations within right-wing civilizational discourses and the 'soft power' and humani-tarian discourses of American liberals."

—Stephen Sheehi, author of *Islamophobia: The Ideological Campaign against Muslims*

Islamophobia
and the Politics of Empire

Deepa Kumar

Haymarket Books
Chicago, Illinois

Published in 2012 by Haymarket Books
PO Box 180165
Chicago, IL 60618
www.haymarketbooks.org
773-583-7884

ISBN: 978-1-60846-211-7

Trade distribution:
In the US, Consortium Book Sales and Distribution, www.cbsd.com
In Canada, Publishers Group Canada, www.pgcbooks.ca
In the UK, Turnaround Publisher Services, www.turnaround-uk.com
In Australia, Palgrave Macmillan, www.palgravemacmillan.com.au
All other countries, Publishers Group Worldwide, www.pgw.com

Cover design by Josh On. Cover image of a US Army Apache helicopter over the minaret of the 14th of Ramadan mosque in downtown Baghdad, Iraq, Wednesday, November 16, 2005. AP Photo. © Mohammed Hato.

Published with the generous support of Lannan Foundation and the Wallace Global Fund.

Printed in Canada by union labor.

Library of Congress cataloging-in-publication data is available.

10 9 8 7 6 5 4 3 2

MIX
Paper from
responsible sources
FSC
www.fsc.org   FSC® C103567

Contents

Section 1: History and Context

Introduction   1
    Acknowledgments

1. **Images of Islam in Europe**   9
    Early Contact with Islam
    Al-Andalus and Muslim Rule in Europe
    The Crusades and the Reconquista
    From Polemic to Indifference
    The Ottomans
    Romanticism and the Enlightenment

2. **Colonialism and Orientalism**   25
    Napoleon and "Enlightened" Colonialism
    The Characteristics of Orientalism
    American Imperialism

3. **The Persistence of Orientalist Myths**   41
    Myth One: Islam Is a Monolithic Religion
    Myth Two: Islam Is a Uniquely Sexist Religion
    Myth Three: The "Muslim Mind"
        Is Incapable of Reason and Rationality
    Myth Four: Islam Is an Inherently Violent Religion
    Myth Five: Muslims Are Incapable of Democracy and Self-Rule

Section 2: Political Islam and US Policy

4. **Allies and Enemies: The United States and Political Islam**   63
    Islam and Modernization
    Saudi Arabia and the King of Islam
    Iran and Afghanistan: Irrational Mullahs and Freedom Fighters
    Israel's Enemies
    Islamists and the Post–Cold War Era

5. **The Separation of Mosque and State**   81
    Orientalist Myths
    The De Facto Separation of Religion and Politics
    Modernization and Secularization
    The Failures of Islamic Revivalism
    Radical Secular Nationalism

6. **Political Islam: A Historical Analysis**   **93**
    What Is Political Islam?
    The Growth of Political Islam
    Political Islam: Mixed Fortunes
    Political Islam in an Anti-Imperialist Framework

7. **The Foreign Policy Establishment and the "Islamic Threat"** **113**
    The Neocons
    The Israel Connection
    Humanitarian Imperialism
    September 11 and the Bush Doctrine
    Obama and Liberal Imperialism

Section 3: Islamophobia and Domestic Politics

8. **Legalizing Racism:**
    Muslims and the Attack on Civil Liberties   **139**
    Terrorizing Arabs and Muslims
    Surveillance, Detention, and Deportation
    Preemptive Prosecution
    The Terrorism Spectacle
    Theories of Radicalization

9. **Green Scare: The Making of the Domestic Muslim Enemy**   **159**
    Manufacturing the Green Scare
    The "Ground Zero Mosque" Controversy
    The Rise of the Islamophobic Network

10. **Islamophobia and the New McCarthyism**   **175**
    The New McCarthyites
    "Education" and Media Propaganda
    Mainstream and Liberal Enablers
    Systemic Racism

Conclusion: Fighting Islamophobia   **193**

List of Acronyms   **201**

Notes   **203**

Index   **225**

Section 1

History and Context

Introduction

On September 11, 2001, I watched the televised spectacle of the Twin Towers crashing down with a sense of horror. I was deeply sorry for the innocent people who were being made to pay the price for the ravages of empire, and I was worried about whether any of my friends or relatives were in the towers. But almost immediately, I started to feel a sense of dread over what was to come: what would the United States do in response? I wondered, with a deep sense of apprehension, how many more innocent people would be killed around the world in the years to follow.

When I went to school that day, one of the first people I encountered was a colleague who jeered, "Are you happy?" Momentarily stunned, I could only stammer that I was not, and that I had just learned that some people I knew might have been in the Twin Towers at the time of the crash. Later that day, I stopped by the local Winn-Dixie grocery store, where the checkout clerk could barely conceal his contempt toward me. Eventually he flat-out asked me to apologize for what had happened that day. Again, I was taken aback. I didn't know how to reply. As a normally outspoken activist, I wasn't used to this sense of muteness; I just stood there and looked at him, temporarily dumbfounded. The only thing I knew beyond a shadow of doubt at that moment was that my response, when it did come out of my mouth, would *not* reveal that I was neither Muslim nor Arab. When I regained my composure, I asked him if he had heard of Timothy McVeigh and the other Christian fundamentalists who had similarly murdered innocent people. I asked him if he thought all Christians were responsible for these acts. He didn't reply.

1

I heard shortly afterward that a young Arab student at a neighboring university had been beaten up and that the campus police had simply looked the other way. Notices were posted in our apartment complex asking people to report "suspicious" behavior and people. A Sikh Indian man wearing a turban was killed in Arizona. In the months that followed, tens of thousands of Muslims were "interviewed" by the state, and thousands were imprisoned, tortured, and deported; a whole process of demonization had begun. With wide public support, the military machine was deployed to rain death on innocent Afghans. Anti-Muslim racism— or Islamophobia—was becoming the handmaiden of empire.

I knew then that I had to organize, speak, and write about this injustice. This book is the product of ten years of such engagement with activists in the antiwar movement, students and colleagues at universities across the United States, and feedback from various independent media editors on my articles about Islamophobia. It is a collective product, in this sense—driven by the need to produce knowledge that can effectively push back against the racist propaganda and help to strengthen social movements against war and racism.

First, a note on what this book is *not* about. This is not a book about the religion Islam. I am not a scholar of religion and do not claim to have any special erudition on this subject. This book is about the image of "Islam," that mythical creation conjured out of the needs of empire that has led even progressives to claim that Muslims are more violent than any other religious group. It is about the "Muslim enemy" and how this construction has been employed to generate fear and hatred.

Even before I began my study of the history of Islam, of Muslim-majority countries, and of the relationship between East and West, I knew instinctively that the Islamophobic rhetoric that passed as common sense in the United States was dead wrong. I grew up in India in a home where the neighbors on both sides were Muslims, and the *azan* (the Islamic call to prayer) was an everyday sound. India is home to more than a hundred million Muslims—more than most Arab nations—and, knowing from experience that Muslims are just as complex as any other group of people, I react viscerally to the stereotypes that pass as credible knowledge in the United States, the country where I have spent my adult life.

I am grateful to the dozens of Middle East studies scholars and others before me who have studied the "Muslim world" for advancing my knowledge of this subject and helping me to expose the underlying racism inherent in the logic of Islamophobia. My contribution to this corpus is a focus on Islamophobia in the American context, on which there is very little work (I use the term "American" to refer to the United States in this book only for stylistic purposes, and with apologies to my Central and South American readers). Drawing on my academic training as a cultural theorist, I situate the rhetoric of Islamophobia within the broader political, historical, legal, and societal context from which it emerges to show that anti-Muslim racism has been primarily a tool of the elite in various societies. There is some debate on whether the term "Islamophobia" is adequate to denote the phenomenon of cultural racism against Muslims. While it does have some limits, I continue to use this term not only because it is now widely accepted but also because in this book I study specifically the fear (and hatred) generated against the "Muslim threat."

The book therefore begins by looking at the first instances in the West when Muslims were constructed as threats to Europe. This takes place in the eleventh century in the context of the Crusades and the reconquest of the Iberian Peninsula. The chapter then goes on to outline the historic relationship between East and West from the eighth to the eighteenth centuries. Such a long view allows us to see that the image of Muslims and Islam in Europe has gone through a series of shifts and changes that corresponded to changes in the political and social realms. Thus, contrary to the idea that the East-West relationship has always been characterized by conflict or a "clash of civilizations," I show that anti-Muslim prejudice was consciously constructed and deployed by the ruling elite at particular moments. While ordinary people in Europe did accept these ideas, for instance during the Crusades, they have also resisted them. This fluidity is all but erased by Orientalist scholars like Bernard Lewis, the author of the term "clash of civilizations." Lewis flattens history to argue that

> the struggle between these rival systems [Christianity and Islam] has now lasted for some fourteen centuries. It began with the advent of Islam, in the seventh century, and has continued virtually to the present day. It has consisted of a long series of attacks and counterattacks, jihads and crusades, conquests and reconquests.[1]

For Lewis, the relationship between the "Christian West" and "Muslim East" is primarily driven by conflict; this fundamental characteristic of the East-West encounter therefore necessarily persists into the late twentieth century. Chapter 1 sets out to debunk this conception by locating the image of Islam in Europe in its proper historical context. Chapter 2 focuses on the nineteenth and twentieth centuries, a period of massive colonization by the Great Powers. England and France in particular conquered large parts of the Middle East and North Africa. They justified this process of colonization by recourse to a body of ideas called "Orientalism." In the nineteenth century, various European nations set up centers for the study of the Orient from which there emerged a huge body of Orientalist scholarship integrally tied to imperialism and colonization. In this chapter, and throughout the book generally, I focus mainly on the Middle East and North Africa, because it was these regions, due to their proximity to Europe, that largely informed the development of an elite Western vocabulary about "Islam." After World War II, the United States took over from France and England, both literally and metaphorically. It began to exercise its hegemony in the region through the borrowed language of Orientalism, but also through the vocabulary of capitalist modernization, which was better suited to the new form of imperialism initiated by the United States. Chapter 3 examines the persistence of Orientalist (and some medieval) views in the twenty-first century. It outlines five taken-for-granted racist narratives about Muslims that flourish today and shows that these myths have a longer history.

The next section is about the American approach to Islam on the political stage. It demonstrates that Islamists have not always been viewed as threats to the United States. Two chapters deal with this history, chapters 4 and 7. Chapter 4 outlines the contradictory policy pursued by the US political elite toward the parties of political Islam. During the Cold War and up until the Iranian revolution of 1979, the United States enthusiastically supported forces that could Islamize the Middle East and serve as a counter to those that posed a challenge to its domination—secular nationalists and the left. In the period after the 1970s, policy makers forged alliances with those Islamists who were on the side of US imperialism and militated against those who refused to play this role. Even after 9/11, when Islamists in general were projected as the arch enemy of the United States, the aforementioned approach would continue.

Chapters 5 and 6 look at the phenomenon of political Islam on its own terms. Chapter 5 shows that the parties of political Islam are not the natural outgrowths of Muslim-majority societies, as some have argued. As in Christian-majority societies, the (misnamed) "Muslim world" has also seen a separation of religion and politics. Understanding this history allows us to see that political Islam is a contemporary phenomenon. Chapter 6 shows that Islamism, often called Islamic fundamentalism, is the product of particular historic conditions in the late twentieth century that also spurred on the growth of Christian, Hindu, and Jewish fundamentalisms.

Chapter 7 sets out to examine post–Cold War thinking within the foreign policy establishment and the path that led up to the era of the "War on Terror." The chapter unpacks two dominant modes of thought in policy circles—those of the neoconservatives and of the realist/liberal camp. Despite the differences between these wings on questions of rhetoric and strategy, they share a common commitment to US imperialism. Their points of contention revolve around the best ways to maintain US dominance and global hegemony. These differences, however, fell to the wayside in the immediate aftermath of 9/11, when conservative/neocon and liberal Islamophobes came together to prosecute the War on Terror. Since then, the United States has been willing to work out deals with the Taliban or with the Egyptian Muslim Brotherhood.

The final section of the book looks at the uses of Islamophobia in the domestic context. Chapter 8 outlines the ways in which the legal system has been bent after 9/11 to prosecute Muslim citizens and immigrants, particularly those of Middle Eastern and South Asian descent. It must be noted that even before 2001, Arabs and Muslims were persecuted by the legal apparatus and treated like potential terrorists. The aftermath of 9/11 witnessed the convergence of domestic and foreign policy, resulting in the construction of the overarching "Islamic terrorist" enemy that must be fought abroad and at home. The corresponding "green scare" (green is the color of Islam) is similar to the various anticommunist "red scares" that marked US domestic politics in the twentieth century. When a nation goes to war with an external enemy, it inevitably turns against those it sees as incarnations of that enemy within its borders: the situation of Muslims in the United States today bears a strong resemblance to that of Japanese Americans during World War II. Statistically, Americans are more likely to die from a bolt of lightning than from an act of "terror." The focus on "radicalized" Muslim Americans serves not to keep the American people safe, but to whip up a sense of fear and paranoia which can then be used to squash dissent and win consent for violations of civil liberties at home and wars abroad.

Chapter 9 looks at the shift inward to "homegrown terrorism" at the end of the decade and outlines the part played by President Obama and the Democratic Party in creating an opening for the far right. The chapter focuses specifically on the controversy generated by the proposal to build an Islamic community center two and a half blocks from the site of the former World Trade Center. The misnamed "Ground Zero mosque" controversy showed the dynamic at work: while the far-right Islamophobes sparked hatred against Muslims, liberals and Democrats fanned the flames. The net result strengthened the racist bigots and enabled a surge in Islamophobia not seen since 9/11. This was the first palpable victory for the Islamophobic and Zionist right, which had been involved in various campaigns since 9/11. The politics of liberal Islamophobia at the top of society enabled the extreme Islamophobia of the right. The far right was then able to capitalize on this atmosphere of racism, building its own ranks through the mechanics of scapegoating. Similarly, politicians used Islamophobia to garner votes and political leverage.

Chapter 10 looks specifically at the right-wing Islamophobic warriors—the new McCarthyites—and their connections to the security establishment, the media, the academy, and the political class. In this chapter I argue that the right-wing Islamophobes are not a fringe minority but rather part and parcel of the structures of mainstream American society. Like Senator Joseph McCarthy before them, the new McCarthyites play a collective role in ramping up fear and hatred against Muslims, with the full consent of both the Republican and Democratic parties. Just as McCarthy was enabled by a political system that found his antics useful in the prosecution of the Cold War, the new McCarthyites of today are useful in pushing the envelope and advancing the War on Terror.

Finally, the conclusion looks at ways in which Islamophobia can be fought and resisted. I argue that Islamophobia is about politics rather than religion per se; it therefore needs to be fought on that terrain. There was much hope in the Muslim American community and among sections of the left that an Obama presidency would mitigate, if not eradicate, anti-Muslim racism. Yet, as this concluding chapter shows, this hope for change did not materialize: Obama wholeheartedly adopted and codified Bush-era policies. After years of betrayals by the Democratic Party, sections of the Muslim American community, along with their allies in the antiwar movement and other social movements, came together to push back against anti-Muslim racism. Local movements to defend unjustly targeted Muslim Americans started to coalesce into a nation-wide movement. The NYPD's harassment of Blacks and Latinos were connected by Muslim rights organizers with the anti-Muslim surveillance campaign, forging bonds of multiracial solidarity. I conclude by advancing the argument that it is only through such efforts, and through a politics of international solidarity that links domestic attacks on Muslims with the goals of imperialism, that Islamophobia can be successfully defeated.

I could not have picked a better year than 2011 to work on this book. The early part of the year saw the birth of the "Arab Spring": in a matter of weeks, ordinary people in Tunisia and Egypt deposed long-hated US-backed dictators. The ensuing media coverage in the United States exposed Americans to images of Arabs and Muslims they had never seen before, at least not on such a consistent basis. The self-activity of ordinary Arabs and Muslims went a long way toward shattering long-held Islamophobic stereotypes; pro-union protestors in Madison, Wisconsin, carried picket signs that read "Hosni Walker" and "Fight like an Egyptian." In a few short months, people in the Middle East and North Africa did more to combat Islamophobic caricatures through their activities than all of the books that have been written on the subject. And so it is to the brave women and men of the Arab Spring that I humbly dedicate this book.

Acknowledgments

Over the last decade I have been fortunate to interact with many intelligent, passionate, and wonderful people who have pushed me to think about this topic in ways that I would not if I had written this book sealed off in an ivory tower. Every question, every comment, and every interaction with hundreds of people at talks, meetings, and workshops in the United States and abroad has impacted and shaped this book. And so I must begin by acknowledging them, even if I cannot list every single person by name.

Those who have labored intensely on the book include, first and foremost, Paul D'Amato, the managing editor of the *International Socialist Review*. Earlier versions of some of the chapters appeared in the *ISR*, and they benefited from Paul's labyrinthine knowledge of all things important (and unimportant!). He also read chapters 1, 2, 3, and 7 and offered useful feedback. Ahmed Shawki, the editor of the *ISR* and another incredible thinker, must be thanked for his support of the project and for catching several errors. Lance Selfa read chapters 4, 7, and 10, and his deep knowledge of the US political establishment was invaluable. Two amazing lawyers, Steve Downs and Amna Akbar, read and vetted chapter 8 on the legal apparatus. A version of chapter 3 was published in the *Journal of Communication Inquiry*; my thanks again to the anonymous reviewers.

I must also thank Yoshie Furuhashi, my friend from graduate school, for publishing my first article on Islamophobia in *MRZine*. She informed me that it received more than ten thousand hits in the first few days. I took this as a sign that I should perhaps continue to write about the topic. I want to also thank my students Hoda Mitwally and Bryan Sacks for being so willing to help me dig up a reference or cross-check a fact. And last but not least, my copy editor, Sarah Grey. Anyone who has worked with a good copy editor knows how important and integral they are to the process—Sarah was the best. While everyone named here engaged with and shaped the book in ways big and small, what errors remain are of my own doing.

Finally, a big thanks to all my dear friends for their kindness and support during a rough year, particularly Helen Scott, Megan Behrent, Anjali Ganapathy, Srinivas Reddy, Ashley Smith, Sarah Grey, Joe Cleffie, Susan Menahem, Lee Wengraf, Susan Dwyer, Virginia Harabin, and Regina Marchi.

Chapter 1

Images of Islam in Europe

In the immediate aftermath of 9/11, sales of the Koran shot up dramatically in the United States. People who otherwise would not have had much interest in Islam turned to its holy book to find explanations for why the attacks had occurred. What prompts this automatic association between the actions of some individuals and their religion? Arguably no one turned to the Bible, either the Old or New Testament, to understand why Timothy McVeigh bombed a federal building in Oklahoma City. Why then are Arabs and Muslims seen primarily through the lens of Islam?

To answer this question we must turn to the dominant images of Islam and Muslims in the West. In particular, this chapter looks at the ways in which ruling elites in Europe throughout history have constructed particular images of the "Muslim enemy" to advance their political ambitions. In short, the history of "Islam and the West," as it is commonly termed, is a story not of religious conflict but rather of conflict born of *political* rivalries and competing imperial agendas.

This is not to suggest, however, that the encounter between "East" and "West" has always been bitter and hostile. I put "East" and "West" in quotes to recognize the fact that there is no monolithic East, just as there is no singular West. Rather, the peoples who lived in the geographic locations that we call Europe and the Near East in the period under study in this chapter, from the eighth to the eighteenth centuries, were marked by cultural, linguistic, ethnic, class, national, and other forms of difference. This chapter, like the book as a whole, eschews a simplistic understanding of Europe and the Near East as "rival systems" based on religious affiliation.

The West, therefore, has had not just one image of Islam but multiple images. For instance, ordinary Europeans who encountered their counterparts in the Near East sometimes found much to admire and respect; yet it would be wrong to underestimate the hold that any society's ruling ideas have on its people. Even while ordinary people can and do resist dominant ideas, those who rule a society tend to set the terms of discussion. By the same token, when elites change their minds about a certain topic, it produces a corresponding shift in the larger society.

The image of Islam in Europe has gone through a series of such shifts. Far from being a simple "clash of civilizations," the East-West encounter is complex, dynamic, and contradictory. This chapter outlines the changing historical circumstances that have produced different images of Islam and Muslims in the West.

Early Contact with Islam

Islam emerged in the seventh century in the Hijaz region of Arabia, which includes the cities of Mecca and Medina. This region was a major hub for trade activity, and the Arabs who lived there were in constant contact with their Christian Byzantine and Persian Sassanid neighbors. It was in this context that Muhammad, a trader by profession, began to devote time to spiritual matters. Muhammad worked for his older, wealthy wife, whose caravans traded with Syria. Muslims believe that in the year 610, while Muhammad was on a retreat in the hills near Mecca, the angel Gabriel appeared to him to deliver a message from God. Over the course of the next two decades (610–32 CE), Muhammad had several such revelations, and on that basis he propagated a new religion called Islam. The word *Islam* means "the act of submission"; a Muslim is someone who submits to God's will. The Koran, the holy book of Islam, is a compilation of the Word of God revealed to Muhammad, his prophet.

At first there were very few converts to Islam. The people of Mecca initially greeted Muhammad with hostility. This came in part from the message he preached, which was that God expects people to share their wealth with those needier than them. In 622 Muhammad and his followers left Mecca to travel to Medina, a journey referred to as the *Hijra*. Here Muhammad became a spiritual and a political leader and attracted a growing community of believers; by the time of his death in 632, Islam had spread beyond the Hijaz and into other parts of Arabia.

Within two decades of Muhammad's death, Arab Muslim armies not only defeated the Sassanid dynasty (which had ruled Persia and the neighboring regions for centuries) but also took over parts of the Byzantine Empire's territories. The expansion continued under the Umayyad dynasty (661–750 CE) into North Africa, and then into Europe in the early eighth century. Their conquests began in Spain, continued through the entire Iberian Peninsula, and reached into Italy.

This incursion into Europe drew alarm. At this stage, however, the Muslim invaders were seen as just another menace—no different from the other armies menacing the borders. Norman Daniel characterizes the first four hundred years of contact (between 700 and 1100 CE) as the "age of ignorance." During this period the West "knew virtually nothing of Islam as a religion. For them Islam was only one of a large number of enemies threatening Christendom from every direction, and they had no interest in distinguishing the primitive idolators of Northmen, Slav, and Magyars from the monotheism of Islam. . . . There is no sign that anyone in northern Europe had even heard the name Mahomet."[1]

This lack of information about Islam did not, however, stop the elites in Northern Europe from developing an image of the people they called the Saracens. The Venerable Bede, an eighth-century Bible scholar, expressed the dominant view at the time, arguing that the Saracens were the children of Hagar, one of Abraham's wives. Hagar's son Ishmael was associated with the Saracens, and his brother Isaac was understood to be the forefather of the Jews (and therefore the Christians).[2] Despite this familial association, the Saracens were still reviled as barbarians.

In Muslim-ruled Spain, however, there was a mix of ideas. "Derogatory and abusive myths about the Saracens were widespread among the Christian and Jewish masses. But these myths were mixed with more reliable impressions based on actual daily contact."[3] Muslim rule over the Iberian Peninsula (Spain, Portugal, and parts of southern France) lasted for eight centuries before the Christians finally drove their Muslim rulers out in 1492. During this period, Christians and Jews were tolerated as "people of the book" and were allowed to practice their religion if they paid a fee. This sustained contact mitigated and tempered the more hostile images.

Al-Andalus and Muslim Rule in Europe

While the rest of Europe was enduring a period of cultural stagnation known as the Dark Ages, al-Andalus, as the Iberian Peninsula came to be known under Muslim rule, saw the growth and development of human knowledge. The works of various great societies, from the Greeks to the Persians, were translated into Arabic in the many libraries created by Muslim rulers (not only in al-Andalus but also in Baghdad under the Abbasid dynasty). One great seat of learning was Córdoba in Spain. Here, as elsewhere, tremendous advances were made in the fields of philosophy, medicine, astronomy, architecture, and even urban development. While the rest of Europe stagnated in darkness, the citizens of Córdoba enjoyed streetlights and running water.[4]

In the context of a flourishing civilization, it is not surprising that negative attitudes toward the "Moors" (Spanish Muslims) would dissipate. Speaking to these changing attitudes, one Christian writer complained:

> The Christians love to read the poems and romances of the Arabs; they study the Arab theologians and philosophers, not to refute them but to form a correct and elegant Arabic [sic]. Where is the layman who now reads the Latin commentaries on the Holy Scriptures, or who studies the Gospels, prophets or apostles? Alas! all talented young Christians read and study with enthusiasm the Arab books; they gather immense libraries at great expense; they despise the Christian language as unworthy of attention. They have forgotten their language. For every one who can write a letter in Latin to a friend, there are a thousand who can express themselves in Arabic with elegance, and write better poems in this language than the Arabs themselves.[5]

María Rosa Menocal, who has studied the intersections of Jewish, Christian, and Muslim thought in al-Andalus, argues that this society, particularly its intellectual and artistic realms, was characterized by *convivencia*, or coexistence in relative peace. And while this age was not free of conflict—as Menocal's detractors have noted—it nevertheless serves as an example of tolerance and relative harmony between peoples of various faiths. In fact, Park51, the Islamic community center in lower Manhattan whose construction sparked controversy in 2010, was originally named Cordoba House as a tribute to this spirit of *convivencia*.[6] This controversy is discussed further in chapter 9.

Intellectually, Europe owes a debt of gratitude to scholars in the Near East. Various Muslim empires not only initiated a period of translation of the great works of various cultures but also oversaw a period of development. For instance, Muslim scholars built on Persian and Greek scientific concepts, and their work then paved the way for the Renaissance and the development of modern science.[7]

Europe finally began the process of moving out of the Dark Ages in the early twelfth century, and intellectuals flocked to the various libraries of the Muslim empires to regain lost knowledge. This period saw the retranslation of the great works of humanity from Arabic back into European languages. Through this process, European intellectuals came to absorb the profound contributions made by Near Eastern thinkers. As Zachary Lockman writes,

> Translated Arabic writings on medicine, mathematics, astronomy and other sciences were for centuries used as textbooks in medieval Europe, while the writings of Muslim philosophers like Ibn Sina (980–1037, known in the West as Avicenna) and Ibn Rushd (1126–98, known as Averroes), and Jewish philosophers who wrote mainly in Arabic like Maimonides (Rabbi Moses ben Maimon, 1135–1204), were eagerly read and discussed and influenced several generations of medieval Christian philosophers and theologians.[8]

Although the Latin Church rejected Ibn Sina's work, such contributions opened the door to more accurate understandings of Islam and Muslims. One person who contributed significantly to this was Peter the Venerable, who among other things had the Koran translated. Yet while access to the Koran (as well as other translated Arabic texts) generated a more realistic picture of Islam among non-Muslims, the Church also quoted it selectively to construct anti-Muslim propaganda.[9]

The Crusades and the Reconquista

The period of European intellectual growth in the eleventh century was accompanied by growth in commerce and trade. Markets and towns began to spring up. By this point, however, Muslims were no longer one enemy among many; the other pagan raiders (such as the Normans and Magyars) that had relentlessly invaded Christian Europe in the ninth and tenth centuries had been converted and integrated. The only enemy that remained was the Muslims. This is not to suggest, however, that Europe was united and at peace. Rather, Islam became a convenient "other" to mobilize support for the territorial ambitions of various rulers. In Spain, Christian rulers in the north began a war to retake the Iberian Peninsula from the "Muslim enemy" in what came to be known as the Reconquista (reconquest).

In the East, the Christian Byzantine Empire (or Eastern Rome) suffered a series of defeats at the hands of the Muslim Seljuq Turks. The emperor wrote to Pope Urban II to seek Europe's help against the Turks. His call was heeded. Urban launched a holy war (known as the Crusades) in 1095 and called upon all Christians in Europe to unite and fight against the "enemies of God." This charge wasn't simply, or even primarily, about religion. As John Esposito explains, "For the Pope, the call to the defense of the faith and Jerusalem provided an ideal opportunity to gain recognition for papal authority and its role in legitimating temporal rulers, and to reunite the Eastern (Greek) and Western (Latin) churches."[10] Religion became the screen behind which social and economic conflicts were played out. To be sure, it was not just Muslims who were killed by the crusaders: systematic pogroms were carried out against Jews in Europe, and Christians in the Byzantine Empire were also mercilessly slaughtered. Additionally, at various points Muslims and Christians cooperated with one another, and turned against their own sides, out of self-interest.

European rulers took up the call to Holy War for a variety of different reasons. "Christian rulers, knights, and merchants were driven by the political, military, and economic advantages that would result from the establishment of a Latin kingdom in the Middle East."[11] Additionally, Europe consisted of a number of rival feudal regimes that constantly fought each other. The Crusades served as a means to reduce this intra-European conflict and to deflect attention onto an external enemy. When Urban launched the First Crusade, he proclaimed: "Let those . . . who are accustomed to wantonly wage private war against the faithful march upon the infidels. . . . Let those who have long been robbers now be soldiers of Christ. Let those who once fought against brothers and relatives now rightfully fight against the barbarians. Let those who have been hirelings for a few pieces of silver now attain an eternal reward."[12] Using religion to cement identity and loyalty, the papacy sought to create a united Christian Europe over which it could hold spiritual authority. Those who heeded this call and joined the crusader armies, however, were driven by everything from religious zeal to the rewards of plunder.

Thus, the image of the Muslim enemy and of Islam as a demonic religion started to come into focus in this context in the late eleventh century. Mobilizing the population for a holy war required religious arguments; it became necessary to acquire information about Islam, its teachings, the life of the prophet Muhammad, and so on in order to argue against them. Here the works of Peter the Venerable and others provided useful fodder for the Church to attack Islam as a heresy and Muhammad as a false prophet.

What Christians now confronted was a religion that was similar to theirs but that challenged the primacy of their belief system. The God of Christianity is the same God of Abraham worshiped in Islam, but Christianity claims that God's revelation in Jesus marked the end of revelation and of prophecy. Islam makes a similar claim but argues that Muhammad was the last prophet who received the final and correct Word of God.

This was not the first time Christianity had encountered such a challenge. Jews, similarly, do not accept the Christian version of revelation and prophecy. However, Jews weren't marching armies into Christian capitals. They were not a threat to the elites in the way the Muslim empires were. Thus, as Richard Southern suggests, it was easy for Christianity to dismiss the Jewish challenge because of the "economic and social inferiority of the Jews."[13] In other words, Jews did not have the social, economic, or political power to threaten Christendom. Furthermore, Christians had access to "an embarrassing wealth of material for answering the Jewish case."[14] Such material was now collected for the case against Islam.

Norman Daniel has conducted one of the most authoritative studies on the image of Islam generated by the intellectual elite in the West from the early twelfth century to the middle of the fourteenth. His book *Islam and the West* shows that key among their various lines of attack was the argument that Islam's revelations were "pseudo-prophecies," based not only on the authority of Christian scriptures but also on the notion that Muhammad could not be a prophet. Instead, Muhammad was cast as "a low-born and pagan upstart, who schemed himself into power, who maintained it by pretended revelations, and who spread it both by violence and by permitting to others the same lascivious practices he indulged himself."[15] We see at this stage the association of Islam with violence, a theme that would recur over the centuries. The thrust here was that those who didn't come under Muhammad's spell, as the "simpleminded" Arabs had, were either subjugated with violent force or enticed with sexual indulgences.

On what grounds did the Church claim that Islam attracted followers through sexual deviance and perversion? For Christians, marriage meant a union with one partner, dissoluble only by death—they thus pointed to Muhammad's multiple wives as proof of his perversion. (Abraham's multiple wives, however, were left out of the debate.) Islam permitted men to take four wives, allowed divorce, and even allowed divorced women to remarry. Christians viewed this with horror. In both scholarly and popular accounts, all sorts of venomous (and entirely fictional) stories began to circulate:

> Muhammad was said to be a magician, a sorcerer who used his evil powers to produce fake miracles and thereby seduce men into embracing his false doctrines; he was a renegade Christian priest, perhaps even a cardinal, whose frustrated lust for power led him to seek revenge on the church by propagating his own pernicious teachings; he was sexually promiscuous, an adulterer, and promoted licentiousness in order to ensnare men into depravity; his death was as disgusting and shameful as his life, for he was devoured by dogs, or suffocated by pigs during an epileptic fit.[16]

Such outrageous and apocryphal stories began to circulate with apparently no need for evidence of any sort. (You can find still some of them today being propagated by the likes of Glenn Beck.) The result was that Islam was debased and constructed as a dangerous enemy.

What was particularly dangerous about this enemy was that not only was it taking over Christian lands but, worse still, it was succeeding in converting people to Islam. When Muslim armies advanced on European lands from the seventh to the eleventh centuries, many non-Muslim subjects (including Christians and Jews) converted to Islam. For instance, non-Orthodox Christians who were persecuted by the Greek Church welcomed Muslim rule. Over a period of several centuries, many converted.

Islam, therefore, was presented as a serious threat. It had to go, and this meant mobilizing an army to retake the Holy Land, rid Spain of the interlopers, and reestablish Christian hegemony. Such a task necessitated the kinds of demonic and highly negative images discussed above. Even during this period, though, pockets of more sympathetic representations and relations existed. The culture of al-Andalus was one such exception, as was the attitude among Christian scholars in the rest of Europe following the period of retranslation.

In addition, direct contact with Muslims produced images that went against the grain. Commerce between Muslim and Christian traders, while not amicable, was at least conducted on terms of mutual respect. Similarly, on the battlefield, the crusaders loathed the infidels but praised their military prowess and told stories of the bravery of Muslim warriors.[17] The emperor Saladin, who retook Jerusalem from the crusaders and was therefore an archenemy, was also admired for his chivalry. An abundance of stories were written about him, and his name was given to European children for generations thereafter. Nevertheless, most scholars of the Middle Ages agree that the dominant view of Islam and of Muslims during this period was extremely negative. In short, it was the "crusading" spirit—the combination of military conquest with religious fervor—that characterized European attitudes at the time.

From Polemic to Indifference

In the fourteenth and fifteenth centuries, as Europe began to come out of the Middle Ages and into the modern era, its polemical construction of Islam changed. As Islam was less and less seen as an existential threat, an attitude of indifference crept in. This shift was the product of a number of developments. First, the never-fully-achieved project of a united Christian Europe started to break down even further around this time due to the rise of nationalism and proto-nationalist identifications. Christians were beginning to define themselves as French, English, Spanish, and so on. As Maxime Rodinson writes, "The plan for the expansion of a united Christian Europe gave way, once and for all [starting around the fourteenth century], to nationalistic political projects."[18] Such internal divisions among Christians deflected attention away from their external enemy. Second, the renaissance of European culture further weakened the authority of the Church. The key source of anti-Muslim religious zeal, the Church, was no longer able to foment holy wars; the Crusades came to an end. Third, the Mongols had now entered the picture and posed a threat to Europe. This recognition of lands beyond Europe, and of threats beyond the Muslims, meant that the world could no longer be divided neatly into Christian vs. Muslim in a narrow, simplistic way. The confluence of these factors led to a more tolerant view of Islam.[19]

This period, marked as it was by relatively peaceful relations between East and West, the flourishing of trade, and a general attitude of indifference, was soon to be punctuated by a new enemy: the rising Ottoman Empire.

The Ottomans

Osman, the founder of the Ottoman Empire, turned against Mongol rule in the late thirteenth century and began a period of conquest. In the century that followed, Ottoman armies expanded into the eastern Mediterranean region and the Balkans. Just as during the early conquests of the Muslim armies in the seventh and eighth centuries, some people in Christian states welcomed the Turks in order to escape religious persecution, this time at the hands of the Roman Catholic Church. The Ottoman policy of "live and let live" stood in contrast to the intolerance that Orthodox Christians and other religious minorities faced under the Church. Balkan peasants captured this mood with the saying "Better the turban of the Turk than the tiara of the Pope."[20]

In 1453 the Ottomans captured Constantinople, the capital of the Byzantine Empire, and brought an end to Christian rule in the East. They now turned their attention to other parts of Europe, conquering Belgrade in 1523. These incursions deep into Europe brought the new Muslim enemy into focus. However, this time the enemy was viewed in secular terms and seen as a political rather than a religious threat (even though the term "Turk" became synonymous with Muslim). Two periods followed: the first, a period of admiration for the new Ottoman enemies, who were seen as a great European power; the second, a complete reversal of this mood, as the Ottomans began a period of decline relative to Europe.

Phase One: Contradictory Views of the Ottomans

The new Muslim enemy was now seen as part of Europe rather than as an outsider. The threat it posed to its neighbors was seen not as a religious one; rather, it was the threat represented by a powerful, arguably the most powerful, European state. Indeed, the Turks were by and large considered to be ethnically European. One theory suggested that they were, like the French and the Italians, descendants of the Trojans.[21] This theory bears some semblance to the Abraham-Hagar story in that Muslims are seen as a part of Europe's history; even while they are enemies, they are still a part of the family, so to speak.

Such Ottoman European genealogies were accepted by some and rejected by others. Nevertheless, various European figures made alliances with the Ottomans. A French king allied himself with a Turkish sultan against the Habsburg Empire; the Pope similarly forged an alliance opposing the Habsburg emperor's plans for a crusade against the Ottomans.[22] Jews fleeing Europe, particularly after their expulsion from Spain in 1492, found a home in the Ottoman Empire. This was true too of Protestants and other dissident Christians seeking to escape Catholic persecution. In short, the diversity that marked al-Andalus found its reflection in the Ottoman territories; Christians and Jews not only lived in an atmosphere of tolerance but also experienced prosperity.

Europe, by contrast, was going through a bitter and violent conflict between Protestants and Catholics. The first half of the sixteenth century saw the emergence of the Reformation. This internal dissent within Christianity created a climate where Islam came to be seen as yet another schism, albeit a dangerous one. Thus, even while Martin Luther, who led the Protestant Reformation, had negative things to say about Islam, he viewed the Vatican as the greater enemy. For Luther, only after the defeat of Catholicism could Islam be beaten.[23] Defenders of Catholicism attacked Protestantism by comparing it to Islam, in some instances seeing it as worse than Islam. Along the way, the Ottomans became involved in this struggle on the side of the Protestants against their common enemy, the Habsburgs, who were the key defenders of Catholicism.

The image of the Ottomans in this period was contradictory. On the one hand, in popular literature the Ottomans were depicted as cruel and violent, in ways that drew on earlier caricatures of Muslims; there was also a morbid fascination with the sexual lives of the Turks and intense curiosity about the harem. On the other hand, however, among those who understood the Ottoman system of administration, there was appreciation for its efficiency as well as the overall grandeur of the empire.

The sixteenth century also saw the emergence of some of the first studies of the Orient to adopt a more open-minded and disinterested tone. At the broader level, the Renaissance led to the scientific revolution of the sixteenth and seventeenth centuries, marking a shift to studying the natural world though the use of empirical and scientific methods (as opposed to religious ones). This would impact how Islam was studied in various newly constituted Oriental centers in Paris, Oxford, and Rome. This "more objective understanding of the Middle East," Rodinson explains, arose from factors such as "geographical proximity, close political relations, increasing economic interactions, [and] the growing number of travelers and missionaries who journeyed to the East."[24]

However, as the Ottoman Empire started to decline, particularly after its defeat in Vienna in 1683, the attitude of admiration and even of tolerance and neutrality it had enjoyed dissipated.

Phase Two: Oriental Despotism

During the seventeenth century, as the Ottoman Empire began to lose its military superiority over Europe, European travelers to Ottoman lands found more to criticize than to respect. The Turks, Zachary Lockman writes, were now depicted as "boorish, ignorant, dishonorable, immoral, ineffectual, corrupt and irrational. The older image of the Ottoman state as an efficient, just, virtuous and tolerant meritocracy faded away, to be replaced by a depiction of that state as corrupt, oppressive and brutal."[25] In part, this was accurate: the Ottoman system had in fact seen a decline, as described by its own chroniclers.

But Europe's contempt toward the East had more to do with its new image of itself. European thinkers during and after the Renaissance imagined their history as an unbroken line of continuity from ancient Greece and Rome to the present—in the process exorcising the Islamic history of Europe. Europe now imagined itself as superior, the heir to the democratic political systems of the Greeks and Romans, and therefore very different from the despotic regimes that it now saw as characterizing the East. In contrast to the democratic West, the Ottomans came to be seen as the manifestation of "Asian despotism." Ottoman integration into Europe was therefore short-lived, and the Muslim enemy again became Europe's "other."

The French writer Montesquieu, writing in 1748, explained that Asia was destined to be despotic because of the way its hot climate affected the temperaments of its people. He argued that in cooler regions such as Europe the people tended to be active and therefore braver, whereas in the warmer climates of Asia the people were inactive and therefore servile and effeminate.[26] It followed from this that democracy was more at home in the former, while the servile people of the East were capable only of despotism. While Montesquieu's bizarre and ridiculous theory is long out of style, the notion of "Oriental despotism" and the belief that the people of the Middle East and North Africa are best suited to dictatorships has endured.

The origin of this myth is based in Europe's transformation and its subsequent rise to global dominance. Up until 1500 or so, Europe was a marginal player on the world stage relative to other great powers (such as the Ottomans, Chinese, and Indians). It overcame its backwardness thanks in no small part to the rise of capitalism. The question of the origins of capitalism is a complex and hotly debated issue, and I will not discuss it here. For our purposes, let me state that the growth of capitalism conferred various advantages—technological, military, communication, and so on—which led first to European dominance over world trade and then eventually to colonialism and imperialism.

By the eighteenth century, the once-invincible Ottomans lost their ability even to resist European incursions into their territory. The "Muslim world," no longer a military threat, saw its image shift again—this time into the realm of the exotic. In the early part of the eighteenth century, the epic collection of folk tales *One Thousand and One Nights* was translated into European languages. Its stories of the "Muslim world" as an exotic and fantastic land populated by genies, harems, and all things enchanting and amusing to Westerners had a great influence on how Europe perceived the Near East. During the Enlightenment, this view shifted yet again as some accurate accounts of Islam began to emerge.

Romanticism and the Enlightenment

The trend toward the exotic was fueled by the growth of Romanticism, an artistic and philosophical movement of the eighteenth and nineteenth centuries. The image of an exotic Orient associated with "sensuality, promise, terror, sublimity, idyllic pleasure, [and] intense energy" can be found in the works of musicians, painters, novelists, and philosophers from Mozart to Byron, Hugo, and Goethe.[27] To be fair, the Romantics did not only look to the East for the exotic: they also looked to their own past, drawing from Gothic tales and stories of European barbarians. Rodinson summarizes the Romantic vision of the East as "characterized by fierce and lavish scenes in a wild array of colors; harems and seraglios; decapitated bodies, women hurled into the Bosporus in sacks; feluccas and brigantines displaying the Crescent flag; round, turquoise domes and white minarets soaring to the heavens; viziers, eunuchs, and odalisques; refreshing springs under palm trees; *giaours* with their throats slit; captive women forced into submission by their lustful captors."[28]

This wild, sensual, and exotic image of the Orient would coexist with a more accurate representation of Islam during the Enlightenment, the philosophical movement that argued against Christian dogma and for reason and rationality as the means to achieve human progress. However, the Romantic movement rejected the Enlightenment philosophers' emphasis on rationality and instead valorized emotion, intuition, and imagination. For Romantic poets, philosophers, novelists, and painters, the East was a source of great wisdom and spiritual advancement. They contrasted this image with their own societies, which had lost these qualities in the mad rush to industrialization and capitalist modernity, and drew on Eastern styles of literary expression, architectures, and other such creative arenas.

The Enlightenment saw the birth of scholarship on Islam that was both realistic and sympathetic.[29] For instance, in contrast to the vicious medieval demonization of Muhammad, several philosophers published tracts arguing that Muhammad was not an impostor. Voltaire defended Muhammad as a great thinker and founder of a rational religion even as he (and other Enlightenment critics of organized religion) condemned Islam quite acerbically. Daniel explains Voltaire's contradictory stances: "We must say that Voltaire first thought an attack on Islam useful for an attack on religion generally; and later saw the advantage of treating the facts less passionately, in order to recommend natural religion at the expense of Christian belief."[30] To be sure, the Enlightenment produced contradictory views on Islam and Muslims.

As the next chapter will detail, theories of race began to emerge during this period, and many leading lights of the Enlightenment—such as Montesquieu, Kant, Hegel and Hume—expressed what today are shockingly racist views. The philosopher Emmanuel Chukwudi Eze, in his anthology of race in Enlightenment philosophy, argues that while some thinkers were undoubtedly racist, others advanced theories of race that were neutral—and still others were antiracist. Enlightenment thinkers classified human beings into races and in the process produced a schema in which whiteness came to be associated with cultural and racial superiority, while "unreason and savagery was conveniently located among the non-whites."[31] With regard to Muslims, Rodinson argues that the "eighteenth century saw the Muslim East through fraternal and understanding eyes"; during the Enlightenment, "the Muslims were not singled out as being different from other men."[32] This attitude would shift with the rise of European colonialism and the birth of Orientalism—a new body of ideas that served to justify conquest. We turn to this in the next chapter.

◆ ◆ ◆

This chapter outlined some of the key shifts in the European image of Islam from the eighth to the eighteenth centuries. This journey through history shows us that at first, between the eighth and eleventh centuries, Muslim incursions into Europe were viewed no differently from other pagan invasions. In fact, the Saracens were believed to be descendants of Abraham and therefore from the same "family" as Christians and Jews. Yet once other pagans integrated into Christian Europe, the powerful Muslim enemy became an "other" that had to be vanquished through holy wars. The papacy sought to unite a fractious Europe under the banner of Christianity as a way to advance its power.

Even in the eleventh century, however, as the Church was propagating hostile images of Islam to mobilize for the Crusades and the reconquest of the Iberian Peninsula, a favorable image also came into being through the work of European scholars. As they began to retranslate the great works of human knowledge, they came to appreciate the contributions of Eastern scholars. Muslim rule in al-Andalus not only helped foster enormous intellectual leaps, it also marked a period of *convivencia* or tolerance when Muslims, Christians, and Jews lived in relative peace.

When Europe, spiritually united under the leadership of the Vatican, began to fracture along national lines, the focus shifted away from the Muslim enemy. The fourteenth and fifteenth centuries therefore saw a turn away from polemic toward indifference—until the Ottoman Empire began to advance into Europe in the early sixteenth century, heralding a new threat. This time, however, the enemy was seen as a secular and political threat rather than a religious one. The Ottomans were presented as Europeans of sorts and admired for their many accomplishments; European rulers forged alliances with them against other European rivals. To be sure, such alliances of convenience across religious lines go back even to the era of the Crusades.

The next shift in perception occurred when Europe arose from its long period of historical decline relative to other powers to begin a period of ascendance. The rise of Europe and the relative decline of the Ottomans turned admiration into contempt. The East in general and the

Ottomans in particular were seen as inferior to the West and capable only of producing despotic societies. This polemical image then shifted into an exotic one during the Romantic era. This fantasy coexisted with the more accurate visions of Islam produced during the Enlightenment.

In short, contrary to the myth that the West and the East have always been in conflict, conflict has in fact coexisted with cooperation. Far from the notion that "East is East and West is West and never the twain shall meet," what we have seen is that the histories of the East and the West, to the extent we can even talk about a singular East and West, are deeply intertwined. At the very least we have to say that such broad geographical and religious characterizations as "Islam and the West" are extremely problematic—not least because the Christian Byzantine Empire thrived in the lands designated as "the East" up until the fifteenth century, and Muslim rule in al-Andalus lasted for about eight hundred years. Thus, the notion of a transhistoric "clash of civilizations" between a united Christian West and a Muslim East is highly flawed.

The history outlined in this chapter also shows that "the West" has not uniformly harbored negative images of Islam. During moments of conflict, political elites mobilized Islamophobia as a means to advance their larger agendas, whether papal supremacy over Europe or the expansionist ambitions of Christian rulers. Islam-bashing has been a useful tool in power politics for a very long time. In the following centuries, during the era of modern colonialism, the demonization of Islam and Muslims continued. This time, however, it was given new legitimacy in the academy and turned into a science.

Chapter 2

Colonialism and Orientalism

When the film *Sex in the City 2*, set in Abu Dhabi, was released in 2010, several reviewers rightly panned it for its racist stereotypes of Arabs and Muslims. It was as if the producers of the film had gone back to the 1920s, revived the Ali Baba film template, added a few iPhones and five-star hotels as a nod to the modernity of Abu Dhabi, and left everything else more or less intact. How do we understand this view of the Middle East as a place that does not change—a place where, despite high technology and consumer luxuries, the people remain static and essentially "Muslim"?

This view of Islam emerges from a body of work known as Orientalism that came into being in the context of European colonization, which reached its peak in the nineteenth and twentieth centuries. While the Ottoman Empire held on to most of its territories during the eighteenth century, in the nineteenth its grip began to loosen.

Imperial nations, particularly Austria and Russia, started to take over Ottoman territories. Additionally, various Christian provinces under Ottoman rule broke away to form new states, notably Greece. The legendary Ottoman Empire was crumbling.

Other Muslim states seemed equally unable to prevent the onslaught of empire. France invaded and occupied Algeria in 1830, and in 1881–83 seized Tunisia as well. In 1882 Britain colonized Egypt, and in 1898 it took over the Sudan. The Ottoman Empire finally collapsed after World War I. The victors of the war divided its territories, and the Middle East in general, amongst themselves. They drew arbitrary borders around new states—Lebanon, Syria, Transjordan, Iraq, and Palestine among them—which France and Britain dominated through the mandate system. After World War II, the United States began to take over the reins from the old colonial overlords.

It was in this context that Orientalism, an entire field of scholarship dedicated to studying the "Orient," was born. While institutes for the study of the Orient had been established earlier, they became a growth industry in the nineteenth century. A large body of scholars dedicated themselves to the project of learning the various languages of the East, translating a range of books, and systematically building up knowledge of the Orient.

This chapter looks at the image of the "Muslim world" in the nineteenth and twentieth centuries as reflected through the language of Orientalism, examining its assumptions and the ways in which Orientalism has served as the handmaiden of colonialism. We will begin by looking at its emergence in France and Britain, and then turn to the United States.

Napoleon and "Enlightened" Colonialism

France was an early pioneer of Orientalist thought. In 1795, the School of Living Oriental Languages was established in Paris. When Napoleon invaded Egypt a few years later, he was able to take with him Orientalists whose knowledge could be put to use for colonial purposes. Napoleon's invasion of Egypt in 1798 stands out as the first instance when knowledge about the native people became central to a colonizing mission.

This is not to say that knowledge about the enemy was not essential in earlier periods. Even during medieval times, European rulers gathered accurate information about Muslim kingdoms through spies, officials, and informants in order to develop martial strategies. They did not, of course, share this knowledge with the public. Instead, they used the vitriolic rhetoric of the Holy Wars to motivate the Crusades and the Reconquista.[1] While this general method persists even in the twenty-first century, what Napoleon's invasion inaugurated was the systematic use of scholarly knowledge to serve the needs of empire, both abroad and at home.

This model of enlightened colonialism has three aspects. First, the colonizer must prepare thoroughly before launching the invasion so as to be well set up to handle obstacles. Second, it should enlist scholars to work alongside soldiers in the colonizing process. Napoleon took with him about 160 scholars to help with the day-to-day process of colonial administration and create a body of knowledge about Egypt for French use. Third, the colonizing nation must develop a justifying rationale. France, having just thrown off the yoke of its oppressive feudal monarchy, believed its mission to be one of restoring Egypt to its former greatness. We can see here the precursors of what would come to be known as *mission civilisatrice*, or the "civilizing mission."

Napoleon was well prepared for this mission, as Edward Said tells us in his classic work *Orientalism*. Having been fascinated by the Orient from an early age, he had read European writings on the subject extensively, both recent and classical. Said focuses in particular on the French traveler Comte de Volney's two-volume exposition *Voyage to Egypt and Syria*. Napoleon found Volney's assessment of the Near East as a locale for French colonialism particularly useful, as well as his list of obstacles that the colonial mission might encounter. One such obstacle was distrust among Egyptians toward Europeans. Napoleon went on to use *Voyage* as a colonizing manual.

In his manifesto, which was widely circulated in Egypt, Napoleon tried to win the hearts and minds of Egyptians:

> Peoples of Egypt, you will be told that I have come to destroy your religion. This is an obvious lie; do not believe it! Tell the slanderers that I have come to you to restore your rights from the hands of the oppressors and that I, more than the Mamluks [who ruled Egypt at the time], serve God . . . and revere His Prophet Muhammad and the glorious Quran. . . . Formerly in the land of Egypt there were great cities, wide canals, and a prosperous trade [sic]. What has ruined all this, if not the greed and tyranny of the Mamluks? . . . Tell your nation that the French are also faithful Muslims. The truth is that they invaded Rome and have destroyed the throne of the Pope, who always incited Christians to make war on Muslims.[2]

Other than the obvious fabrications about the French being Muslims and destroying the papacy, what is noteworthy about this manifesto is its attempt to win over Egyptians through praise for Islam. Napoleon repeatedly insisted that he was fighting for Islam. He invited sixty Muslim scholars from al-Azhar to his quarters and impressed them with his knowledge of and respect for the Koran. Everything that Napoleon said was translated for popular consumption into Koranic Arabic. This strategy worked: the people of Cairo lost their distrust of the French colonizers.[3]

When Napoleon left Egypt, he gave strict instructions to his deputy that Egypt was to be administered according to the model he had set: Orientalists were to be consulted before policies could be enacted, and the Muslim religious leaders he had won over also needed to be part of the arsenal of colonial rule. Napoleon charged his small army of scholars with the task of gathering vast amounts of firsthand information about Egypt. As Said writes, a team

> of chemists, historians, biologists, archaeologists, surgeons, and anti-quarians [became] the learned division of the army. Its job was no less aggressive: to put Egypt into modern French. . . . Almost from the first moments of occupation Napoleon saw to it that the Institut [the Egypt Institute set up by him] began its meetings, its experiments—its fact-finding mission, as we would call it today. Most important, everything said, seen, and studied was to be recorded.[4]

This work resulted in the publication of *Description of Egypt*, a compendium in twenty-three volumes published between 1809 and 1828. Its detailed information on every aspect of Egyptian society, from monuments to facial structures, was created for use not by Egyptians but by the French. While there is much accurate and valuable information in the *Description*, the important point that Said makes is that such vast knowledge was amassed without the input of the native people. This account of Egypt, Said argues, served to displace Egypt's own sense of itself and its place in the world in favor of a French colonial vision of the same. It was ultimately created to help the French dominate the Egyptians.

The French, naturally, did not see their conquest in such base terms as control and domination. Rather, as the quote from Napoleon's manifesto suggests, their goal was to restore Egypt to its glorious past of "great cities" and "wide canals." France would, they thought, save a once-great country from ruin and show the natives what they once were and could become again under French tutelage. This paternalistic logic became more developed as the European colonial mission grew; Rudyard Kipling immortalized it in his 1899 poem "The White Man's Burden." Its French variant, *mission civilisatrice*, was used to great success to win domestic consent for colonial conquests in a nation founded on the ideas of *liberté, égalité, fraternité* (liberty, equality, and fraternity).

The French occupied Egypt only until 1801. It was interimperialist rivalry with Britain that ultimately forced them to leave, but Egyptians had also quickly realized that the French did not have their best interests at heart. Nevertheless, this method of colonization was seen as a model to be emulated. After Napoleon, Said writes, the "very language of Orientalism changed radically"; from then on "the Orient was reconstructed, reassembled, crafted, in short, *born* out of Orientalists' efforts."[5] The Orient was no longer strange and exotic but a region that could be understood and controlled. And Orientalist scholarship was the key that would unlock the secrets of the East.

The Characteristics of Orientalism

Nineteenth-century Orientalist scholars did not necessarily see themselves as agents of empire; they considered themselves, by and large, to be producing disinterested knowledge. Some, however, advised the French government and played an important role in enabling colonization—such as Silvestre de Sacy, an important Orientalist who influenced generations of scholars. Whether consciously or not, Orientalists produced a body of work that aided the project of imperialism. Before we consider some of the assumptions that undergird Orientalism, it is useful to distinguish nineteenth-century colonial rhetoric from its precursors.

Prior to the nineteenth century, European colonialism was explained primarily through the lens of Christianity. In the sixteenth and seventeenth centuries, Europeans justified their slaughter and exploitation of the "Indians" in the New World through the argument that the Indian "savages" were wild animals, idolaters whom God had ordained to be dominated by Christians.[6] They similarly justified their enslavement of Africans through the book of Genesis, arguing that Africans were a cursed people (drawn from the myth of the curse of Ham) whose black skin color marked their curse. The "curse" conveniently meant that even African slaves who converted to Christianity could still be retained as slaves.[7]

The shift from religious to "scientific" justifications began in the eighteenth century. Enlightenment philosophers divided human beings into various races or "species" with distinct characteristics. Over the course of time, this classificatory system led white Europeans to conclude that they were superior to other "darker, colored peoples," who were both "ugly" and at best "semi-civilized."[8] This was an important component in the early development of racism as an ideology to justify slavery

and conquest.[9] Additionally, as chapter 1 explained, the eighteenth century saw the development of notions of European superiority, particularly
through the association of the West with democracy and the East with
despotism. Yet, as Rodinson argues, "in the eighteenth century, an un-
conscious sense of Eurocentrism was present but it was guided by the
universalist ideology of the Enlightenment and therefore respected non-
European civilizations and peoples."[10] By the nineteenth century, however, this Enlightenment universalism was rapidly being replaced by an
emphasis on differences between people and civilizations. Europe developed what Etienne Balibar calls an "imperialist superiority complex."[11]

This emphasis on differences took ideological form in the body of
thought that has come to be known as Orientalism. Orientalism has a
few characteristic features. Drawing on the work of Zachary Lockman
in *Contending Visions of the Middle East*, as well as others, I outline four
key features of Orientalism. First, it is based on a civilizational view of
history—the idea that civilizations come into being, prosper, and then
go into decline. Second, because it emerged from philology, the historical
and comparative study of language, it assumes that everything one needs
to know about a civilization can be found in its texts and languages.
Third, Orientalism sees Islam and its classical texts as key to understanding contemporary Muslims and their societies. Fourth, it draws on theories of race and the notion that Muslims are a distinct race.

A widely accepted theory in the nineteenth century was that
human society was divided into different and distinct civilizations which
existed in isolation from each other, each driven by its own core set of
values. This theory held that the West, as a unique civilization with roots
in ancient Greece, had certain qualities that differentiated it from all
other civilizations. These included "freedom, law, rationality, science,
progress, intellectual curiosity, and the spirit of invention, adventure and
enterprise."[12] Every other civilization was then defined in relation to
this notion of a superior "West." Predictably, the world of Islam was
characterized as premodern, backward, primitive, despotic, static, undemocratic, and rigid.

Closely associated with civilizational theories is the notion that a
people can be understood through its languages and key texts. Philologists like Sacy advocated the notion that the study of a society's written
texts could yield insights into the timeless essence of a civilization. Orientalists would therefore learn Arabic, Persian, and Turkish and translate

and analyze the texts of the East. Rather than examine the historical context of Muslim societies, philologists simply pursued textual analysis. It is no wonder then, as Rodinson notes, that despite the "tremendous amount of accurate information and precise documentation, which the specialists were able to assemble, the rift between their intellectual efforts and the world of objective reality continued to widen."[13]

It followed from this that Islam, as defined by its classical texts, was the key lens through which Muslim-majority societies could be understood. If women were oppressed it was because of the teachings of the Koran; if Muslims supposedly lacked an entrepreneurial spirit it was due to "Islamic tradition"; if modernization was rejected, again the Koran was to blame. In short, a whole host of characteristics associated with the West but allegedly absent from the "Muslim world" could be explained by recourse to religious texts and the mentalities they supposedly created. In this book, the term "Muslim world" has been put in quotation marks precisely to challenge the notion that Islam is the single most important factor in defining the people who live in the Middle East, North Africa, and elsewhere, or that there is a single undifferentiated entity called the "Muslim world." Instead, I try to show that like elsewhere in the world, religion is one factor among others that impact the lives of people who live in Muslim-majority societies (a term I prefer to "Muslim world").

In addition to civilizational theories, the Orientalists drew on the theories of race discussed above that placed European Caucasians at the top of a racial hierarchy. As Rodinson explains:

> The Oriental may always have been characterized as a savage enemy, but during the Middle Ages, he was at least considered on the same level as his European counterpart. And, to the men of the Enlightenment, the ideologues of the French revolution, the Oriental was, for all his foreignness in appearance and dress, above all a man like anyone else. In the nineteenth century, however, he became something quite separate, sealed off in his own specificity, yet worthy of a kind of grudging admiration. This is the origin of the *homo islamicus*, a notion widely accepted even today.[14]

Starting from this idea that Muslims are a race, Orientalists claimed to be able to explain the "Muslim mind" or the "Arab mind." Because race-based theories assume that the members of a race are all alike, scholars within this tradition could make sweeping generalizations about how Muslims think and behave. Most of all, the "Muslim mind" was disparaged; as the British poet Rudyard Kipling wrote, "You'll never plumb the Oriental mind. And even if you do, it won't be worth the toil."[15]

It followed from this logic of civilizational and racial superiority that the West had to lead lesser nations and peoples. In the late nineteenth century, when Kipling wrote "The White Man's Burden," he was simply reinforcing an idea that was by then widespread. Kipling wrote of the inherent superiority of the West and its "burden" to civilize and tame the peoples of the East. Characterized as "half devil, half child," the colonized were seen both as evil and barbaric and as childlike and therefore in need of protection. When the poem was originally published, Kipling used the subtitle "The United States and the Philippine Islands" as a way to urge the Americans to take on the same responsibilities as the British.[16]

And take them on they did. An American journalist writing in 1921 brought together Orientalist assumptions about civilization and race in the following way:

> Out of the prehistoric shadows the white races pressed to the front and proved in a myriad of ways their fitness for the hegemony of mankind. Gradually they forged a common civilization; then, when vouchsafed their unique opportunity of oceanic mastery four centuries ago, they spread over the earth, filling its empty spaces with their superior breeds and assuring to themselves an unparalleled paramountcy [sic] of numbers and dominion. . . . At last the planet was integrated under the hegemony of a single race with a common civilization.[17]

Woodrow Wilson, seen as visionary for championing self-determination, put it as follows:

> In order to trace the lineage of the European and American governments which have constituted the order of social life for those stronger and nobler races which have made the most notable progress in civilization, it is essential to know the political history of the Greeks, the Latins, the Teutons, and the Celts principally.[18]

In sum, the Orientalist view of the East as it emerged in the nineteenth century was based on a racial and civilizational vilification of Muslims. This is not, however, to suggest that Orientalist scholarship existed or was used in colonial contexts without contradiction. There were Orientalists who rejected notions of racial superiority; at the same time, however, they agreed that race was a useful category of analysis. There were those who admired Islam and others who disparaged it; some actively aided the colonial mission while others saw themselves as producing objective knowledge. Orientalist ideas were used differently in various contexts. Put simply, the relationship between Orientalist thought and the project of empire-building is complex.

However, it is undeniable that the aforementioned assumptions underlying all Orientalist scholarship lend themselves well to the call for colonial conquest. The worldview proposed by the Orientalists is one in which the "West" is seen as a dynamic, complex, and ever-changing society that cannot be reduced to its key religion or any other single factor, while the "Orient" or the "world of Islam" is presented as unchanging, barbaric, misogynistic, uncivilized, and despotic. The only logical conclusion that flows from this is that it is the responsibility of the West to intervene in these static societies and bring about change. The West had acquired a superiority complex and the rest of the world would have to submit to its dictates.

These ideas may have served to justify French and English conquest of the Middle East and North Africa in the nineteenth and twentieth centuries, but it was the United States that breathed new life into them after World War II. Even today, variations of these ideas can be found in American society. For instance, books like Raphael Patai's *The Arab Mind*,[19] which was used by the US military to devise the torture techniques used in Abu Ghraib and elsewhere, are a reassertion of *homo islamicus*. Modern-day Orientalists like Bernard Lewis and Samuel Huntington have argued that the conflict between the United States and the Middle East is a "clash of civilizations." According to Huntington, who has done much to popularize this notion, "Western ideas of individualism, liberalism, constitutionalism, human rights, equality, liberty, the rule of law, democracy, free markets, the separation of church and state, often have little resonance in Islamic societies."[20] In the following chapter, we will explore the continuity of the classical Orientalist corpus. Here we turn to American imperialism and its vision of empire and language of domination.

American Imperialism

Prior to the nineteenth century, very little was known in the United States about the "Muslim world." America's conquests focused more on continental expansion into the West and Southwest; other parts of the world did not matter very much. In the eighteenth century, Americans' key sources of information about the Middle East were *One Thousand and One Arabian Nights* and the King James Bible.[21] The political elite that founded and oversaw the American nation "after 1776 regarded the Muslim world, beset by oriental despotism, economic squalor, and intellectual stultification, as the antithesis of the republicanism to which they had pledged their sacred honor."[22]

Greater familiarity with the Middle East in the nineteenth century came from visitors to the Holy Land and from missionaries. Mark Twain, who went on to become a staunch anti-imperialist, wrote in 1869 about his trip to the Holy Land in a book titled *The Innocents Abroad*, which sold nearly a hundred thousand copies.[23] While Twain witheringly (and hilariously) critiqued his fellow travelers for their hubris and lack of cultural sensitivity—a characteristic of American tourists that would continue into the next century and become grist for the Hollywood mill—he also had harsh words to say about Muslims. He called them "a people by nature and training filthy, brutish, ignorant, unprogressive [and] superstitious," and saw the Ottomans as "a government whose Three Graces are Tyranny, Rapacity, [and] Blood."[24]

Romantic notions of the Orient dominated popular culture. Illustrated versions of *The Arabian Nights* were widely sold, as were books about the Prophet that presented the Arab world as backward and savage. In addition to novels and travelogues, a series of other popular media such as fairs and exhibitions, photographs, and theme parks transferred Europe's exotic image of the East to the United States.[25] In nineteenth-century Europe the Orientalist image and the exotic one coexisted, and the US audience readily adopted the latter. For instance, the American painter Frederick Bridgman produced dozens of sexually charged paintings of the East in line with those of his mentor, the French painter Jean-Léon Gérôme, famous for his paintings *The Snake Charmer* and *The Slave*.[26] Hollywood would further these exotic images in early silent films such as *The Arab* (1915), *Cleopatra* (1917), *Salome* (1918), and *An Arabian Knight* (1920), among others. Rudolph Valentino played a "Lawrence of Arabia"–type sheik in two films, *The Sheik* (1921) and *The Son of the Sheik* (1926), which among other things presented the East as sexually charged.

Outside of culture, in the realm of politics, little systematic knowledge was accumulated about the East. The American Oriental Society was founded in 1842, but it was not until World War II that the United States began to approach the study of the Middle East systematically, as Europe had.[27] Prior to this point, the relatively few US scholars who studied Islam and the East did so primarily through the lens of Orientalism and were situated in departments or institutes of "Near East studies" or "Oriental studies."[28] European Orientalists held cultural prestige within the field.[29]

The end of the Second World War changed this situation, as the United States emerged from the war as the strongest Western power. It set out to take the place of Britain and France in the Middle East and establish its dominance over the region. To do so, however, the United States needed information to guide its policy. At first, it could rely only on young men who had grown up in the region, children of missionaries or university professors, known as "Arabists." But in the context of the Cold War, and with the development of national liberation movements, the elites needed reliable information to further their interests in the region. The government and private foundations began to sponsor and fund "area studies" programs and departments that focused on the study of not only the Near East but also more broadly Asia, Africa, and Latin America. It was in this context that US universities turned toward the production of knowledge instrumental to serving the needs of empire. Two approaches guided the study of the Middle East: Orientalism, which was still dominated by philologists, and social scientific research, from which a new model known as "modernization" would be developed.

Prominent Orientalist scholars from Europe crossed the Atlantic to take up academic positions at US universities during the postwar era. H. A. R. Gibb, who was central to the development of the Orientalist approach in the United States, left Oxford to take a position at Harvard University in 1955. Gustave von Grunebaum, the Austrian Orientalist, influenced a new generation of scholars at the University of Chicago and then UCLA.[30] Between them they brought Orientalist modes of analysis to the United States and continued the work of influential late-nineteenth-century Orientalists like Ernest Renan. Gibb, for instance, argued that the "Arab mind" and the "Muslim mind" had an essence that could be grasped by reading the classical texts of Islam. Grunebaum argued that a static Islamic culture could help explain all contemporary phenomena. Such sweeping generalizations, characteristic of Orientalist scholarship, were influential in the United States because they provided a quick and easy way to grasp a large and complex region.

In the ensuing decades, Orientalism was challenged by social scientific research to such a degree that Gibb acknowledged some of the shortcomings of the Orientalist method and urged social scientists and Orientalists to work together.[31] However, despite the publication of a number of works critical of its assumptions and methods in the period after the 1970s, Orientalism survived. Bernard Lewis, the British Orientalist, can be credited with continuing the legacy and influence of Orientalism. Lewis accepted a position at Princeton University in 1974 and has been a key figure in Orientalist thought in the United States ever since.

The United States, however, could not simply accept *in toto* the language of the old empires. Its own anticolonial history meant that there were voices in the political sphere that resisted the mantle of imperialism. Even though it entered the imperial arena with the Spanish-American War of 1898, the "issue of self-rule was so deeply emplaced in the national psyche," Sidney Lens writes, that "an anti-imperialist opposition . . . began to form."[32] The Anti-Imperialist League, founded in November of 1898, included not only figures like Mark Twain but also prominent mainstream politicians. This trend of opposition in the mainstream was mitigated over the course of the twentieth century; nevertheless, it gave rise to an image of the United States as being a different kind of world power—different, that is, from the "old-style imperialism" of Europe.

This dynamic was played out concretely in the postwar era. The upheavals of World War II weakened the older empires and created a bipolar world oriented around two new powers, the United States and the Soviet Union. In this context, the United States hoped to loosen the aging imperial powers' grips on their colonial territories. The Truman and Eisenhower administrations therefore claimed to support anticolonial national liberation movements; concretely, they announced their intention to aid developing nations by supporting projects that would build infrastructure and foster economic growth. But this economic aid came at a price— they demanded political allegiance. For instance, the United States first sought to bring Gamal Abdel Nasser's Egypt under its wing through promises of financial aid. Nasser flirted with the Soviet Union, though, and the Eisenhower administration punished him by reneging on its promise to provide funding for the construction of a dam in Aswan. Nasser promptly nationalized the Suez Canal, which led Britain, France, and Israel to launch a war on Egypt. The United States (and the USSR) then intervened on Nasser's side, allowing Egypt to finally get rid of its former colonial master—Britain. This example reveals the carrot-and-stick approach that the American elite employed again and again during the Cold War: using monetary incentives to win allies, punishing them when they strayed, but also acting to weaken the hold of former colonizer nations when possible.

Secretary of state John Foster Dulles said of the Suez crisis that what "the British and French have done is nothing but the straight, old-fashioned variety of colonialism of the most obvious sort."[33] In contrast, the United States crafted a new model of imperialism on the basis of what Melani McAlister has called "benevolent supremacy." This model was premised on the notion that an American-dominated world would ensure liberty and democracy for all through the mechanism of free-market capitalism. Henry Luce, publisher of the magazines *Life* and *Time*, captured this new global role for the United States in an editorial titled "The New American Century." He argued that the United States was a "Good Samaritan" that would bring about "Freedom and Justice" around the world in the postwar period.[34]

McAlister states that, at the policy level, "benevolent supremacy" meant linking "US economic and military strength to a program that was anticommunist, anticolonial, and supportive of free markets."[35] The policy of anticolonialism was about supplanting the old colonial powers and was therefore highly selective. The United States supported anti-colonial struggles in some cases where its aims coincided with those of the anti-colonialists but thwarted other struggles (for instance, it came in on the side of France in Algeria and Indochina), and it had a few of its own colonies in the Caribbean and the Pacific. Above all, newly decolonized nations were not to oppose economic imperialism and the United States' access to markets and investment opportunities around the world. Sidney Lens explains that Washington's strategy revolved around three goals: to establish an "open door" policy that allowed the United States to enter into otherwise blocked-off markets and to establish multinational trade as the pillar of economic policy; to weaken and isolate forces that opposed the open door (which included the former colonial powers as well as radical nationalists and communists); and to gain, as President Kennedy put it, "influence and control" over pliant governments, typically right-wing, through "grants and loans with conditions attached to them, military aid, equipment and training of puppet armies, military pacts, CIA-sponsored revolts, and on occasion, when these other methods were inadequate . . . direct intervention by U.S. armed forces themselves."[36]

This new form of imperialism required a new language; that language was called "modernization theory." Area studies in the United States were dominated by this approach from the 1950s to the 1970s. Modernization theory draws on the work of Max Weber, distinguishing between "traditional" and "modern" societies. Traditional societies were agricultural and rural, slow to change, and politically authoritarian. Modern societies, on the other hand, were seen as industrial, quick to change, and politically democratic and egalitarian. The scholars who developed this approach offered various explanations for why traditional societies did not progress; some pointed to cultural factors, others to economic ones. At the end of the day, it was agreed that change would not come from within these societies but had to be brought from outside.

In short, it was a new way to divide the world into "us" and "them." According to the theorists of modernization, "our" society was dynamic, scientifically oriented, rational, supportive of individual development, democratic, and egalitarian, whereas "their" societies were static, hidebound, despotic, and authoritarian. What was needed, then, was Western intervention to "help" traditional societies make the transition to modernity. This view was not so different from earlier Orientalist notions, but it was wrapped in the credibility of social science. Modernization theorists didn't speculate about contemporary societies based on classical texts: they conducted empirical research and gathered data which was evaluated using quantitative data analysis techniques. This time it was real science—it had to be correct!

Daniel Lerner, author of the highly influential book *The Passing of Traditional Society: Modernizing the Middle East*, argued that people who live in modern societies are distinguished by their personalities, which he explained in psychological terms. Modern individuals have "empathy," which allows them to see themselves in the shoes of others and therefore to visualize and make possible social mobility. Traditional individuals do not have this capacity and are therefore in need of Western influence to help them shed their old, static ways.[37] Lerner's method of analysis was based on social scientific methods and the use of quantitative data. In the field of mass communication, Everett Rogers published *Diffusion of Innovations*, which studied how new ideas could be spread in traditional societies. Rogers concluded that those who were not open to "innovation" introduced by the West were best understood as "laggards."[38] In short, those who resisted Western propaganda/"innovation" were seen not as individuals acting in their own interests but rather as hidebound traditionalists blocking progress.

While Orientalism and modernization theory each had its own research traditions and methods, both shared a polarized view of the world: the East was inferior and the West was superior. Since neither theory could see change coming about internally in Eastern societies, both argued for Western intervention, which they claimed would benefit native/traditional peoples. Overall, few if any questioned the premise that research on the Middle East (and in area studies in general) should be tailored to meet the needs of the US government. This was the dominant trend until the 1970s. At that point, various factors, particularly the impact of successful national liberation struggles on the field of Middle East studies, led to a flurry of books and articles critical of both Orientalism and modernization theory.

Despite these critiques, the Orientalist and modernization schools of thought continued to flourish. In fact, they came together in the form of Samuel Huntington, the Harvard political scientist. In an essay published in the influential journal *Foreign Affairs* in 1968, Huntington drew on modernization theory to justify the United States' massive bombing of the Vietnamese countryside. Later, in the post–Cold War world, Huntington developed Lewis's concept of the "clash of civilizations" and helped to popularize Orientalist scholarship.

◆ ◆ ◆

This chapter focused on the birth of Orientalism in Europe during the period of modern colonialism, discussing the ways in which Orientalism as a body of thought was tied directly to the project of imperial conquest. While the story starts in Europe, it continues in the United States, which took over the mantle of colonial overlord in the "Muslim world" after World War II. The United States envisioned itself as a different kind of world power than "old Europe," and its imperial interests were projected through the lens of "benevolence." In essence, this meant anticommunism and free-market capitalism. Modernization theory emerged in this context to serve the needs of the "new" empire. Yet Orientalism's prestige and the emigration of Orientalist scholars from Europe to area studies programs in the United States meant that it too was influential in the political sphere.

Chapter 4 will look concretely at how the United States used both theories to develop policy in the Middle East. In particular, we look at its "Islam policy" and the ways in which it related to Islamist organizations.

It is now well known that the United States viewed the parties of political Islam as allies during the Cold War. In the 1980s, however, Israeli right-wingers and a group of foreign-policy hardliners called the neoconservatives began to project "Islamic terrorism" as a global threat akin to the Soviet Union (see chapter 7). In the post–Cold War period, these arguments—bolstered by Lewis, Huntington, and others—started to gain so much ground that the Oklahoma City bombing was first pinned on "Islamic terrorists" before the homegrown Timothy McVeigh was identified. In the immediate aftermath of this incident, and building upon the attempted bombing in 1993 of the World Trade Center, the omnibus Counterterrorism Act ratcheted up the climate of fear against Arab and Muslim "terrorists" (see chapter 8). Even so, at the level of foreign policy, the first Bush and the Clinton administrations eschewed this "clash of civilizations" rhetoric in favor of a "balance-of-forces realist" stance. It was not until the events of 9/11 that domestic and foreign policy converged to project the overarching Muslim threat. In the following chapter, we will see that this was not a hard task, given that Orientalist assumptions about the "Muslim world" were accepted and even taken for granted by the liberal establishment.

Chapter 3

The Persistence of Orientalist Myths

At a campaign stop during his run for the presidency in 2008, Republican candidate John McCain was confronted by an elderly white woman who said that she did not trust Barack Obama. McCain nodded in agreement until she added that Obama was an Arab. McCain replied: "No ma'am, no ma'am, he is a decent family man, citizen, that I just happen to have disagreements with."[1] Underlying this exchange was a whole host of assumptions about Arabs: that they are bad, cannot be trusted, are not American (Arab Americans don't count), are not decent people, and don't value family. Despite the seeming disagreement, McCain and his supporter shared an implicit view of Arabs as foreign terrorists.

Obama—the "liberal" candidate—responded to charges that he was a Muslim and a terrorist by insisting that he was a Christian. On the campaign trail, he asserted that he has attended the same Christian church for two decades, that he was sworn into office using his family Bible, and that he constantly pledges his allegiance to the flag in the Senate.[2] In short, he did nothing to challenge the association of Muslims and Arabs with terrorism, tacitly accepting the anti-Muslim logic that passes for conventional wisdom in mainstream US politics.

Since the events of 9/11, politicians and the media have not just promoted Islamophobia—they've turned the dial up to eleven. This rhetoric was not invented after September 2001; it has a long history, as we saw in the previous two chapters. This chapter will examine some images of Muslims that have persisted to the point of becoming "common

41

sense"—ideas which are believed to be true and so obvious that they need no verification. In particular, we will look at five myths about Islam and Muslims. I use the term "myth" for both its meanings—as a traditional story of supposedly historic events that shed light on the worldview of a people, and as a false and questionable story. Myths about Islam in the twenty-first century are indeed historical, but they are based on a distorted or selective interpretation of the past. The goal of this chapter is to outline how these Islamophobic myths evolved out of Orientalist thought and earlier traditions, and then debunk them.

Myth One: Islam Is a Monolithic Religion

In the eleventh century, when the image of the Muslim enemy was beginning to crystallize, religious scholars commissioned by the European elite made few attempts to understand the various branches of Islam and their actual practice by Muslims around the world. Instead, they wanted to expose Muhammad as an impostor and Islam as a false religion. Not much time was invested in learning how Islam had incorporated the cultural practices of the empires and peoples it conquered or how it was transformed by different cultures taking various forms in various regions.

While today only those on the far right would claim that Islam is a false religion, it is often taken for granted that Islam is homogenous. This is in large part because Orientalists, like their medieval counterparts, propagated the myth that Islam is a monolith that can be fully understood through its classical texts. Only working from such an assumption can anyone make claims about a static entity called "Muslim civilization" with a core set of unchanging values, or about the "Muslim mind" (viewed, of course, in the singular, as though all Muslims shared a hive mind). It is only by denying the diversity of Islamic history and practices that one can then argue that Islam has certain inherent, unchanging characteristics that render it antidemocratic, violent, sexist, and so on. The myths discussed in this chapter emerge from this core assumption that Islam is a monolith.

Even a cursory look at the practice of Islam around the world shows this myth to be patently false. One and a half billion people around the world are Muslims—85 percent are Sunni and 15 percent are Shi'a.[3] Within these two main denominations, there are many more branches. Muslim-majority countries and regions span the globe, from Indonesia to Bangladesh to several central Asian countries, the Middle East, and

North Africa. In most of these countries Islam is the dominant religion, hence the term "Muslim-majority countries." But these countries are also home to Christians, Jews, and people of other faiths, as well as atheists. India, a predominantly Hindu country, is home to more than a hundred million Muslims.

Islam looks different in each of these regions and countries, largely because as it spread, people imbued it with their own local customs and traditions. The Sufi Islam practiced in northern India is quite different from the Shi'a Islam practiced in Lebanon, which is in turn different from the Sunni Islam practiced in Pakistan. Even within a single branch of Islam there are customs and practices that vary by region and across time. Thus, the Islam of seventh-century Arabia is different from the Wahhabism that exists today in Saudi Arabia. Religious texts may be more or less fixed, but all of the world's religions, including Islam, have changed and adapted based on historical transformations.

Much of the current Islamophobic rhetoric seeks to demonize Arabs in particular. As we saw in the example at the start of this chapter, Obama was "accused" of being an Arab, which is shorthand for "Muslim" in some quarters. Let us note, therefore, a simple point: all Muslims are not Arabs, and all Arabs are not Muslims. Arabs are people who speak Arabic, share certain common cultural traditions, and claim a common Arab ethnic identity.[4] Geographically, the Arab world has traditionally been divided into two parts: the Maghreb or the West, which includes Morocco, Libya, Algeria, Tunisia, Sudan, and other countries west of the Nile, and the Mashreq or the East, which includes Egypt, Syria, Lebanon, and all the countries to the east of the Nile up to, but not including, Iran. Because of linguistic and cultural differences, Iranians and Turks are not considered Arabs.

Thus, if we actually look, even briefly as we have above, at the diversity of the people who follow Islam, we find not only that there is no biological or ethnic basis for *homo islamicus* but that the notion of a monolithic Islam immediately falls on its face. So too does the Orientalist claim that there is a transhistoric "Islamic civilization" which is based on a core set of values and from which one can explain a host of contemporary phenomena. Yet this is precisely the logic we will find at work in the following myths, which assert that Islam is inherently sexist, irrational, violent, and undemocratic. The homogenization of Islam and of Muslims is so taken for granted that it functions as the basis of all of the other myths. Said noted that the influential Orientalist Grunebaum "produced a solid *oeuvre* that concentrated on Islam as a holistic culture about which, from beginning to end of his career, he continued to make the same set of essentially reductive, negative generalizations."[5] This pattern can be found not only in scholarship but in popular culture as well.[6]

Myth Two: Islam Is a Uniquely Sexist Religion

While sexually repressed Europe was fascinated and titillated by Muslim marriage customs even during medieval times, there was no systematic discussion of women and Islam until the nineteenth century. Commenting on Europe's nineteenth-century obsession with Muslim women, one scholar stated that there "is no subject connected with Islam which Europeans have thought more important than the condition of Muslim women."[7] The dominant narrative that emerged was one that presented Muslim women as severely subjugated, oppressed, and little more than slaves. Just as the Muslim despots tyrannized their subjects, it was argued, they also tyrannized their wives and daughters. As various scholars have shown, in reality the European men who wrote about the plight of Muslim women had little access to these women to verify their assumptions. Coterminous accounts by Western women of the Muslim women they encountered reveal a more complex reality.[8] Nevertheless, this narrative of the oppressed brown woman serviced the colonial enterprise. Western men could now ride off in their jodhpurs and pith helmets to rescue them.

One pith-helmeted English gentleman who rose to the occasion was Evelyn Baring, first Earl of Cromer, more famously known as Lord Cromer. When Britain invaded and occupied Egypt in 1882, Cromer was entrusted to oversee the occupation. He wrote that "Islam as a social system has been a complete failure. . . . The degradation of women in the East is a canker that begins its destructive work early in childhood, and has eaten into the whole system of Islam." The solution was that Muslims "be persuaded or forced into imbibing the true spirit of western civilization."[9] At home, this champion of Egyptian women's rights worked feverishly to deny British women the right to vote as a founding member and president of the Men's League for Opposing Women's Suffrage. This was not a contradiction for Cromer, who was a social conservative at home but an enlightened colonizer abroad. As a colonial overlord, he was not putting forward a statement of principle but rather simply deploying arguments useful to the colonial mission.

More than a century later, it should come as no surprise that President George W. Bush, whose policy record was firmly antiwoman, should masquerade as the rescuer of Afghan women. One of Bush's first acts after coming to power was to cut funding to international groups that provide abortion services to women, yet he billed the war on Afghanistan as necessary to rescue Afghan women: "We have obviously serious problems with the Taliban government. They're an incredibly repressive government, a government that has a value system that's hard for many in America . . . to relate to. Incredibly repressive toward women."[10] Perhaps it was the "incredible" part that impressed Dubya, for his own life is steeped in sexist assumptions and practices. At any rate, a whole slew of female politicians, and even feminist organizations such as Feminist Majority, came out in support of the war. Laura Bush, temporarily morphed into a feminist crusader, claimed: "Because of our recent military gains in much of Afghanistan, women are no longer imprisoned in their homes. They can listen to music and teach their daughters without fear of punishment. Yet the terrorists who helped rule that country now plot and plan in many countries. And they must be stopped. The fight against terrorism is also a fight for the rights and dignity of women."[11] In reality, conditions for women in Afghanistan, particularly in rural areas, deteriorated after the US invasion. This point was made quite strongly by women's rights advocate Malalai Joya, the youngest woman ever elected to the Afghan parliament; the United States responded by barring her entrance into the country for a speaking tour in 2011 until public protest erupted.[12]

Despite this reality, the logic that Muslim women are oppressed and therefore need to be rescued by the West continues to hold ground. The Islamic veil has been the subject of much controversy. Seen ubiquitously as a symbol of Muslim women's oppression, the veil has been banned, scorned, or otherwise used to advance the aforementioned colonial argument. In April 2011, the French government recycled this argument when it banned women from wearing the veil in public—running roughshod over religious freedom in the process. Absent from this discourse are the voices of Muslim women themselves, who could construct an alternative narrative—one which speaks to a self-conscious choice made by autonomous individuals. As I have argued elsewhere, such a move would entail a shift in the terms of discussion: instead of being portrayed as voiceless victims, Muslim women would become actors capable of changing their own circumstances.[13] Needless to say, this will not do—at least not for imperial nations that are hell-bent on "rescuing" Muslim women whether they like it or not.

However, once we have dispensed with imperial chicanery, the next logical question is whether Islam is uniquely sexist. To advance this argument, one may point to the fact that women's rights have been severely curtailed by right-wing Islamist regimes such as the Taliban in Afghanistan and the Conservative Alliance in Iran. We might respond to this point in two ways. First, the parties of political Islam adapt religion to serve their political goals in much the same way as American fundamentalists have used Christianity to attack women's rights. Second, *all* of the world's major religions are to a greater or lesser extent sexist. Singling out Islam for its sexist practices in the mainstream media and public discourse is not a historical oversight but a systematic attempt to construct "our" values and religion as being enlightened in contrast with "theirs."

One could, for instance, point to sexism in the history of Christianity and in Christian-majority societies quite easily. The Christian creation myth tells us that Eve was created out of Adam's rib, and that women's pain in childbirth is a punishment for Eve's disobedience to God. Women who were thought to be witches were burned at the stake not only in Europe but in colonial America, barely three centuries ago. Nicaragua, Chile, El Salvador, and Malta, all predominantly Catholic countries, ban abortion without exception, even if the woman's life is in danger.[14] The United States has yet to elect a female head of state, while Muslim-majority countries like Pakistan, Bangladesh, and Indonesia have already done so. What is worse is that the "enlightened" United States continues to curtail women's rights. Only 13 percent of US counties offer abortion services. Several states have passed laws that allow pharmacists to refuse to fill birth control prescriptions, including emergency contraception. And at the same time that women's rights to control their bodies have been restricted, attention on the fetus has increased. These restrictions on women's rights are due in no small part to the influence of the Christian Right on US politics. This is similar to the dynamic in many Muslim-majority countries, where the emergence of Islamist groups has led to a decline in women's status.

Even if we examine Islam on its own terms, there is much debate about the role of women. The Koran, like any religious text, lends itself to multiple interpretations. There are passages in the Koran that grant women the same rights as men to divorce and that permit them to own and inherit property, marking a step forward for women in Arab society at the time.[15]

There are, however, also passages that condone polygamy and that restrict women's inheritance rights to only half of what men receive.[16]

Scholars like Leila Ahmed and Asma Barlas have argued that Islam is not inherently misogynistic. They point to the egalitarian passages in the Koran that suggest equality between men and women. Barlas argues that sexist interpretations of the Koran are products of particular societies that needed religious authority to justify gender inequality.[17] Ahmed states that prior to the institutionalization of Islam, women in Arab society participated in warfare and religion and had sexual autonomy. Montgomery Watt even goes so far as to argue that Arab society at the time was predominantly matrilineal.[18] However, Maxime Rodinson rejects this analysis, describing Arabia in this period instead as a patrilineal society where polyandrous practices, combined with substantial social roles for women, prevailed in certain regions.[19] Prophet Muhammad's first wife Khadija was a wealthy woman who was forty when she proposed to the twenty-five-year-old Muhammad. Khadija had been married twice before and was widowed; it was Muhammad's first marriage.

As Islam spread, it adopted the cultural practices of various empires, including those of the neighboring Persian and Byzantine empires. The Christians who populated the Middle East and the Mediterranean had more rigid customs associated with women. In the Christian Byzantine Empire, the sexes were segregated. Women were not to be seen in public, were veiled, and were given only rudimentary education. As the expanding Islamic empire incorporated these regions, it also assimilated these cultural and social practices.[20] In other words, the particular misogynistic practices that Islam came to adopt were largely inherited from the Christian and Jewish religious customs of the neighboring societies Muslims conquered. The significant point here is that sexist attitudes toward women, far from being unique to Islam, were prevalent among Christians and Jews as well.

The women of this region had seen their rights curtailed under Western influence before. Ahmed shows that a similar fate befell Egyptian women when the Greeks conquered Egypt in 333 BCE.[21] In Greek society, women led segregated lives, cared for the young, and were "veritable children" under the law. The Greek philosopher Aristotle believed that the male "is by nature superior, and the female inferior, and the one rules and the other is ruled."[22] By contrast, in Egyptian society, women had a high status, especially upper-class women. In the New

Kingdom (1570–950 BCE), Egyptian women and men were considered equals under the law. Women had the right to inherit, own, and manage property, marriage laws were egalitarian, and women could move freely and without seclusion. That doesn't mean it was not a male-dominated society—but the bonds of oppression were looser than those found in Greek society.

So much for the Orientalist myth of liberty and women's rights as enduring "core values" of the West from ancient Greece to the present. In reality the great "liberal" Western tradition is not only mired in sexism but—as the case of Egypt shows—has even played a part in curtailing women's rights in the East. Moreover, it is crucial to remember that the rights that women *do* enjoy anywhere in the world today are the result of struggles waged by women (and men) for those rights. It took no less than a hundred years of bitter struggles for women to win the right to vote in the United States.

Myth Three: The "Muslim Mind" Is Incapable of Reason and Rationality

In a 2006 speech, "Faith, Reason, and the University," Pope Benedict XVI equated Catholicism with reason and Islam with violence and a lack of reason. Paraphrasing a fourteenth-century Byzantine emperor, he argued that when a religion (like Islam) is spread through violence it goes against reason and also against nature, for "not to act in accordance with reason is contrary to God's nature."[23] In making this argument, the Pope joined a long line of Orientalists who have argued that reason, rationality, and science are alien to the world of Islam.

The French Orientalist Ernest Renan, who championed science and reason, stated in his 1883 essay "Islam and Science" that "early Islam and the Arabs who professed it were hostile to the scientific and philosophic spirit."[24] In a lecture at the Sorbonne, he said:

> Anyone with any knowledge of current affairs can see quite clearly the actual inferiority of the Muslim countries, the decadence of the states governed by Islam, the intellectual barrenness of the races that derive their culture and education from that religion alone. All those who have traveled to the East or to Africa have been struck by the totally narrow mind of the true believer, the kind of iron band around his head that closes him off completely from science and

makes him quite incapable of learning anything or opening his mind to any new ideas.[25]

Renan made sweeping generalizations about the "narrow minds" of people who live in the East and in Africa, who because of their adherence to Islam are an intellectually barren race. What we see here are not only racist assertions about Muslims but also the idea that Islam has stunted scientific growth. When challenged to explain the flourishing of science in Islamic empires in the Middle Ages, Renan replied that the Arabs, like other "Semites," were incapable of science. The Abbasid caliphate, he added, was essentially Greek and Persian, even if it used Arabic. Thus, it was the "Aryans" who were responsible for this flowering of science.[26]

Cromer, whom we encountered in his pith helmet earlier in Egypt, had this to say in his two-volume book *Modern Egypt*:

> The European is a close reasoner; his statements of fact are devoid of ambiguity; he is a natural logician, albeit he may not have studied logic; he is by nature skeptical and requires proof before he can accept the truth of any proposition; his trained intelligence works like a piece of mechanism. The mind of the Oriental, on the other hand, like his picturesque streets, is eminently wanting in symmetry. His reasoning is of the most slipshod description. Although the ancient Arabs acquired in a somewhat higher degree the science of dialectics, their descendants are singularly deficient in the logical faculty. They are often incapable of drawing the most obvious conclusions from any simple premises of which they may admit the truth.[27]

Unlike Renan, Cromer is kind enough to admit that Arabs and Muslims once grasped the "science of dialectics"—but today, he claims, they are completely deficient in logic and reasoning. While this caricature persists even in the early twenty-first century, as the Pope's statement made clear, biological racism of the kind seen above has more or less been replaced by cultural racism.[28]

While today such blatantly racist arguments as Cromer's are advanced only by those on the far right, it isn't hard to see how the overall logic of irrationality pervades many discussions. Often, those who are seen as "terrorists" are presented as crazed, irrational, and fanatical: as individuals who commit untold horrors with no clear reason or motivation.[29] Palestinian suicide bombers, for instance, are presented as rabid lunatics rather than as people driven to extreme measures under conditions of occupation.[30] Terrorists cannot be reasoned with; rather, we are told, they are driven by irrational motivations and must therefore be put on "kill lists."

The debate on whether Iran should be allowed to have nuclear weapons draws from these arguments. Republican candidate and former New York City mayor Rudolph Giuliani argued that "the reality is the use of military force against Iran would be very dangerous. . . . It would be very provocative. The only thing worse would be Iran being a nuclear power. It's the worst nightmare of the Cold War, isn't it? The nuclear weapons in the hands of an irrational person, an irrational force. Ahmadinejad is clearly irrational."[31] These lines of demarcation are familiar: "irrational" Iran and the "rational" West. Little discussion is devoted to why Iran, as a rational political actor, might want to acquire nuclear weapons; it is, after all, surrounded by nuclear powers such as India, Pakistan, China, Russia, and Israel, and by US bases in Qatar, Iraq, Turkey, Uzbekistan, and Afghanistan, any of which might harbor nuclear weapons.

There are many ways to debunk this myth about Islam, science, and rationality, and many excellent books and articles that tear to shreds the very concept of biologically defined races and the spurious connection between biology and intellectual capacity. (See, for instance, the various excellent critiques of the book *The Bell Curve*.)[32] Here, however, I will expand in more detail on the point raised in chapter 1—that the West would not have gone through the Renaissance had it not been for the scientific contributions made by the Abbasids and the kingdoms of al-Andalus.

During the seventh century, while Europe was mired in the Dark Ages, Islam came onto the scene and Muslim armies established a vast empire that stretched from Central Asia through parts of Europe all the way to the Atlantic Ocean. The Muslim rulers of the Umayyad and Abbasid dynasties (661–1258 CE) recognized the advanced development of the kingdoms and cultures they had conquered and took it upon themselves to assimilate and adopt these cultures. They established libraries and translation centers where the great works of science, medicine, and philosophy, both Eastern and Western, were collected and translated. This age of translation was followed by a period of great creativity as a new generation of Muslim thinkers and scientists built upon this knowledge and made their own contributions.

The Persian scholar Ibn Sina—known in Western histories as Avicenna—laid the basis for the study of logic, science, philosophy, politics, and medicine. Ibn Rushd systematized Aristotle's thought so as to introduce rationalism and antimysticism to a new audience; he also went beyond Aristotle to promote rational thought as a virtue in itself. Ibn Rawandi wrote several books questioning the basic principles not only of Christianity and Judaism but of Islam as well. Ibn Rawandi belonged to the Mu'tazilite sect, which went so far as to question whether the Koran was really a collection of the revelations that Muhammad received from God. They used rationalist thinking, fragments of Greek philosophy, and their own observations to develop theories to explain the physical world.[33] In short, science thrived in the world of the Islamic empires.

When Europe emerged from its period of stagnation, its Renaissance in art, culture, and the sciences drew on this enduring legacy as European thinkers flocked to the great Muslim libraries, not only to relearn their own history and tradition but also to absorb the further development of this tradition by Muslim thinkers.[34] This history is either ignored or revised by past and present-day Orientalists, who present the "West" as a mythical entity that apparently developed in isolation from the rest of the world.

It is also significant that the Pope, in denouncing Islam for lacking reason, failed to bring up the Catholic Church's hostile opposition to the scientific revolution and to the birth of nonreligious and rational ways of understanding the world. The scientific revolution and, more broadly, the Enlightenment stood in opposition to Christian dogma and were viewed as a threat by the Church. Scientists who employed reason and rationality to explain the physical world were severely punished. Giordano Bruno, who championed the Copernican system of astronomy, was imprisoned for eight years by the Roman and Venetian Inquisitions for refusing to recant his beliefs. He was later burned at the stake. Galileo was similarly brought before the Inquisition and placed under house arrest for the rest of his life.

The Pope's speech is deeply rooted in Orientalist myths; it presents a particular vision of a rational and enlightened "West" while obscuring Christianity's own history of violence. He quotes the Byzantine emperor Manuel II Paleologus, who said, "Show me just what Mohammed brought that was new, and there you will find things only evil and inhuman, such as his command to spread by the sword the faith he preached."[35] It is ironic that Joseph Ratzinger—who was elected Pope Benedict XVI after serving as head of the Vatican office of the Congregation for the Doctrine of the Faith (formerly known as the Inquisition)—could denounce the spreading of religion through violence and face little or no criticism. This is in no small part due to another deeply entrenched myth: that Islam is at its core a violent religion.

Myth Four: Islam Is an Inherently Violent Religion

Barely moments after the Twin Towers came crashing down, US politicians and pundits began to associate that act of violence with Islam in ways not dissimilar to earlier Orientalist constructions. From the public speeches of mainstream political figures to the rants of right-wingers such as Ann Coulter to the proclamations of the Pope and others, a slew of comments too numerous to list here connected the actions of a handful of extremists to the religion of Islam.

This myth has a long history. As we saw in chapter 1, its origins go back to the eleventh century and the start of the Crusades. One contemporary echo can be found in a cartoon of the Prophet Muhammad published in the Danish newspaper *Jyllands-Posten* in 2005. This cartoon featured the Prophet with a bomb on his turban, implying that Islam came into being with violence at its core. Muslims around the world protested angrily, but thanks to the actions of a small number of Islamists, the protests were interpreted in the West not as legitimate offense against an ancient slur but as a dogmatic response to the publishing of an image of the Prophet. Liberal columnists endorsed this position, defending the cartoonists on the grounds of free speech, and many US newspapers carried the cartoon on the same grounds, without recognizing or acknowledging that the cartoon itself endorsed the myth of an inherently violent Islam.

The association of Islam with violence has only continued under the Obama administration. After Major Nidal Hassan turned a gun against his comrades and killed thirteen of them at Fort Hood in November 2009, the dominant explanation in the media linked Islam to violence.[36] One article in *Forbes* even went so far as to suggest that Hassan's actions could be better understood through the phrase "going Muslim," which describes a process whereby a Muslim "discards his apparent integration into American society and elects to *vindicate his religion* in an act of messianic violence against his fellow Americans" (italics added).[37] The essence of the argument is that Muslims are like ticking time bombs programmed by their religion to inevitably turn to violence and as such do not belong in American society. The "Ground Zero mosque" controversy in 2010 extended this association. Those opposed to the construction of an Islamic community center in downtown Manhattan argued that any symbol of Islam was offensive to the 9/11 victims' families. This argument is premised on the notion that Islam itself was to blame for the events of 9/11, rather than particular fundamentalist interpretations of the religion.

In his book *"Islam" Means Peace*, Amitabh Pal debunks this myth by pointing to the rich tradition of nonviolence in Islam. The book not only cites pacifist passages from the Koran and the Hadiths but also casts a spotlight on nonviolent protest movements in Muslim-majority societies which are largely unknown.[38] To this must be added Christianity's history of violence, if for no other reason than to question why it is so often sidelined, particularly in contrast to Islam's constantly cited history of violence. The claim that Islam was spread through war in the initial stages after its emergence in Arabia is indeed accurate. In the two decades after the Prophet's death in 632 CE, Muslim armies defeated its two great neighbors, the Byzantine and Persian (Sassanid) Empires, conquered large segments of their land, and set up an Islamic empire. They were able to defeat these two powerful empires because constant warfare between the Byzantines and the Persians over the previous century had left the people war-weary. In other words, war was a constant fact of life at the time. In fact, some villages welcomed the Muslim armies. Once in power the Muslim invaders gave their subjects the choice of either converting to Islam or paying a tax (unlike their Orthodox Christian counterparts, who persecuted heretics and ruled through fear, intimidation, and terror).

Christianity too rose to dominance through conquest and conversion, first in the Roman world and then in the neighboring areas of Europe, Armenia, Arabia, eastern Africa, and central Asia.[39] As previously noted, the Crusades, waged by European Christians from the eleventh century to the thirteenth, were another violent chapter in Christianity's history. During the First Crusade in 1099, crusaders launched a killing spree after taking control of Jerusalem, murdering almost the entire population of Muslim men, women, and children. The Jews, who fought side by side with the Muslims to defend the city, were not spared either. The crusaders set fire to a synagogue in which Jews had taken refuge and made sure that every one of them burned to death.[40] This was not an anomaly: crusaders passing through Germany en route to Jerusalem had murdered Jews in cold blood. Christians were among the victims. When the crusaders attacked Constantinople in 1203, "for three days and nights, the Crusaders murdered, raped, looted or destroyed everyone and everything they could get their hands on. Untold thousands perished; many more were brutalized, maimed and left homeless."[41] King Richard of England (known as Richard the Lionheart) beheaded thousands of men in full view of their armies after a battle. In contrast, after Saladin, the sultan of Egypt, successfully retook Jerusalem from the crusaders, he forbade acts of vengeance and violence against the crusaders, gave Jews state money to rebuild synagogues, and left churches untouched.[42] This is consistent with the manner in which the Muslim empires treated Christians and Jews. During five hundred years of Muslim reign in Jerusalem, from the seventh century to the eleventh, Christian churches were left alone and Jews were permitted to return and resettle in the area. This harmony was violently interrupted by the Crusades, when Christian armies wreaked havoc in the region, destroying synagogues and mosques and killing Jews, Muslims, and Christians.

Christian empires were no less brutal toward their own populations. This ranged from the persecution faced by non-Orthodox Christians in the Byzantine Empire to the Vatican's intolerance toward non-Catholic Christians and Jews. Still to come was the Inquisition, a series of movements orchestrated by the Catholic Church and Christian orthodoxy to reassert the Church's economic control over Europe. The Spanish Inquisition, for instance, is remembered for its utter brutality, mass torture, and the burning of men and women at the stake. Many Jews and Christians fled Europe to escape the Inquisition and sought a new home under the Muslim Ottoman Empire (1299–1922). Ottoman society was far more tolerant; Jews and Christians lived peacefully there, and some attained high positions in the bureaucracy (sometimes even without converting to Islam).

Looking at Christianity's brutal history today, one might well advance an argument that all Catholics are bloodthirsty fanatics. Indeed, this logic would be analogous to the argument that Islam is inherently violent and that Muslims have a "predisposition" toward violence. Yet such a generalization is unthinkable. To my knowledge, no mainstream newspaper or magazine has drawn a straight line between the Crusades and the Nazi Holocaust of Jews, let alone between the birth of Christ and various acts of terrorism committed by Christian fundamentalists. Furthermore, as Talal Asad argues, the same people who call the actions of suicide bombers unjustified legitimize the American wars in Iraq and Afghanistan, which have caused the deaths of hundreds of thousands. In short, only the violence of certain groups is highlighted and coded as a product of those groups' religious affinity.

Myth Five: Muslims Are Incapable of Democracy and Self-Rule

As we have seen, the notion of "Oriental despotism" was developed in the eighteenth century by writers like Montesquieu, who argued that the hot climate of the East made Orientals supine and submissive and thus unable to resist tyranny. The Orientalists gave this theory academic credibility by stating that despotism was one of the core values of "Islamic civilization." And modernization theory would make it even more scientific by suggesting that "traditional" societies were characterized by hierarchical systems of power. Since, these theorists argued, change would never come from within, it was the burden of the West to civilize, modernize, and democratize the East. This "white man's burden" argument has been used, in different forms and guises, by every imperial power since.

Arthur James Balfour, who famously penned the Balfour Declaration recognizing Zionists' claim for a state in Palestine, put it this way in 1910:

> First of all, look at the facts of the case. Western nations as soon as they emerge into history show the beginnings of those capacities for self-government . . . having merits of their own. . . . You may look through the whole history of the Orientals in what is called, broadly speaking, the East, and you never find traces of self-government. All their great centuries—and they have been very great—have been passed under despotisms, under absolute governments. All their great contributions to civilization—and they have been great—have been made under that form of government. Conqueror has succeeded conqueror; one domination has followed another; but never in all the revolutions of fate and fortune have you seen one of those nations of its own motivation establish what we, from a Western point of view, call self-government.[43]

Balfour went on to add that Britain was in Egypt therefore not only for the sake of the Egyptians but "for the sake of Europe at large." This was the burden of the great British Empire, he concluded, and they must bear it with grace and dignity.

What then if the ungrateful native should choose self-rule over the enlightened colonial overlord? What was Balfour's Britain to make of the movements for national liberation then starting to emerge in Egypt, India, and other colonized nations? Such struggles for self-determination had to be explained away. One way this was done was to assert that the leaders of these movements were misguided agitators who could not understand what was in their own best interests. As Cromer argued, "the real future of Egypt . . . lies not in the direction of a narrow nationalism, which will only embrace native Egyptians . . . but rather in that of an enlarged cosmopolitanism."[44] In other words, the subject people should shut up and realize that they are better off as members of the global British Empire.

Echoes of such attitudes were to be found in the United States as well. In 1907, President Theodore Roosevelt, who shared Balfour's and Cromer's views of Egyptians, stated that they were "a people of Moslem fellahin who have never in all time exercised any self-government whatever." A firm believer in race hierarchies and the "white man's burden," he asserted that Muslims were an inferior people: "It is impossible to expect moral, intellectual and material well-being where Mohammedism is supreme."[45] Often these ideas were used to explain why it was that "democracy-loving" imperialists couldn't bring democracy to the countries they colonized—the people just weren't ready for it. At other times it was suggested that colonialism paved the way for self-rule and that without such Western influence democracy would not have taken root in the East.[46]

Almost a century later, the George W. Bush administration, after it failed to unearth WMDs in Iraq, would use this myth to argue that the United States needed to stay in order to bring democracy—a proposition that received widespread public support. I was part of an antiwar coalition that opposed the upcoming war on Iraq until the actual invasion; once Bush declared that the United States would stay to rebuild the country and establish democracy, though, I found almost unanimous agreement in the coalition that this was indeed the right thing to do. The United States has similarly stated at various points that one of its goals in Afghanistan is "nation-building"—and liberals as well as antiwar feminists accepted this logic.[47] In reality, the United States has never had an interest in bringing democracy to the people of the Middle East, or to any other people for that matter. If anything, it has a long and sordid record of wrecking democratic movements and replacing them with dictatorships.[48]

This trend can be observed in the Middle East in the postwar period. After World War II, the Middle East and North Africa were rocked by national liberation struggles. Between 1932 and 1962, Egypt, Iraq, Syria, Lebanon, Libya, Morocco, Tunisia, and Algeria all succeeded in shaking off the hold of their colonial masters. In the wake of these struggles there was a widespread desire for reform and change in the region, and new political and social forces emerged. Secular Arab nationalism gained a stronghold, but socialist and communist parties also vied for political influence. The United States publicly supported national liberation struggles but nevertheless intervened when it saw an opportunity to weaken the hold of Britain and France; its interests did not (and do not) lie in supporting democratic movements on their own terms. In fact, secular nationalists who failed to comply with American interests were reviled. John Foster Dulles, as Eisenhower's secretary of state, called Nasser and other Arab nationalists like him "pathological" for their suspicion of the West and referred to the secular nationalist Iranian leader Mohammed Mossadegh as "a wily Oriental."[49] Eisenhower himself believed that secular nationalists were little more than Oriental despots. He said: "If you go and live with these Arabs, you will find that they simply cannot understand our ideas of freedom and dignity. . . . They have lived so long under dictatorships of one form or another, how can we expect them to run successfully a free government?"[50]

In truth, the United States had little interest in "bringing democracy" to the region. Its activity in the Middle East is motivated by one chief objective: namely, to control the oil wealth of that region, at any cost. Consequently, its foreign policy has been directed toward preventing the emergence of any government or movement that might threaten its dominance in the region, as discussed in the previous chapter. In order to achieve this aim it has consistently supported dictators and repressive regimes (such as the Saudi monarchy and others in the Gulf) that can be relied upon to act in the interests of the West. It has further funded, trained, and armed the military and security forces of its dictatorial allies so as to prevent domestic challenges to their rule. This strategy has largely been successful until fairly recently; over the years, various movements for progressive change have been squashed by US-backed dictators. Should that fail, the United States continues to maintain powerful naval forces and military bases in the region.

When necessary, and where possible, the United States has intervened militarily, such as in 1958 when US Marines briefly entered Lebanon to block an attempt by Arab nationalist forces to topple the pro-Western government in power. It also supported Islamist groups that opposed secular nationalists and communists in various countries, as we will see in the next chapter. Covert CIA operations have served as another handy tool, using assassination attempts, coups, and other such means to dispose of unfriendly governments and political organizations. In 1953, the CIA toppled Mohammed Mossadegh, who had been democratically elected to power in Iran in 1951. Mossadegh's crime was nationalizing the oil industry. He was replaced by Reza Pahlavi, the Shah, who ruled with an iron fist, murdered and tortured tens of thousands of political dissenters, and abolished all political parties but his own.[51] In this, the United States was simply taking a page from Britain, which similarly militated against constitutional and democratic movements in Persia (and Egypt) at the turn of the nineteenth century.[52]

Despite the hot weather, people in the Middle East and North Africa have fought for self-rule and progressive reforms. Yet when they have done so, instead of receiving American support, they have seen their democratic aspirations quashed. This effort continues: in 2011, another wave of mass struggle burst onto the historic stage in the Middle East and North Africa. In a matter of weeks, grassroots movements in Tunisia and Egypt swept from power two pro-Western dictators who had ruled with an iron fist for decades. Democracy and political freedom were key demands in the Arab uprisings of 2011. The United States' response was at first to stand by its dictatorial allies. When it became clear that they would be swept aside, it embraced the grassroots movements rhetorically. In reality, the United States has either tried to co-opt sections of the resistance (Libya) as a way to limit the scope of change, or supported the forces of counterrevolution, from the Egyptian army to various Gulf states (Saudi Arabia and Qatar in particular are leading the counterrevolutionary efforts).

Despite the wave of movements against dictatorship, the doddering old Orientalist Bernard Lewis continued to maintain that democracy will not work for Arabs; a consultative system that comes out of traditional Islamic culture would be better. As he put it, "We, in the Western world particularly, tend to think of democracy in our own terms—that's natural and normal—to mean periodic elections in our style. But I think it's a great mistake to try and think of the Middle East in those terms and that can only lead to disastrous results, as you've already seen in various places." Echoing an older argument, he added that "they are simply not ready for free and fair elections. . . . I think we should let them do it their way by consultative groups."[53] Lewis was speaking here to Western leaders; he seemed to be advising them that the "problem" of the various people's movements cannot be solved through Western-style elections because the "language of Western democracy is for the most part newly translated and not intelligible to the great masses."[54] Even in the twenty-first century, the natives, the unwashed masses, still don't know better. Their systematic organizing and Twitter-based publicity for free elections, more political parties, and greater political freedom are best ignored; instead the West, which still knows best, should guide them to accept Islamic forms of governance for which they are better suited. Old habits die hard.

◆ ◆ ◆

These five myths have dominated the national political conversation ever since the events of 9/11. Both liberals and conservatives accepted the logic of these myths and propagated them in the years after 2001. To be fair, not all liberals or left-wingers support Islamophobia; some have indeed written and spoken out against anti-Muslim racism. However, these voices are a tiny minority in the United States. Particularly with the rise of the Obama administration, mainstream liberalism has wholeheartedly adopted the notion that the United States can indeed act as a force of humanitarianism around the world, and has given its consent to the War on Terror.

From their support for the Afghan war to their acceptance of the notion that the United States would bring democracy to Iraq, liberal imperialists have endorsed and participated in propagating the myths outlined in this chapter. Still, there are differences between liberal and conservative imperialists. For instance, conservative imperialists argue that Islamist organizations around the world are united in a conspiracy to overthrow the West and establish a caliphate from North Africa to Southeast Asia. Liberal imperialists do not see such a pan-Islamic threat and are willing to work with moderate Islamists. In the following chapters I will flesh out and differentiate the forms of Islamophobia that emerge from conservative and liberal corners.

First, though, we will turn our attention to the new Muslim enemy— the "Islamic terrorist." It is important to start by noting that Islamist groups were not always seen by the US government as enemies. As we will see in the following chapter, during the Cold War the United States supported the parties of political Islam against secular nationalist and leftist parties it believed to be in the pocket of the Soviet Union. At the same time, the Iranian revolution of 1979, which deposed the US-backed Shah and brought a Shi'a Islamist government to power, meant that the United States had Islamist enemies at the same time as it had Islamist allies. In a nutshell, the foreign policy establishment's view of political Islam has been neither uniform nor consistent. It is to this history that we turn next.

Political Islam and US Policy

Chapter 4

Allies and Enemies: The United States and Political Islam

In 1945, President Franklin Delano Roosevelt met King Saud on board the USS *Quincy* in the Mediterranean. The topic of oil came up—and US-Saudi relations, begun in 1933 when the first oil concession was granted, became even more "special." Over the following decades, the United States helped Saudi Arabia to modernize its society and bolster its security apparatus, while the oil-rich nation allowed the United States to control its black gold. A front-page story in the *New York Times* captured the encounter as follows:

> When King Abdul Aziz Ibn Saud, 65-year-old monarch of Arabia Deserta [sic], left his country for the first time to visit President Roosevelt his voyage was a fantastic pot-pourri of contrasting scenes of the modern world with the ancient westward journey by the Three Wise Kings of the Orient.[1]

The timeless Orient had come into contact with the modernity of the United States. To draw out this contrast, the article went on to talk about harems, sheep, banquets, swords and daggers, ceremonial robes, tribes, and Islam. In one short article, the *Times* was able to bring together the image of the exotic and unchanging Orient with that of the United States as modernizer. This motif would set the terms for the next few decades.

Interestingly, what is absent from the mainstream account of US-Saudi relations is the fact that, beginning in the 1950s, the United States tried to project the king of Saudi Arabia as an "Islamic pole of attraction" against the secular nationalism of Egypt's Nasser. In the context of the Cold War, the United States had two objectives in the Middle East: to control the flow of oil and to keep the Soviet Union out. After an initial period when it tried to bring radical secular nationalists into the fold, it turned against them. This meant cultivating all forces that could counter radical secular nationalism and communism. At the top of this list were the Islamists.

Readers unfamiliar with this history might be surprised to learn that Islamists were not always seen as enemies. Instead, policymakers adopted a checkered approach driven by Cold War interests. At first, up until the 1970s, the political elite allied with Islamists. In the 1970s, though, this approach changed in response to various factors, including the Iranian revolution of 1979. After this, and up until the end of the Cold War, they had it both ways: Islamists were enemies in some cases, but not in others. The United States used the Holy Warriors in Afghanistan (the predecessors of al-Qaeda) to fight a proxy war with the Soviet Union. At the same time, particularly in the wake of the 1979 hostage crisis, Ayatollah Khomeini in Iran came to personify all things Islamic and evil. *Realpolitik* dictated that the United States must cut against some Islamists but ally with others against its main Cold War enemy.

After the collapse of the Soviet Union, the United States' new post–Cold War vision again meant that it worked with the Islamists who were willing to grease the wheels of *pax Americana* and militated against those who resisted. Only in 2001 did a uniform consensus emerge among the political elite, at least rhetorically, that Islamists were now the key enemy against whom an endless War on Terror must be waged. Like their medieval and modern-era counterparts in Europe, the American elite have allied with Muslims when it suited them and turned them into enemies when necessary. In this chapter, I outline American attitudes toward political Islam and the use of Islam on the political stage in the period between 1945 and 2001.

Islam and Modernization

As one of two superpowers on the world stage, the United States had a steep learning curve in the postwar period. The Council on Foreign Relations (which publishes the influential journal *Foreign Affairs*) organized a series of conferences in the late 1940s and '50s to hash out a strategy for responding to the wave of decolonization struggles sweeping Africa, the Middle East, and Asia.[2] These study groups brought together members of the US government and the few experts who existed at the time. As stated in chapter 2, this period saw the growth and development of "area studies" programs at various universities to meet the knowledge needs of the US government. The end result was policy that was influenced by both modernization theory and Orientalism.

In 1949, President Harry Truman launched his Point Four Program, which promised financial and technical aid to developing nations. The administration had a particularly dismal view of the people in Muslim-majority countries that, according to Douglas Little, is captured by the following quote from British ambassador to Iraq Sir John Troutbeck: "Seeing little but squalor and stagnation around him, [the Arab] will not admit to himself the obvious answer, that he belongs to a peculiarly irresponsible and feckless race."[3] In order to prevent what was believed to be the natural racial tendency of Arabs toward political and religious extremism, it was argued, economic assistance was vital. Modernization theorists raised the alarm of revolution. Walt Rostow, author of *The Stages of Economic Growth: A Non-Communist Manifesto* and among the most influential modernization theorists, helped the Kennedy and Johnson administrations develop policy; he also influenced Henry Kissinger, who followed his precepts.[4]

The dominant thinking was that once freed from the colonial yoke, Muslim-majority countries, if left unchecked, would veer out of Western control and likely into the clutches of the Soviet Union. This was not an acceptable outcome. At first, policymakers sought to bring radical nationalists like Nasser and Mossadegh onto their team. When this failed they had to devise new strategies. Eisenhower, who replaced Truman, developed a Middle East policy that took these circumstances into consideration. The Eisenhower Doctrine, unveiled in 1957, promised financial and military assistance to countries in the Middle East that were under threat "from any nation controlled by international communism."[5] In short, in addition to financial incentives, Eisenhower put the military option on the table.

One lesser-known aspect of the Eisenhower Doctrine was the "Islam strategy." This strategy consisted of bolstering Islamist organizations against secular nationalists and trying to create an Islamic pole of attraction in King Saud of Saudi Arabia. In a letter to a confidant in the early fifties, Eisenhower said that "we wanted to explore the possibilities of building up King Saud as a counterweight to Nasser. The king was a logical choice in this regard; he at least professed anti-Communism, and he enjoyed, on religious grounds, a high standing among all Arab nations."[6]

Some administrators even began to develop the notion of Saud as a kind of "Islamic Pope."[7] A year after Eisenhower wrote his letter about Saud, he received Said Ramadan, the son-in-law of the Muslim Brotherhood's founder Hassan al-Banna, at the White House. Even though the Brotherhood had resorted to violent actions, killing several Egyptian officials, it was to become a part of the United States' strategy in the Middle East.[8]

The Orientalists who helped shape this strategy were convinced that the secular ideologies of nationalism and communism would hold little weight in the "Muslim world." At a conference organized and sponsored by the government at Princeton University in 1953, Orientalists, policy-makers, and various native informants concluded that the United States must use religion to win hearts and minds, ignoring the popularity of secular nationalist movements.[9] US propaganda efforts at the time thus emphasized the Christian and religious roots of American culture in contrast to the godlessness of the USSR.[10] The National Security Council reasoned in 1952 that the "three monotheistic religions in the area have in common a repugnance to the atheism of communist doctrine and this factor could become an important asset in promoting Western objectives in the area."[11]

During the 1950s, the Muslim Brotherhood was used against Nasser in Egypt, and a group of clergy against Mossadegh in Iran.[12] If Mossadegh's nationalization policy represented the potential for what secular nationalists in power might do to Western oil interests, Nasser represented Washington's nightmare scenario in the region. Though Egypt does not possess oil, Nasserism, with its emphasis on pan-Arab unity, sought to unite the technologically advanced urban countries and their large, highly skilled working classes with the vast wealth of the oil-producing countries. The combination of Cairo and Riyadh would have severely hampered Western domination over the oil resources. Thus, in addition to hatching coup plots against Nasser and carrying out various assassination attempts on him (such as poisoning his chocolates),[13] the CIA began to cultivate the Muslim Brotherhood and to rely increasingly on Saudi Arabia as a counterbalance. As one senior CIA official put it, the

> optic was the Cold War. The Cold War was the defining clarity of the time. We saw Nasser as socialist, anti-Western, anti-Baghdad Pact, and we were looking for some sort of counterfoil. Saudi efforts to Islamicize the region were seen as powerful and effective and likely to be successful. We loved that. We had an ally against communism.[14]

This strategy, however, flew in the face of reality and was doomed to fail. Had the Orientalists actually bothered to study the facts on the ground, they would have concluded, as Walter Laqueur did in 1956, that what "is decisive is that Islam has gradually ceased to be a serious competitor of Communism in the struggle for the souls of the present and potential *elites* in the countries of the Middle East."[15] If that was true of communism, it was even more so of nationalism. Shockingly, Arabs, like other people, were capable of separating religion in their private lives from politics. This is, of course, a shock only to those mired in Orientalist traditions, and in the following chapter we will see that this separation of politics and religion has a long history in the ironically misnamed "Muslim world."

Despite this reality, however, the strategy of cultivating Islamists continued without contradiction until the 1970s. It must be noted, however, that the Islam strategy was not uniformly accepted or even widely known. What was clear was that the Arab nationalists were enemies who had to be quashed by any means necessary.[16] Though Eisenhower's Islam strategy failed to accomplish this goal, Israel's crushing victory in the 1967 Six Day War opened new possibilities. In the war, Israel humiliated and defeated not only Nasser's Egypt but the other neighboring states as well. Arab nationalism was thrown into crisis, and in the political vacuum this created, Islamism was able to grow and develop (as will be discussed in greater detail in chapter 6). Thus began a period of contradiction in which the United States pushed back some Islamists while promoting others.

This contradictory stance dovetailed with the United States' new security paradigm under the "Nixon Doctrine," announced in 1969. The Nixon administration rested its Middle East policy on building up three regional strongmen: Israel, the Shah's Iran, and Saudi Arabia. Officially, it was known as the "twin pillar" strategy, but in addition to Iran and Saudi Arabia, Israel, and later Egypt and Turkey, helped secure US interests in the region. An alliance with Saudi Arabia meant US support for the kingdom's attempts to Islamize politics in the region. Meanwhile, it stood by the "secular" and "modernizing" Shah's regime, which faced an emerging opposition movement in which Islamic clerics played a leading role.

Although the Iranian revolution of 1979 was the pivotal moment that shifted US attitudes against what the West labeled "Islamic fundamentalism," certain incidents prefigured this shift. These incidents persuaded the United States that Islamists could not always be trusted to act in the interests of the West. In 1973, Egyptian president Anwar Sadat, Nasser's successor, led a war against Israel under the banner of Islam.[17] Whereas Nasser had mobilized pan-Arab nationalism, Sadat turned to religion. His domestic strategy involved promoting the Muslim Brotherhood as a way to weaken and isolate the secular nationalists. Islam was therefore a useful tool for him in the same ways it was for the United States. In fact, Sadat went on to become the West's darling after making peace with Israel, until the forces that he helped unleash turned against him and assassinated him in 1981.

Muammar Gaddafi also deployed Islamic symbols and language to legitimize his rule in Libya in the early 1970s. A vocal opponent of the West, he proclaimed that Libya was an Islamic state and that he intended to promote Islamic "radicalism" and "terrorism" around the world.[18] The United States frowned upon Gaddafi but at the same time gave its consent to King Faisal of Saudi Arabia as he attempted to Islamize politics in the region. The logic was that the kind of top-down Islamism promoted by Saudi Arabia could be controlled from above and therefore made to work in the United States' interests, whereas Gaddafi's variant could not.

Saudi Arabia and the King of Islam

While King Saud was an ineffective "Islamic Pope," his younger half-brother Faisal played this part quite well. When he was still a prince, Faisal grasped the efficacy of using religion to advance political agendas. The US government viewed him as the dream combination of "modernization plus Islam." He continued the modernizing reforms initiated by his predecessors but crushed all nationalist resistance that might thwart US interests. He developed a pan-Islamism based on three objectives: to promote cooperation among Muslim states, to fight the Soviet Union and communist organizations in the Arab world, and to Islamize the Palestinian question.[19] In short, he sought to reconfigure politics in the region through the optic of Islam as a way to consolidate Saudi hegemony.

The crushing of secular nationalism in 1967 and Nasser's death a few years after created an opening for Faisal. The war of 1973 further bolstered Saudi Arabia's image in the Arab world. The Saudi-led oil embargo that followed the war elevated its prestige to such an extent that it was able to seize the initiative from secular nationalism and put its homegrown brand of Islam, Wahhabism, on the map. Wahhabism is an ultraconservative interpretation of Sunni Islam which has functioned historically to sanction the rule of the al-Saud family. In the 1970s, the Saudi ruling elite used its vast oil resources to promote Islamism and Wahhabism on the world stage in a variety of ways:

- It set up a massive network of charity and good works, which allowed Islamist groups to provide solutions to the economic crises gripping various countries.
- It used the World Muslim League (set up in 1962) to counter secularism.
- It brought together a number of countries in the region under the Organization of the Islamic Conference in 1969 to set an agenda consistent with the Saudi outlook.
- It created an Islamic financial system that tied various African, Asian, and Middle Eastern countries to the oil-rich nations.[20]

While the World Muslim League and the Organization of the Islamic Conference were the political means for establishing Saudi hegemony, the Islamic financial system laid the economic basis for the growth of Islamism. Under Saudi guidance, the vast amounts of money pouring into Arab oil-exporting countries in the early 1970s were directed into a network of banks that were under the control of the Islamic right and the Muslim Brotherhood. These banks then funded sympathetic politicians and parties, media companies, and the business ventures of the devout middle class. They also financed Muslim Brotherhood operations in Egypt, Kuwait, Pakistan, Turkey, and Jordan.[21]

The West wholeheartedly supported this banking system. Not wanting to be left out of the tidal wave of petrodollars now flowing through Islamic banks, Western banks pitched in to provide expertise, training, and technological know-how. The key American players included Citibank, Chase Manhattan, Price Waterhouse, and Goldman Sachs. The rise of the Islamic banking system coincided with the development of the neoliberal model in the West. The neoliberal guru Milton Friedman and his disciples at the University of Chicago forged close ties with the Islamists. As Robert Dreyfuss put it, "Islamic finance repeatedly relied on right-wing economists and Islamist politicians who advocated the privatizing, free-market views of the Chicago school."[22] At the end of the day, through its various political, religious, and economic institutions, Saudi Arabia played a key behind-the-scenes role in furthering the cause of Islamism with the blessing of the United States.

Iran and Afghanistan: Irrational Mullahs and Freedom Fighters

As the 1970s drew to a close, the United States came face to face with the reality of what can happen when former allies turn into enemies. This did not, however, stop its plan to employ the Afghan *mujahedeen* (Islamist guerrilla warriors) in a proxy war against the Soviet Union. Thus began a period of contradiction when members of the Reagan administration spoke from both sides of their mouths. On the one hand, they used harsh language to denounce Iran; on the other, they referred to the Afghan mujahedeen as "freedom fighters."[23] This contradiction was also reflected in popular culture—the film *Rambo III* is dedicated to the "brave Afghan mujahedeen fighters," while *Not Without My Daughter* depicts Iran as a misogynistic, totalitarian state.

The Iranian revolution of 1979 overthrew the US-backed Shah and brought to power Ayatollah Khomeini, who denounced the United States as the "Great Satan." As mentioned above, Mossadegh, who came to power in the elections of 1951, had nationalized Iran's oil industry and dealt a blow to British petroleum interests. Initially, the political elite saw Mossadegh as a means to establish greater control over Iran's oil resources and elbow Britain out. However, when Mossadegh rejected their plan to allow American oil companies into the country, his American would-be friends turned against him. The CIA organized a coup (known as Operation Ajax), relying on the support of the Islamist clergy, particularly Khomeini's mentor Ayatollah Abolgassem Kashani, who could mobilize large numbers of people from Tehran's slums against the secular nationalist Mossadegh.[24] Kashani received substantial sums of money from the CIA and had very close ties to it. It was this initial groundwork, laid by the CIA and Kashani, that helped position Khomeini for his role in the 1979 revolution.

The Iranian revolution was the product of deep discontent among workers, students, peasants, and traders (or *bazaaris*) against the Shah. The left played a role in the uprisings in the military as well as in the student protests. However, it failed to provide leadership for the movement as a whole for various reasons, including the part played by the United States in weakening the communists and other leftists. Iran's workers, in particular its oil workers, were the key muscle that brought the Shah down but were unable to play an independent role. This allowed Ayatollah

Khomeini to maneuver between various factions over the course of two years and finally to take power for the Islamic Republican Party.[25]

Not only was the Shah—a key pillar in US policy in the region—defeated, but fifty-two Americans were taken hostage for 444 days. This was a blow to US hegemony in the region, and soon the terms "terrorist," "fanatic," and "extremist," which earlier had been used to describe secular nationalism, were projected onto Islamism. Khomeini came to symbolize all things evil and irrational. As Fawaz Gerges writes, it "was under the impact of the Iranian revolution, then, that Islamism replaced secular nationalism as a security threat to US interests, and fear of a clash between Islam and the West crystallized in the minds of Americans."[26] Strategically, the United States wished to quash the revolution—the last thing it wanted was a successful model of anti-US Islamism that could be emulated by other Islamists in the region.[27]

This did not, however, stop support and funding for the mujahedeen in Afghanistan, or approval for General Mohammad Zia ul-Haq's broad program of Islamization in Pakistan.[28] It also did not prevent the Reagan administration from arming Iran during the Iran-Iraq war, at a point when it appeared that Iraq might win the war. The covert operation that came to be known as Iran-Contra involved secretly supplying arms to Iran and using the proceeds to fund the right-wing Contras in Nicaragua against the popular Sandinista government. The logic behind this continued support for Islamists was that the main enemy was the Soviet Union: if Islamists could be used to weaken this Cold War enemy, so be it. The United States also tried to weaken the Soviet Union by supporting Islamists in various Central Asian republics.[29]

Funding for the mujahedeen began in mid-1979, well before the Soviet invasion.[30] Zbigniew Brzezinski, President Carter's national security advisor, explained this funding and support prior to any act of Soviet aggression in a now-famous interview:

> According to the official version of history, CIA aid to the mujahideen began during 1980, that is to say, after the Soviet army invaded Afghanistan [in] December 1979. But the reality, secretly guarded until now, is completely otherwise: indeed, it was July 3, 1979, that President Carter signed the first directive for secret aid to opponents of the pro-Soviet regime in Kabul. And that very day, I wrote a note to the president in which I explained to him that in my opinion this was going to induce a Soviet military intervention. . . . The day that the

Soviets officially crossed the border, I wrote to President Carter: We now have the opportunity of giving to the USSR its Vietnam War.[31]

Financial and technical support for the mujahedeen was predicated on a strategy of drawing the USSR into a protracted war that would sow internal dissent and divert resources, just as Vietnam had done for the United States. The plan worked: soon thereafter, the Soviet Union invaded Afghanistan. The invasion led Carter to announce his "doctrine" in 1980, in which he declared that the United States would go to war if an "outside force"—the USSR—threatened Persian Gulf oil supplies. But the real proxy war took place in Afghanistan.

In order to defeat the Soviet Union, the United States supported groups with reactionary social goals with full knowledge of their violent and repressive tendencies, just as it had in the Congo, Chile, Guatemala, and Indonesia, among others. Gulbuddin Hekmatyar of the group Hezb-e-Islami, for instance, received large sums of American aid even though, as journalist Tim Weiner notes, Hekmatyar's "followers first gained attention by throwing acid in the faces of women who refused to wear the veil." Weiner's CIA and State Department sources described Hekmatyar as "scary," "vicious," "a fascist," and "definite dictatorship material."[32]

When Ronald Reagan took office in 1981, he picked up where Carter left off. With the help of Pakistani intelligence, the Reagan administration armed and trained the mujahedeen from Afghanistan and elsewhere in camps set up in Pakistan and Afghanistan. He justified such support through the 1980s by arguing that the mujahedeen are "our brothers," and "we owe them our help."[33] One such brother was a Saudi businessman named Osama bin Laden. It was at these camps that bin Laden made the contacts that enabled him to form al-Qaeda in the early 1990s. Throughout the 1980s, the United States supplied large quantities of arms such as C-4 plastic explosives, long-range sniper rifles, wire-guided antitank missiles, and Stinger anti-aircraft missiles, as well as extensive satellite reconnaissance data on the location of Soviet targets.[34] The United States not only armed and trained the Islamists but, with the help of its allies (Saudi Arabia, Egypt, Israel, and Pakistan), pumped some three billion dollars into the region, more than any other aid program to insurgent groups.

The CIA undertook a program of recruitment and toured people like Osama bin Laden and Sheik Azzam (the spiritual leader of the mujahedeen and one of the founders of the Palestinian group Hamas) around the region.[35] Azzam also traveled the length and breadth of the United States, visiting twenty-six states.[36] The men recruited through such activity were then trained at various military locations in the United States. Official training began under the Carter administration and included the CIA personnel, military soldiers, and Pakistani ISI operatives who later trained the mujahedeen in Afghanistan and Pakistan.[37] The trainers of the Afghan holy warriors passed on more than sixty deadly skills, including how to stab an enemy from behind, how to strangle an enemy, how to use karate chops to kill, how to use sophisticated timers, fuses, and explosives, how to use a remote-control device to set off bombs, and psychological warfare techniques.[38]

The main source of volunteers for the Afghan jihad was the Arab world. Thousands of people who came to be known as the "Afghan Arabs" poured in from Egypt, Saudi Arabia, Algeria, and several other countries. Until that point, militant Islamists in these countries had no program outside of isolated acts of urban terror. In fact, most were seen as outlaws in their countries of origin. The Afghan war served to unite them, train them, and give their movement life.[39] As Fawaz Gerges writes:

> In Afghanistan was assembled the first truly global army of Islamic warriors—the Afghan Arabs. Never before in modern times had so many Muslims from so many different lands speaking so many tongues journeyed to a Muslim country to fight against a common enemy—Egyptians, Saudis, Yemenis, Palestinians, Algerians, Sudanese, Iraqi Kurds, Kuwaitis, Turks, Jordanians, Syrians, Libyans, Tunisians, Moroccans, Lebanese, Pakistanis, Indians, Indonesians, Malaysians, and others.[40]

For the first time it seemed as if a global "community of believers" had come together to fight against infidel encroachment, thanks to the United States and its allies in the region.

The Soviet Union's retreat from Afghanistan in 1989 marked a high point for the global Islamist movement and legitimized the extremist tactics of the militants in eyes of others who now looked to them as a way forward. Their job complete in Afghanistan, the holy warriors now dispersed to other regions such as Bosnia, Kashmir, and elsewhere to carry on their jihad.[41] The former CIA asset bin Laden, in alliance with the Egyptian Ayman al-Zawahiri, formed al-Qaeda and turned the Afghan jihad into global phenomenon.[42]

Another consequence of the Soviet-Afghan war was the emergence of the Taliban and various militant Pakistani Islamists. With the backing

of Benazir Bhutto's government in Pakistan, the Taliban, an Islamist formation mostly identified with the Pashtun ethnic group, began to take
control of Afghanistan in 1994. After a vicious two-year struggle, they
finally captured Kabul in 1996. Once in power, they applied their Deobandi philosophy—a particularly conservative approach to Sunni
Islam—not only to their own community but to Afghanistan as a whole.
The various mujahedeen groups that had held power had already started
to Islamize Afghan society, but the Taliban took it to a new level. Women
were forced to wear the veil and were not allowed to take jobs; men had
to grow beards and wear certain types of clothing; television, music, and
movies were strictly forbidden; and a force of religious police was set up
to enforce these rules. The United States, despite its pious lip service to
freedom and democracy, was more than happy to forge a relationship
with the Taliban in order to establish a pipeline to oil and natural gas resources in the Caspian Sea.[43] In short, the American government was
willing to work with Islamists when it was convenient, even well into
the 1990s.

To round out the discussion of United States policy toward political
Islam in the 1980s, we now turn to the part played by Israel. Starting in
the late 1970s, a coalition of US conservatives, Orientalists, and right-
wing forces in Israel attempted to introduce the language of the new
global "terrorist" enemy into the lexicon of the foreign policy establishment. Chapter 7 discusses these connections in greater detail; the next
section provides a historical overview.

Israel's Enemies

Israel has been viewed positively in the United States ever since its founding in 1948. In popular culture, from Anne Frank's *Diary of a Young Girl*
to Leon Uris's *Exodus*, the plight of Jews during the Nazi Holocaust and
Zionist aspirations for a homeland were viewed sympathetically. In contrast, Arabs were depicted in films like *Lawrence of Arabia* as incapable of
realizing self-determination without the help of the West. The 1967 war
only confirmed the view that Arabs were inferior to Israelis. In policy
circles, the war was frequently used to show, as one CIA study put it,
that "many Arabs, as Arabs, simply weren't up to the demands of modern
warfare and that they lacked understanding, motivation, and probably in
some cases courage as well."[44] While the United States had strategic al-

liances with various Arab nations, the image of the Arab in popular culture was largely derogatory and stereotypical.[45]

In Israel, negative views of Arabs were equally common all the way back to the Zionist literature of the 1890s, which depicted the local Palestinians as donkeys. As the early Zionist poet Hemdah Ben-Yehuda put it, "How beautiful is Israel without Arabs." However, Zionist ideology was not explicitly anti-Muslim until the 1970s.[46] Rather, hostility toward Arabs and Muslims was part and parcel of the Zionist program of creating an exclusive Jewish state in which all Gentiles were unwelcome. Two sets of developments changed this state of affairs: one internal and the other external.

Israeli politics shifted to the right in the mid-1970s as the parties of the religious right started to play a more prominent role in mainstream politics. This shift inaugurated the use of more prejudicial language against Arabs and Muslims in the public sphere. In addition to religious groups, the ultranationalists and settler communities with the most vitriolic attitudes toward Muslims played a part in this process.

In 1979, Benjamin Netanyahu, as head of the Jonathan Institute, a "private foundation dedicated to the study of terrorism,"[47] organized a pivotal conference in Jerusalem at which political leaders from around the world came together to discuss "terrorism" as a new world threat. (This international effort is discussed in greater detail in chapter 7.) Even at this stage, though, *realpolitik* triumphed. Borrowing a page from its American allies, Israel had a permissive attitude toward the Islamists. In 1973, the Muslim Brotherhood set up the Islamic Center (*al-Mujamma' al-islami*), the precursor to Hamas, and in 1978 it was recognized by the Israeli state. Shaul Mishal and Avraham Sela argue that the "communal activities of the Mujamma' acted as a kind of security valve in relation to Israeli authorities."[48] The Mujamma' undertook a mosque-building program with the consent of Israel, so that between 1967 and 1986 the number of mosques in the Gaza Strip doubled from seventy-seven to 150. In the context of the Intifada of the late 1980s, the number of mosques grew to two hundred by 1989. Some have argued that at times Israel even funded the Islamists.[49] The Islamists, in turn, routinely clashed with secular nationalists and far-left forces.

External developments, including the Iranian revolution, the birth of Hezbollah in Lebanon, and the rise of Hamas, eventually forced Israel to rethink this strategy. After the collapse of the Soviet Union, Israeli leaders—with the assistance of their neoconservative allies in the United States—sought to convince the US political leadership that it faced a larger-than-life enemy: Islamic fundamentalism.[50] Their efforts were successful only after September 11, 2001; in the 1980s, despite the rise of Hezbollah and Hamas as threats to Israel, the United States continued to support Islamists against the USSR. The key battleground in this Cold War proxy conflict, as we saw, was Afghanistan.

Islamists and the Post-Cold War Era

The years immediately before 1991 witnessed several victories for Islamists. In addition to the Soviet defeat in Afghanistan, Islamists in various countries gained momentum around that time. In the Sudan, a military coup brought the Islamist ideologue Hassan al-Turabi to power. In Algeria, the Front Islamique du Salut (FIS) won decisively in the first free elections in that country since independence. And in Palestine, the domination of the Palestine Liberation Organization (PLO) over the Intifada came increasingly under threat from Hamas.[51] Ayatollah Khomeini issued a *fatwa* of death against Salman Rushdie for his book *Satanic Verses*, and his call was taken up around the world—particularly in Pakistan and Britain. Islamists were becoming a presence on the world stage.

However, they did not immediately become the key enemies of the United States. The collapse of the Soviet Union and the emergence of a unipolar world, or more aptly a "unipolar moment," meant a reconfiguration of US imperialism. There was much fanfare about the "peace dividend" and a global order characterized by butter, not guns. The United States, we were told, would create and police a "New World Order" in which it would show up anywhere it was needed, like a "globocop," to right wrongs, advance humanitarian goals, and save the day. The 1991 Gulf War demonstrated to the world that the end of "communism" did not mean the end of the US military; instead of fighting the Russians, it would be used against other still-significant threats to international stability—rogue states, failed states, terrorists, and a host of others who refused to acquiesce to *pax Americana*.

The central goal shared by the George H. W. Bush and Bill Clinton administrations was to expand American power and prevent the rise of any potential rival. Like their postwar counterparts, the American leaders of the 1990s sought to integrate the world into a capitalist order under their control. This time, instead of modernization, the model was neoliberalism. In order to ensure what Bush described as the "New World Order," the United States militated against "rogue regimes" that refused to play by American rules and attempted to control regions whose instability could undo the smooth functioning of the capitalist system. Nonstate actors outside American control had to be eliminated.

In the 1990s, like today, the Middle East was perhaps the most strategically important region, chiefly because it houses the world's largest oil reserves—oil being, of course, the lifeblood of the world economy. Virtually every US intervention in the region is related either directly or indirectly to the question of control over the flow of oil. In this context, Islamist groups and nations were cast as allies or enemies based on their degree of acquiescence to US aims. The political elite during the Clinton era, still sore from the Iranian revolution and the upheavals of the late 1970s and 1980s, viewed Iran negatively as the hub of international terrorism and Islamist extremism; it banned trade with Iran and instituted sanctions. Turkey, however, was another matter. When the Islamist party Refah was elected to power in the mid-1990s, the United States was willing to work with it, provided it did not interfere with US interests.[52] And, as mentioned above, Clinton administration officials consorted with the Taliban in relation to a pipeline deal that would, it was hoped, give US companies access to the oil and natural gas reserves in the Caspian Sea. At the end of the day, the Islamists who cooperated with the United States' vision of the world were allies, and those who did not were enemies.

What shifted during this period was that nonstate actors who resorted to terrorist tactics in their war against the West became a thorn in the Americans' side. Beyond al-Qaeda, many of the militants who had fought in Afghanistan either returned home or traveled to Bosnia, Kashmir, and elsewhere to carry on the holy war.[53] Their training and war experience with the CIA and the Pakistani intelligence agency ISI gave them the knowledge they needed to use violent tactics to advance their goals. This was a rather inconvenient outcome for the United States. The 1993 World Trade Center bombing attempt brought home the point that the forces the United States had enabled through the Afghan war could create blowback. This was followed by the Riyadh bombing in 1995, the Khobar bombing in 1996, the American embassy bombings in Kenya and Tanzania in 1998, and the bombing of the USS *Cole* in 2000. These attacks on the United States' diplomatic or military presence in the Middle East and Africa led the US military to a new practice it called "asymmetrical warfare," which treated these new stateless and transnational groups as threats that needed to be monitored and tracked.[54] The Clinton administration designated several groups as "terrorist" and developed a defensive strategy to protect its military and diplomatic installations abroad. Clinton did not rule out the occasional cruise-missile attack, however: he bombed "terrorist" targets in the Sudan and Afghanistan in 1998 in response to the Tanzanian and Kenyan embassy bombings.

Even at this stage, though, "terrorists" did not replace the Soviet Union as the new global enemy of the United States; instead, the dominant thinking in policy circles was that violent Islamists were one force among many that could upset its post–Cold War vision. However, pockets of the ruling elite, particularly the neoconservatives, began to write about "Islamic fundamentalism" as a potential key threat to US interests. The Israeli political class similarly tried to win the United States and Europe to viewing Islamism as their new larger-than-life enemy.[55]

Fawaz Gerges describes this as a debate between "confrontationists" and "accommodationists." The confrontationists argued that Islamism was the new post–Cold War "other" and that the United States needed to confront and challenge this adversary in the "clash of civilizations" that was to follow. The key ideologue leading this charge was Bernard Lewis, who penned his views on Islamism in 1990 in a now-famous essay titled "The Roots of Muslim Rage" in which he raised the alarm about an impending "clash of civilizations."[56] Samuel Huntington then popularized this concept in an essay titled "The Clash of Civilizations?" in *Foreign Affairs*, followed by a book with the same title (minus the question mark). Huntington put forward the thesis that in the new post–Cold War era, conflict would be characterized by cultural differences between various civilizations. He named about seven or eight such civilizations, arguing that the Islamic civilization was among the more dangerous threats to the West.

This argument was reflected in a slew of other articles. For example, journalist Judith Miller, in a *Foreign Affairs* article in 1991, argued that US policymakers should not try to distinguish between "good" and "bad" Islamists because there was a consensus among all Islamists to defeat the West. As she put it: "In Islam's war against the West and the struggle to build Islamic states at home, the ends justified the means."[57] Confrontation, rather than co-optation or dialogue, was the only way to thwart this new enemy. In addition to Lewis and Huntington, Daniel

Pipes (son of the necon Cold Warrior Richard Pipes), Martin Indyk (who served on Bill Clinton's National Security Council), Jeane Kirkpatrick (a onetime Democrat turned dogged Cold Warrior Republican), and others added their voice to this chorus.[58] The "clash" thesis is not a partisan position; confrontationists belong to both political parties. The difference between the accommodationists and confrontationists is not over the goal of US hegemony, it is about strategy and rhetoric, as we will see in chapter 7. For example, accommodationists do not see Islamism as the new monolithic enemy; instead, they draw distinctions between moderate Islamist groups (which can be worked with) and the extremist minority. George W. Bush, toward the end of his second term, took an accommodationist approach toward the Taliban by inviting it to participate in talks with the United States. While Obama took a confrontationist approach by ordering the assassination of Osama bin Laden in 2011, his administration too made overtures to the Taliban.

During the 1990s, the accommodationist line dominated in Washington. The first Bush administration stated that the "US government does not view Islam as the next 'ism' confronting the West and threatening world peace."[59] The Clinton administration continued to operate within this framework. As Anthony Lake, Clinton's national security advisor, put it:

> In the Middle East and throughout the world, there is, indeed, a fundamental divide. But the fault line runs not between civilizations or religions; no, it runs instead between oppression and responsive government, between isolation and openness, and between moderation and extremism.[60]

The Bush and Clinton administrations sought to win over Muslim-majority countries by appealing to universal values of freedom, tolerance, and responsive government. Of course, in practice they did nothing to pressure their authoritarian allies in the Middle East or North Africa to open up their political systems or foster democracy. Instead, they maintained that "openness" and "moderation" would be achieved through neoliberal reforms. In the 1990s, liberal imperialism held the day.

Yet at various moments the confrontationists asserted themselves. The hard-liners pointed to the World Trade Center bombing in 1993 and argued that an international network of Muslim terrorists was out to destroy the West. Building on earlier stereotypes of the Arab terrorist, the right was able to drum up fear and paranoia. It was so successful in these efforts that when a federal building in Oklahoma City was bombed in 1995, the media were quick to jump to the conclusion that Muslims were to blame.

One consequence of the Oklahoma bombing was the 1995 Omnibus Counterterrorism Act, passed in both houses of Congress and signed into law by President Clinton. The act was billed as a means to protect Americans from terrorism and, among other things, made it legal to deport noncitizens suspected of terrorist ties, based on secret evidence which does not have to be disclosed. An "alien" could also be deported for making contributions to international charities that the US government deemed to be funders of terrorism. Thus, even though the Oklahoma bombing was carried out by Timothy McVeigh, a homegrown white Christian fundamentalist, Arabs and Muslims were targeted for blame and vigilante violence. It was only a matter of time before another attack on American soil would swing the pendulum toward the confrontationists, opening the door to the "clash of civilizations" and the USA PATRIOT Act.

◆ ◆ ◆

The one constant underlying the various zigzags in attitudes among the US ruling class is that Islamists were pegged as allies or enemies based on US interests and political hegemony. The debate between confrontationists and accommodationists within the foreign policy establishment does not question the right of the United States to assert its power around the world. Thus, this debate is more aptly characterized as a tactical disagreement between conservative (or, more aptly, neoconservative) and liberal imperialists on how best to realize the aims of empire-building.

In chapter 7, we will examine the logic of these two visions of empire in the post–Cold War era and into the first decade of the new millennium. But what of political Islam on its own terms? What explains the rise of Islamism over the last three decades of the twentieth century? Is this simply the inevitable outcome in lands dominated by Islam? It is to these questions that we turn next. The following two chapters lay out a historical analysis of the Islamist phenomenon which we can then use to examine debates within the foreign policy establishment.

Chapter 5

The Separation
of Mosque and State

The history of Islam begins with the prophet Muhammad and ends with 9/11 and the bombings in London and Madrid: that is, at any rate, the timeline put forward in an introductory book on the world's religions, published by Oxford in 2007.[1] The underlying logic is straightforward—Islam leads to terrorism in a simple and unproblematic way. That such a timeline could pass through the filters at Oxford, many of whose publications on Islam have been cited favorably in this book, is a reflection of the extent to which this logic has become common sense in the post–9/11 world. The underlying assumption is that Islam has always been political, and that the parties of political Islam are a natural outgrowth of the religion.

This chapter sets out to debunk that notion in two parts. First, it lays out the historical separation between the religious and political spheres in Islam. Second, it outlines the trend toward secularism in Muslim-majority countries over the last two centuries. What this history shows is that political Islam's rise to prominence was not inevitable. Chapter 6 will then lay out the particular historical conditions that have enabled the parties of political Islam to grow.

Orientalist Myths

The primary architects of the idea that religion and politics have always been intertwined in the "Muslim world" are the right-wing ideologues Samuel Huntington and Bernard Lewis. Lewis, in the essay mentioned in the last chapter, "The Roots of Muslim Rage," sets out his argument as follows. He begins by pointing to the historic separation of religion and politics in Christianity and then states that such a separation has not occurred in Muslim societies, which, he argues, have not seen the equivalent of the Enlightenment. He asserts that whereas their own historical conflicts forced Christians and the West to learn to separate religion and politics, "Muslims experienced no such need and evolved no such doctrine."[2] As he puts it, "the origins of secularism in the West may be found in two circumstances—in early Christian teachings, and, still more, experience, which created two institutions, church and state; and in later Christian conflicts which drove the two apart." In contrast, there was "no need for secularism in Islam."[3] In his book *What Went Wrong?*, published shortly after 9/11, Lewis develops these arguments further and asserts that "the notion of a non-religious society as something desirable or even permissible was totally alien to Islam."[4]

Huntington, who popularized Lewis's "clash of civilizations" thesis, took this one step further and argued that the "underlying problem for the West is not Islamic fundamentalism. It is Islam, a different civilization whose people are convinced of the superiority of their culture, and are obsessed with the inferiority of their power."[5] What follows from this reasoning is that while certain "civilizations" understand the proper role of religion in society, others do not. Therefore, Islamist groups in contemporary society are a natural outgrowth of an antisecular cultural tendency in "Islamic civilization."

This section sets out to demonstrate why this is an erroneous reading of the history of Islam. While Islam came into being as both a political and religious ideology, since at least the eighth century it has had a de facto separation of political and religious power.[6] Furthermore, there is nothing unique in Islam's political potential. When the papacy sought to unite Europe under the banner of Christianity, it unleashed the Crusades in the name of God. Christianity too has been political since at least the fourth century (when Rome adopted Christianity as its official religion), if not since its founding.

However, the potential for a religion to be used for political purposes needs to be distinguished from its actual role in various societies at specific historical moments. Not unlike Christianity, Islam transformed in various ways to adapt to the needs of the societies in which it was practiced. A brief overview of the birth of Islam and the rise of revivalist movements reveals a simple point: political Islam is better understood as a *contemporary* phenomenon akin to the rise of Christian, Jewish, and Hindu fundamentalisms in the recent past rather than as the natural outgrowth of Islam.

The De Facto Separation of Religion and Politics

The prophet Muhammad, a merchant who traveled widely, understood that if the tribes who populated his city were to gain greater political and economic power in the region, they would need to unite under a common banner. As Tariq Ali notes,

> Muhammad's spiritual drive was partially fueled by socio-economic passions, by the desire to strengthen the commercial standing of the Arabs and the need to impose a set of common rules. His vision encompassed a tribal confederation united by common goals and loyal to a single faith. . . . Islam became the cement utilized by Muhammad to unite the Arab tribes and, from the beginning, it regarded commerce as the only noble occupation.[7]

Islam as envisioned by Muhammad combined spirituality with politics and economics with social mores. He acted as both a political and a religious leader, and his authority in both realms was unquestioned.[8] This was not so with his successors, however. Shortly after his death there were conflicts over who was to be Muhammad's temporal successor (called the caliph). The fourth caliph, Ali, was opposed by several forces including one of the Prophet's wives. Followers of Mu'awiyah (founder of the Umayyad dynasty) are known as Sunni Muslims, while followers of Ali are known as Shi'a Muslims. It was a struggle for political power that led to the first religious division between Shi'a and Sunni.[9]

Within a century after Muhammad's death, Muslim armies went on to conquer vast areas and to establish a powerful empire. It was in this context that a de facto separation of religious and political power began to take shape. While the heirs to the Prophet, or the caliphs, held religious authority, monarchs, sultans, and emirs wielded political power.[10] I use the term "de facto" because there was no formal or legal separation of religion from politics, but rather a separation of the spheres of activity and power, with the religious sphere being subordinated to the political one. Though the Abbasid caliph was the recognized religious leader of this early Muslim empire, he was a mere figurehead who didn't exercise power in any real sense of the term. It was the Turkic warrior-rulers who held political power from the ninth to the thirteenth centuries. The *ulama*, a class of religious scholars, had little choice but to accept this arrangement. However, they understood that if they were to win authority in a context in which the caliph didn't hold political power, they would need to find ways to explain away this practice on religious grounds thereby bestowing legitimacy on the caliph and validating their own authority.[11] Mohammed Ayoob traces the continuity of this practice over many centuries and notes that "the distinction between temporal and religious affairs and the temporal authority's de facto primacy over the religious establishment continued throughout the reign of the three great Sunni dynasties—the Umayyad, the Abbasid, and the Ottoman."[12]

The first Muslim empire, which brought together large numbers of people from various regions, sought to develop a set of laws that could be applied uniformly to all Muslim subjects. This need for a system of organization was the impetus behind the development of the Sharia—a set of rules codified into law. The *ulama* were entrusted with the task of formulating the Sharia. The various Sharia systems that emerged from this effort attempted to describe all human acts and activities and to classify them by permissibility: as forbidden, objectionable, recommended, and so on. These rules encompassed almost all spheres of life, from commerce and crime to marriage, divorce, property, hygiene, and interpersonal relationships.[13] It was the responsibility of the religious establishment to promote adherence to the newly developed Sharia law.

This role of ensuring social discipline through religious law was pervasive, and in this realm the *ulama* did indeed hold power. However, in the realm of politics they had little sway. Instead, in terms of Muslim societies as a whole, the *ulama* played a secondary and subservient role in relation to the political leadership. Thus, even though Islamic treatises that emerged during this period and later have a good deal to say about the nature of good rulers and governments and are loaded with suggestions and advice for rulers, they do not stake out a political role for the clergy. While the clergy insisted that the powerful should rule society in a way that conformed to Sharia law, they viewed their role to be censuring bad rulers rather than acting as rulers themselves.[14] As Ayoob notes, there "was a consensus that as long a ruler could defend the territories of Islam (*dar al-Islam*) and did not prevent his Muslim subjects from practicing their religion, rebellion is forbidden, for *fitna* (anarchy) was worse than tyranny. . . . Political quietism was the rule in most Muslim polities most of the time for a thousand years, from the eighth to the eighteenth century."[15]

A division of labor developed between the "men of the pen" and the "men of the sword." While the former class, which included not only the *ulama* but also bureaucrats (who worked under the leadership of the political ruler), was charged with carrying out the administrative and judicial functions of government, the latter defended and expanded the empire and held political authority.[16] Whereas the prophet Muhammad was both a political and religious leader, the needs of empire necessitated a de facto separation.

While this was the reality of the relationship between religion and politics, leading theologians went out of their way to demonstrate the opposite as a way to uphold their credibility. They have consistently done so through history, thereby creating the impression that religion and politics were more closely intertwined than they actually were. Not surprisingly, Orientalists—whose view of the world is driven by texts—fall easily into the trap of not separating religious claims from actual reality. That said, there are examples of more practically minded theologians, such as al-Ghazali (1058–111), who openly advocated a division of labor between the caliph and the sultan.[17]

Thus, contrary to Lewis's claims about the indivisibility of religion and politics in Islam, Ayoob argues that the "historical trajectory of religion-state relations in Islam . . . has not been very different from that of Western Christianity."[18] What is different is that Islam has not had the kinds of clashes between the state and the religious establishment that have taken place through much of the history of Christianity. There are numerous reasons for this, a discussion of which is beyond the scope of this chapter. Ayoob explains the differences between the Christian and Muslim experiences as follows:

> The religious class [in Islam] did not pose the sort of challenge to temporal authority that the religious hierarchy presided over by the pope did to emperors and kings in medieval and early modern Europe. The dispersal of religious authority in Islam therefore normally prevented a direct clash between temporal and religious power, as happened in medieval Christendom. . . . It also helped preclude the establishment of a single orthodoxy that, in alliance with the state, could suppress all dissenting tendencies and oppress their followers,

as happened in Christian Europe during the medieval and early modern periods. Wars of religion and persecution of "heretical" sects were therefore infrequent in Islamdom in contrast to Christendom. At the same time, it promoted the creation of distinct religious and political spheres that by and large respected each other's autonomy.[19]

In the following section, we look at the ways in which modern secularism was able to take hold in Muslim-majority societies. This too was the product of several factors; we will explore the impact of colonialism and capitalism, which led to secular and modernizing reforms from above as well as national liberation struggles from below, led by secular nationalist forces. These factors and others would play a role in leading the transition toward the secularization of Muslim-majority countries.

Modernization and Secularization

The turn toward secularization and modernization was spurred on by the spread of capitalism and the encroachment of colonialism on various Muslim empires. In fact, it was only during the era of capitalist development that Islam finally ceased to play a central role in social organization. In response to the loss of their territories to European colonial powers, the Muslim rulers of the Ottoman, Egyptian, and Persian Empires introduced programs of modernization, capitalistic reforms, and Westernization. In introducing these changes, the various rulers' shared goal was to find ways to develop their military power; in the process, they also transformed their economic and political systems. The result was a series of military, administrative, educational, economic, legal, and social reforms strongly influenced by the transformations in Europe that led to their ascendance. The intellectual work of the more advanced Muslim empires during the Middle Ages had laid the groundwork for Europe's Renaissance; now Europe's move toward capitalism was adopted by the East. These modernizing reforms gradually displaced Islam as the basis of Muslim society and put secularism in its place.[20] Additionally, a new Western-educated, secular middle class came into being and assumed positions of importance in government, education, and law, which then eroded the *ulama*'s traditional basis for power. It is only in this context that we can understand the "return to Islam" or the various Islamic revivalist movements of the eighteenth and nineteenth centuries, to which we will return shortly.

The first efforts at modernization were initiated from above. The monarchs who presided over Turkey, Egypt, and Iran looked to the West to find ways to develop their military in order to better defend themselves from colonial conquest. The nineteenth-century Egyptian ruler Mehmet Ali, for instance, made a push toward industrial and military development. As the historians Goldschmidt and Davidson note, "Mehmet Ali was the first non-Western ruler to grasp the significance of the Industrial Revolution. He realized that a modernized army would need textile factories to make its tents and uniforms, dockyards to build its ships, and munitions plants to turn out guns and bayonets."[21] This realization resulted in the wholesale restructuring and modernization of Egyptian society.

The Ottomans in Turkey similarly carried out a series of reforms—they built schools, roads, and canals, curbed excessive taxation, and set up a modern financial system. The rulers of the Qajar dynasty in Persia attempted to pass similar reforms in the eighteen and nineteenth centuries but had less success than their Egyptian and Ottoman counterparts. In all three cases, there was also a move to establish a modern state.[22]

One of the outcomes of these early modernizing reforms was the creation of a new class of people: the secular middle class. New schools based on European educational models gave rise to a new intellectual elite that was modern and Western in its orientation. This new secular-minded middle class assumed positions of power within the government and in law and began to displace the *ulama*. This class eventually went on to lead the early national liberation struggles in various countries.

Yet these early struggles, despite their popular appeal, had few successes beyond Turkey. Turkey is significant, though: in 1923, it became the first republic in the modern Middle East.[23] Mustafa Kemal Ataturk instituted a series of reforms, including the formal separation of religion from politics, and carried out what Marxists refer to as "bourgeois democratic tasks"—in other words, the reforms needed to mark the transition from a feudal monarchy to a capitalist democratic order. His key battle was against the old order based on Islamic law and practices. To consolidate his own authoritarian rule, he had to destroy the power and authority of the old ruling classes, which were tied to Islam. In 1924, he abolished the caliphate, closed down the madrassas (religious schools), replaced Sharia law with the Swiss civil code, and expunged the Turkish constitution of any reference to Islam as the state religion. Ataturk was fiercely secularist, and the Turkish army carried on his legacy after his death.

This secularization did not, however, occur in other countries until after World War II. Prior to the war, where nationalist parties did come to power for brief periods, not only did they fail to carry out significant reforms that would ease the conditions under which the majority lived, but they also failed to decisively rid their countries of colonial domination, being satisfied instead with power-sharing agreements. The early nationalist leaderships vacillated between collaborating with imperial powers and protesting imperial domination, conditions that created an opening for radical secular nationalism.[24] We will return to the postwar turn toward radical nationalism shortly.

The Failures of Islamic Revivalism

While at the top of society the response to colonialism was a move toward modernization and secularization, others turned to the fundamentals of Islam—the Koran, the lives of the Prophet and his followers, the example of the early Islamic community—for solutions and models of Islamic reform. These revivalists saw European colonialism and imperialism—particularly in the late nineteenth and early twentieth centuries, when European powers started to make significant incursions into Africa, Asia, and the Middle East—as vital threats to Muslim political and religious identity.[25] The leaders of this revivalist turn tended to be religiously minded middle-class individuals who sought to limit the *ulama*'s control and authority over Islamic texts and who insisted on the right of individual interpretation (*ijtihad*) of the Koran and the Sunna.[26]

The key representatives of this new current were Jamal al-Din al-Afghani, Muhammad Abduh, and Rashid Rida. Together they laid the basis for the Salafiya school of thought.[27] In essence, the Salafists advocate a return to the traditions of the original religious community around the prophet Muhammad (the *salaf*). However, even at this stage, Islamic revivalism and Salafist thought in particular had little to say about the state, beyond its role in applying Sharia. They issued no wholesale condemnation of Muslim governments and therefore no call to overthrow these governments—such a turn within Salafism occurred only later in the twentieth century.[28]

Inspired by the writings of Rashid Rida, Hassan al-Banna founded the Muslim Brotherhood in Egypt in 1928. Around the same time, Mawlana Mawdudi published his Islamist doctrine in the Indian subcontinent.[29]

Mawdudi, a modern Islamist, argued for the formation of an Islamic state throughout all of historic India. This position stood in contrast to the Muslim nationalist leaders who called for a "Muslim state," one which might include secular spaces. Mawdudi rejected nationalism and secularism as Western ideas that were impious and therefore unacceptable. In his book *Jihad in Islam*, published in the 1920s, he called for an Islamic state in which all of society would be run based on Sharia law. He also argued that to achieve this, political struggle (*jihad*) was vital. He founded the Jamaat-e-Islami (JI) party in 1941 to carry out this struggle.[30] The JI continues to exist as a political party of the devout middle classes in Pakistan.

Mawdudi was inspired by al-Banna.[31] Both of their parties engaged in national liberation struggles but rejected secular nationalism. Like the JI, the Muslim Brotherhood in Egypt rejected the demands of nationalists who called for an end to British rule and the creation of a modern state with a constitution. The Brothers argued that there was no need to look to Western models of social order. Instead they championed the slogan still used today: "The Koran is our constitution." The founding Egyptian Brothers then set up branches in several countries, including Lebanon, Jordan, Palestine, and the Sudan.

The revivalist movements and groups discussed above were minor players on the political stage in the nineteenth century and in the first half of the twentieth century. The dominant trend in the Middle East, North Africa, and South Asia during this period was toward secularism and modernization. Thus, despite his best efforts, al-Afghani—the "father" of modern Islamist thought—failed to build a pan-Islamic alliance. Similarly, the secular nationalists in India and Egypt had the support of the vast majority of the population; Islamist currents were marginal.

During the post–World War II era, a new generation of radical anti-colonial secular nationalists took the place of their predecessors. The previous generation had failed to end colonization, and colonial conditions had become unbearable for the vast majority. Even though by 1945 many Middle Eastern and North African countries had been granted formal independence, in reality they were not free. The League of Arab States, formed in 1945, consisted of the supposedly independent countries of Egypt, Syria, Iraq, Yemen, Lebanon, Transjordan, and Saudi Arabia, but all of these countries were in fact under the thumb of the British. The vast majority of ordinary people had grown disillusioned with their countries' leadership. They saw the pro-Western upper and middle classes as incapable of delivering internal reform and despised the landed aristocracy for its collusion with imperial powers and shameless self-promotion.[32] The loss of Palestine in 1948, and the failure of the Arab states to stop the formation of the state of Israel, exacerbated matters. The result was that popular discontent, combined with leftward pressure exerted by various Communist parties in the region, pushed the nationalist movements in a more radical direction. This new phase saw the birth of radical Arab nationalism in the Middle East, with its key leaders (such as Egypt's Gamal Abdel Nasser) referring to themselves and their programs as "Arab socialism."

Radical Secular Nationalism

During the postwar period, radical secular nationalism was the dominant political philosophy in colonized nations from Indonesia to Algeria. Several Orientalists, ignoring this reality (as we saw in the last chapter), asserted that people in Muslim countries—whom they viewed as being deeply entrenched in their religious beliefs—would reject political ideologies like nationalism and Communism. They were wrong. As John Esposito and John Voll argue, although "emerging nationalist movements had significant Muslim components . . . nationalism was not articulated in significantly Islamic terms." This was particularly true in the postwar period, when "the major ideologies of protest and of radical reform were shaped by Western democratic, socialist and Marxist perspectives."[33] These forces then led successful national liberation struggles and introduced secular reforms into their societies.

For instance, Nasser introduced various measures in the form of political, social, and economic reforms under the banner of "Arab socialism." One such measure was meant to quell the influence of the clergy and prevent them from interfering in matters of the state. Another imprisoned members of the Muslim Brotherhood and outlawed the organization. We see here a further separation of religion and politics. Though Nasser claimed that some of Islam's teachings were consistent with his view of "socialism,"[34] Nasserist ideology was secular at its core.

◆ ◆ ◆

All in all, Islamic revivalism might have been confined to the dustbin of history had it not been for the collapse and defeat of secular nationalism in the late 1960s and early 1970s. It is to this failure that we turn next in order to understand the conditions that have allowed political Islam to develop and grow.

In sum, what this brief history of Islam and of Islamic revivalism makes clear is that there is no direct link between seventh-century Islam and the rise of Islamist groups in the latter part of the twentieth century. I have outlined the de facto separation that took place in Islam between the religious and political spheres, and the quietist doctrines that advocated an eschewal of political power. The traditions of secularism and modernization have been dominant for at least the last two centuries in various Muslim-majority regions, beginning with modernizing reforms instituted by various Muslim monarchs, then followed by further changes implemented by secular nationalist leaderships after successful anti-colonial struggles. Thus, political Islam is better understood in light of recent political and economic developments—developments that have given rise to religious movements in other societies as well.

Chapter 6

Political Islam:
A Historical Analysis

I n the last quarter of the twentieth century, religious fundamentalisms of various stripes began a process of ascendance. In India, for instance, Hindu extremists began to gain ground in the political vacuum created by the failures of the secular nationalist Congress Party. This political opening, coupled with the ravages of liberalization, allowed the Hindu right to come to power, and consequently to push through a program of *Hindutva*, the Hinduization of society. In the United States, Christian fundamentalism in the form of the New Right started to impact politics in the late 1970s. Gaining momentum as a backlash against the progressive movements of the 1960s, the fundamentalists succeeded over the course of the next few decades in shifting the terms of debate on most social issues to the right. The same is true of Jewish ultranationalist and fundamentalist organizations in Israel. In short, the entry of religion into politics is not unique to countries where Islam is the dominant religion.

This chapter outlines the particular conditions that have enabled Islamic fundamentalism. First, however, it must be underscored that imperialist nations, particularly the United States, have played an active role in fomenting the rise of Islamism. Since this history was covered in chapter 4, I will not discuss it again here. This chapter focuses on conditions *internal* to various Muslim-majority countries that created a space for Islamism. These include the decline of secular nationalism, which resulted in an ideological vacuum; the failure of the various communist parties to offer a progressive alternative, thereby ceding ground to the Islamists; and economic crises and their exacerbation under neoliberalism, which presented an opening for Islamists and their charitable networks. It then offers a general method for how progressives and the left might view political Islam. In essence, we should neither uncritically support the Islamists nor reject them out of hand; rather, these groups and their actions should be judged on a case-by-case basis grounded in a concrete historical analysis. Let us begin, however, by grasping what is meant by "political Islam."

What Is Political Islam?

The phenomenon under study in this chapter has variously been referred to as "Islamism," "Islamic fundamentalism," and "Islamic neo-fundamentalism," among other names. I will use these terms interchangeably, recognizing that they resonate differently in different countries. In my view, however, the term "political Islam" is the most appropriate, since it refers to the *reinterpretation* of Islam by various individuals and groups to serve particular *political* goals. Thus, Muslim community groups and student organizations do not fall under this category, just as the YMCA would not fit under the rubric of Christian fundamentalism.

Let us look at a few examples of how Islam has been reinterpreted to serve explicit political goals. Ayatollah Khomeini in Iran adapted Shi'a Islam to serve as a means to mobilize the clergy and to lead a popular revolution against the Shah. Up to that point, Shi'a Islam had, for the most part, had a politically passive or quietist orientation. While sections of the clergy were sometimes involved in political activity, there was a consensus for some eleven centuries that the clergy should not control the state. Rather, as Ervand Abrahamian notes, most "viewed the clergy's main responsibilities, which they referred to as the *velayat-e faqih* (jurist's guardianship), as being predominantly apolitical."[1] Khomeini broke radically with this quietist Shi'ite stance in the context of the social upheavals of the late 1960s and '70s; he called for Muslims to overthrow the Shah in the name of Islam and to establish an Islamic state based on Sharia law.[2] He further argued that religious judges had a divine right to rule, thereby steering away from previous quietist tendencies.[3] Khomeini's rereading of Islam served as a means to nudge various sections of society, particularly the quietist clergy, to get behind a program of political revolution.

In the Sunni tradition, we can take the example of the Muslim Brotherhood (MB) in Palestine. From about 1967 they shied away from openly organizing against or confronting the state of Israel, which is why they were favored by the occupation authorities. Historically, this trend has been justified by muslim religious scholars (*ulama*) using two arguments: first, that it is better to have tyranny than anarchy, because the latter would lead to the dissolution of the *ummah*, the community of believers; second, that a Muslim ruler, even a corrupt and unjust one, is necessary in order to defend the land of Islam against infidels. This reasoning has been used time and again through history to justify the reign of corrupt and cruel rulers.

In Palestine, even though the rulers were Zionists, the MB nevertheless shied away from open confrontation after 1967 and sought to "prepare the generations" for an Islamic state. As Khaled Hroub notes, the Palestinian MB used this rationale to justify its policy of nonconfrontation with Israel until 1987 and despite "mounting accusations by other Palestinian nationalist and leftist organizations of cowardice or even of being indirectly in the service of the Israeli occupation, the Palestinian Islamists clung to their strategy of 'preparing the generations' for a long time."[5] However, sections of the MB broke with this quietist line and sought to reinterpret Islam to serve the goals of national liberation. They viewed the struggle to liberate Palestine as a religious struggle (*jihad*), which was obligatory for Muslims to fight because it took place under defensive conditions (occupation, dispossession, colonialism). Furthermore, they saw it as essential for Muslims to fight for the homeland, which they viewed as *waqf*, an inalienable religious endowment.

In 1987, in the context of the first Intifada, the debate between the quietists and the confrontationists broke out into the open and led to the formation of Hamas, a group dedicated to the liberation of Palestine.[6] Here is how one Islamist put it: "Why should Islam be viewed as a separate entity to what is going on in the region, confined to mosques and cut off from social and political life? This question lies in the minds of hundreds of Palestinian youths in the Gaza Strip, youths who are dedicated to Islam and have also participated in resistance to the Israeli occupation. Their answer: let us engage in active resistance to the occupation because the occupation not only affects the land; it also aims to uproot Islam."[7]

In short, within both the Sunni and Shi'a traditions, currents have emerged that have adapted Islam to serve particular political goals. In the

Shi'a tradition this includes, among others, groups such as ISCI (the Islamic Supreme Council of Iraq), the Islamic Dawa (Call) Party, and the Sadrists (followers of Muqtada al-Sadr) in Iraq; Hezbollah and Amal in Lebanon; and the Islamic Republican Party in Iran. The more numerous Islamist groups, however, emerge out of the Sunni branch of Islam, since Sunni Islam is practiced by about 85 percent of all Muslims around the world. They include the various Muslim Brotherhood offshoots that sprang from the original group founded in Egypt, the Afghan Taliban, al-Qaeda, AQAP (Al-Qaeda in the Arabian Peninsula), al-Shabaab of Somalia, and so on. While each of these groups emerges from particular national and regional contexts and is influenced and shaped by these historical conditions, what they share in common is support for the creation of an Islamic state based on Islamic or Sharia law. Yet even with this shared goal, there are various interpretations of Sharia—some more strict than others. Also, there are differences between groups about the methods of creating an Islamic state: for instance, whether it should be based on a vote by the majority (Hezbollah) or imposed from above (Taliban). Finally, Islamist organizations differ in their tactics. Some prefer a more radical and violent approach (such as Islamic Jihad in Egypt or the Pakistani Lashkar-e-Taiba); others, which tend to be the majority, take a reformist and at times parliamentary approach.

Clearly, the parties of political Islam vary widely in their origins, politics, and tactics. Thus, contrary to the views peddled by the neocons and other conservative imperialists, as we will see in the following chapter, nothing resembling a global conspiracy by Islamists to topple the West can be said to exist. How, then, do we understand the rise of the aforementioned parties and groups? In chapter 4 I discussed the part played by the United States. I now turn to the internal conditions that enabled the parties of political Islam to grow.

The Growth of Political Islam

Broadly speaking, a confluence of three factors helped pave the way for the rise of Islamism: the failure of secular nationalism, the weakness of the left, and the onslaught of economic crises. In what follows, I examine each of these in greater detail. While these are the overarching conditions that enable Islamists to vie for hegemony, there are specific local and regional factors that play a role. It is beyond the scope of this chapter to speak to these local conditions.

The Failure of Secular Nationalism

The rise of radical secular nationalism in the post–World War II period, as discussed in the last chapter, marked a progressive turn in anti-imperialist politics in colonized nations. From Indonesia to Algeria, a new generation of secular-minded political leaders at the heads of popular anticolonial movements swept aside the old order and introduced a series of reforms. However, such developments were not universal across all Muslim-majority countries. We see this trend in Turkey, Egypt, Indonesia, Algeria, and Pakistan, but not in Saudi Arabia or the Gulf monarchies, for instance. In the latter, secular nationalist and leftist forces, to the extent that they existed (as in Yemen and to a lesser degree in Saudi Arabia), were pushed back by the monarchs with the support of the West. Nevertheless, it is important to highlight that secularism was arrived at and developed in many Muslim-majority countries, albeit in ways different from the European experience. Here we turn to the failure and decline of these movements.

In a nutshell, secular nationalism was unable to realize the radical economic and political promises made to its polities. The case of Egypt illustrates this point vividly. In 1952, Nasser and a secret association known as the "Free Officers" led a rebellion against King Farouk, on the backs of workers' strikes and student uprisings (as well as region-wide anger over the Palestinian issue), and deposed him. Once in power, they initiated a series of reforms that in essence destroyed the old system that was dominated by feudalism and bourgeois mercantilism.[8] They undertook a program of agricultural reform, industrialization, and the nationalization of various sectors of the economy; they abolished the constitutional monarchy and established a republic, but concentrated power in their own hands. They also passed pro-labor laws in response to the strikes and demonstrations of the early 1950s. Perhaps most important, the Nasserists were able to finally rid Egyptian society of British control. The culmination of this movement was the nationalization of the Suez Canal in 1956. When Nasser defeated British, French, and Israeli opposition to the nationalization of the Suez (with the support of the United States and the Soviet Union), he became a regional hero, and Nasserism was viewed from then on as a model for emulation in the rest of the Arab world.

In 1957, Nasser called for the establishment of a "socialist" order in Egypt. What he meant by socialism was unclear; it varied depending on the context in which he spoke about it.[9] In practice, Nasser, who emerged from the middle class, led a program that curbed the power of large capital through nationalization and concentrated economic planning by the state.[10] "Arab socialism" was in practice state capitalism; it involved state planning combined with authoritarian control and the use of repression to quell opposition. Politically, Nasserism sought to unify and regroup Arab territories into one nation and overturn the arbitrary divisions imposed by the Allied powers after the First World War. The principal enemy was imperialism, particularly the imperialism of the United States, which emerged as the dominant power in the Middle East after the war. While Nasser sought military and financial support from the Soviet Union, he was by no means a stooge of Soviet interests. Nasser's main counterpart in the East was the Arab Socialist Ba'ath Party of Syria and its branches in Jordan, Lebanon, and Iraq. These parties had a similar orientation and class base, but they never achieved the same prominence as Nasserism. Other examples of secular nationalism in North Africa and South Asia include the National Liberation Front (FLN by its French initials) in Algeria, Sukarno in Indonesia, and Zulfikar Ali Bhutto in Pakistan.

However, postwar secular nationalism, despite its radical promises, was ultimately a middle-class ideology that served the interests of its class. State capitalist measures, while moderately successful for a period, were unable to seriously address class inequalities and produce real economic change. Furthermore, in the 1970s many of these countries experienced crises that state capitalist methods were unable to resolve. The result was increased unemployment and growing class inequality—conditions that were only exacerbated with the introduction of neoliberal reforms.

On the political front, the Six-Day War in 1967, in which Israel defeated neighboring countries and annexed their territories in a matter of six days, dealt a deathblow to the political legitimacy of Arab nationalism. As Maxime Rodinson puts it,

> Both Nasserism and Ba'athism failed to achieve Arab unity and to resolve the problem of Israel and the Palestinians. Nowhere was economic performance brilliant, and Nasser's Egypt in particular sank into destitution and cultural decline. The new classes in power were often painfully reminiscent of the old. The June 1967 fiasco raised the question of the adequacy of old ideas for solving the pressing problems of the day. Every major problem, every failure, every crisis

that arose . . . led to feelings that something was lacking in nationalist ideology, that other important ideologies should be looked to as sources of fresh ideas.[11]

The ideological vacuum created by the collapse of secular national-ism and the search for "fresh ideas" created an opening for the Islamists. While the far left could have occupied this vacuum, as the following sec-tion will show, they squandered their credibility and thereby ceded ground to the Islamists.

Again Egypt demonstrates this dynamic well. At about the same time that the economy began to decline, Islamic Associations, called Jamaat al-Islamiyya, started to emerge in student circles in the main cities. The regime of Anwar Sadat helped nurture and support the development of these groups in an attempt to turn sharply away from the secularist and statist policies of the previous period. These associations recruited students who were growing increasingly disillusioned with left politics and trained them in the "pure Islamic life" at summer camps. In order to gain broad support in a climate where the left still had influence, they offered what they called "Islamic solutions" to the crisis facing Egyptian universities.

For instance, students had to deal on a daily basis with an inefficient and overcrowded transportation system. For women, this was particularly difficult, as they were often harassed on crowded buses. The "Islamic" solution was to transport women in minibuses brought explicitly for this purpose. Once this alternative mode of transport became popular, how-ever, the Islamists restricted this service to only those women who wore the veil. The privatization of transport was thus a way of responding "Is-lamically" to a social problem, and of placing women students in a situa-tion where they had few choices but to adopt the veil. A similar approach was used with dress and gender segregation.[12] It was a combination of so-cial services and moral instruction that advanced the agenda of the Islamic Associations. Soon chants of "Democracy" began to clash with "Allahu Akbar" (God is Great) at student demonstrations. In a matter of a few years, the Islamists were dominant on campuses and the left was forced into hiding.[13]

A similar dynamic can be seen in other nations where secular na-tionalism and the left lost political credibility, albeit at different points. It was only in the late 1980s and the 1990s that Hamas was able to suc-cessfully challenge the dominance of the PLO in Palestine. Yet it was not a foregone conclusion that Islamists would occupy the vacuum created by the collapse of secular nationalism. If there was a political alternative to the left capable of leading working-class struggles, it was the various Communist Parties (CPs) in the region.

The Failure of the Communist Parties

In the twenty years after the Second World War, mass movements swept the Middle East and North Africa. In three countries—Egypt, Iran, and Iraq—the working classes played an important role in the mass mobilizations. In the context of rising class struggles, religious and sectarian divisions were sidelined, and the parties of political Islam saw their influence wane.[14] Additionally, in countries like Lebanon, Syria, and Sudan, the CPs played an important role in leading students', peasants', and workers' struggles.[15]

Despite these successes, the CPs were severely hampered by their adherence to Stalinist politics.[16] They vacillated on important questions. When the Soviet Union declared support for the United Nations' partition plan for Palestine, despite massive popular opposition to this plan in the Arab world, the CPs went along with it. Later, when the Soviet Union changed its position and turned against Israel, the CPs simply followed suit. They also shifted between support for and opposition to nationalist parties as Soviet policies changed. After the Second World War, and with the onset of the Cold War, the Soviet Union advised the Arab Communist Parties to sever popular-front alliances with bourgeois nationalist groups and to assert their independence. In practice, this meant opposition to radical Arab nationalism, which was immensely popular. The CPs took a stance against Nasserism and Ba'athism.[17] In Algeria, the CP supported the integration of the Algerian masses into French life, which put it on the opposite side of the struggle for national liberation led by the FLN.[18]

In the 1960s, the CPs once again switched position to accommodate Soviet directives. The CPs of Syria, Lebanon, Iraq, and Jordan issued a joint statement in 1964 calling for "closer unity and cooperation between all the patriotic and democratic trends and . . . all the national forces of the Arab liberation movement."[19] In practice, this meant that the Syrian CP declared the Ba'ath Party one of the "basic revolutionary forces." The Syrian Communists then entered the regime and gave up all political independence. Similarly, the Iraqi Communist Party aligned itself with the

Ba'ath Party and, by association, the war against the Kurds and the repression of Shi'a Muslims.[20] All of these disastrous shifts delegitimized the CPs in the eyes of people who had once turned to them for leadership. Additionally, the parties' uncritical support for various "revolutionary" nationalist parties and regimes meant that when radical nationalism went into decline, the CPs too suffered a loss of credibility. As Phil Marshall notes, "by the late 1960s communist strategy had evacuated the Middle East of any coherent secular alternative to nationalism—and had done so at a time when the region was about to move into a period of increased instability. This left an increasingly disillusioned population without a point of reference for change and opened a political space which religious activism soon started to occupy."[21]

Economic Crisis and the Class Basis of Islamism

In addition to the political crisis of secular nationalism, the 1970s saw the emergence of economic crises that state capitalist economic systems were unable to handle effectively. Further, the turn to neoliberalism and the institution of International Monetary Fund (IMF) structural adjustment programs in various states meant the degradation of social welfare programs. It is here that Islamist organizations with their vast charitable networks were able to make inroads. The dynamic can be understood as follows:

> As a result of structural adjustment, state capacity to co-opt oppositional movements declined and services were increasingly restricted to urban middle class and elite areas. Income distributions polarized. Structural adjustment meant that states were unable to provide previously established levels of services or to ensure adequate supplies of commodities. . . . The political and moral vacuum opened up great opportunities that were seized by Islamists, who established a social base by offering services that the various states have failed to provide.[22]

The main recruits to Islamism in the early 1970s were educated urban youth. Between 1955 and 1970, population growth in Muslim-majority countries approached 50 percent.[23] By 1975, with urbanization and literacy growing steadily, 60 percent of the population was under the age of twenty-four. While these youth, who hailed mostly from families that had recently moved to the cities, had access to education thanks to the reforms instituted by the secular nationalists, they had few opportunities for economic advancement. In some cases, states offered jobs to new graduates and were able to absorb a number of them into roles as state bureaucrats. Yet even this avenue became tenuous as IMF policies of liberalization and government cuts instituted in countries like Egypt and Algeria lowered salaries for intellectual bureaucrats, who then had to find second jobs as taxi drivers or night watchmen to survive.[24]

The frustration and political discontent that grew from this situation led these students toward Islamist ideologies. While some of them had been attracted to nationalism and communism, the failure of these ideologies, combined with economic hardship, pushed them in the direction of Islamism. A sizable number of these young intellectuals, educated in government schools that followed a Westernized curriculum, came from the sciences (engineering in particular) or from teacher training schools.[25] The typical Islamist of this era was an engineer born sometime in the 1950s whose parents were from the countryside.[26] Gulbuddin Hekmatyar, the leader of an ultraconservative faction of the Afghan mujahedeen, was trained as an engineer; Hacene Hashani, the spokesperson for the Algerian Front Islamique du Salut (FIS) in 1991, was an oil engineer; Ayman al-Zawahari of al-Qaeda was trained as a medical doctor.

As such, this intellectual leadership held a modern, urban worldview. Thus, the rise of contemporary political Islam is not the reemergence of a medieval clergy crusading against modernity but rather a modern urban phenomenon born of the crises created by capitalism.[27] As Chris Harman puts it, "Islamism has arisen in societies traumatized by the impact of capitalism—first in the form of external conquest by imperialism and then, increasingly, by the transformation of internal social relations accompanying the rise of a local capitalist class and the formation of an independent state."[28]

While the educated urban youth became the cadre base of the newly emerging Islamist movement, other classes that were threatened by capitalist modernization have also drifted toward Islamism. Chief among them is the devout segment of the middle class, another mainstay of the Islamist movement. One portion of this middle-class bloc consists of descendants of the mercantile classes of the bazaars and souks; another consists of newly wealthy professionals, flush with money from jobs in oil-producing countries.[29] The international Islamic banking and financial system spearheaded by Saudi Arabia, discussed in chapter 4, has financed and promoted the interests of this middle-class base.

If educated urban youth and the devout middle class are the main forces behind Islamism, other classes also support them. At times, in countries like Egypt, Iran, Turkey, and Pakistan, these two classes have received support and funding from landowning classes whose power was diminished by the nationalists.[30] At times they have also had the backing of the big bourgeoisie.

In the 1980s and 1990s, the Islamists made headway among yet another class—the very poor. This category includes declassed refugees and urban slum-dwellers, as well as those historically oppressed and exploited due to their religion. For instance, Hamas has recruited heavily from the refugee camps created by Israel, and while it has the support of businesspeople, the middle class, merchants, and the wealthy, its leadership and cadre are largely drawn from the refugee camps.[31] This is true too of Hezbollah, whose mainstay is the Shi'a poor in the outskirts of big cities like Beirut, in what is known as the "belt of misery." Similarly, the Sadrists in Iraq, both in the 1990s and today, draw much of their support and muscle from the slums of Sadr City.

The devout middle class, which sometimes has the backing of other segments of society, typically tends to be more conservative in its orientation and constitutes the "moderate" Islamist wing. While members of this class share the vision of creating an Islamic state, they prefer to do so under conditions of social stability that advance their economic interests. Urban youth displaced from the middle class due to a lack of opportunity, on the other hand, tend to be open to more confrontational and violent tactics; they constitute the "radical" wing of the Islamist movement. At times these two groups have cooperated with each other; at other times they have gone their separate ways.

Typically, the moderates advocate an Islamization of society from the bottom up through the use of strategies such as preaching and social and charitable networks. They also seek to pressure political leaders and will enter into political alliances to promote Islamization from the top. They are sometimes open to revolt, but only when all peaceful methods of protest have been exhausted. The radicals, however, advocate the concept of revolution—a forceful overthrow of the existing political regime and its replacement by a radically different system.[32] At times those who begin as moderates get radicalized in the context of political persecution. Thus, Sayyid Qutb, an influential Islamist theoretician who belonged to the moderate Muslim Brotherhood, took a radical turn in 1954 after he was imprisoned and tortured by Nasser's government.

These vacillations are typical of movements led by the petty bourgeoisie because, as a class, it lacks the social weight to bring about effective political and economic changes. Placed in a context of economic crisis, the Islamists often make vague anticapitalist appeals against poverty and greed and combine them with attacks on "Western values" and imperialism. In reality, however, this is not anticapitalist ideology. With few exceptions, Islamists are in practice strong advocates of capitalism and neoliberalism and therefore cannot offer real solutions to the people who turn to them as a political alternative.

In sum, the confluence of several political and economic developments in the late 1960s and early 1970s laid the basis for the growth of political Islam.

Political Islam: Mixed Fortunes

Over the last three decades of the twentieth century and into the new millennium, the parties of political Islam have been able to advance and position themselves as players in the political arena. Both the moderate and the radical wings have seen successes as well as setbacks and defeats. For instance, after the Afghan mujahedeen defeated the Soviets in 1989, the politics of radical, violent Islamism gained legitimacy. Yet when the "Afghan Arabs," as they are called, returned to their home countries and carried out a program of violence, such as in Algeria and Egypt in the 1990s, their credibility declined considerably in both contexts.

Similarly, the electoral approach suffered a setback in 1992, when the FIS in Algeria was not permitted to govern after winning elections. This pattern continued in Turkey in 1997, when the Islamists were forced from power by the army. Yet in 2002 the Justice and Development Party (AKP) was able to win elections and hold on to power—not surprising given that it is pro-NATO, pro-United States, and pro-neoliberal.[33] For these reasons, it has been argued that the AKP offers a model for other Islamists to emulate. In 2006, Hamas achieved an electoral victory.

This pattern of ascendance and decline is likely to continue until a left alternative can present itself and arrest this dynamic. The Islamists are able to tap into the real anxieties and economic insecurities faced by the vast majority of people. Their charitable networks, funded by petrodollars, offer some genuine relief to those whose lives are devastated by neoliberalism and imperialism. However, they have no real solutions to the crises endemic to capitalism. Once in positions of power, they flounder and find themselves unable to prevent the outbreak of violence and chaos by more radical elements bent on ridding their societies of "impious" influences. Their puritanical laws and edicts alienate the very people who once supported them, paving the way for their decline.

Political movements led by the middle classes cannot offer real solutions to the problems faced by the vast majority. As Harman argues,

> Islamism, then, both mobilizes popular bitterness and paralyzes it; both builds up people's feelings that something must be done and directs those feelings into blind alleys; both destabilizes the state and limits the real struggle against the state. The contradictory character of Islamism follows from the class base of its core cadres. The petty bourgeoisie as a class cannot follow a consistent, independent policy of its own. This has always been true of the traditional petty bourgeoisie—the small shopkeepers, traders and self-employed professionals. They have always been caught between a conservative hankering for security that looks to the past and a hope that they individually will gain from radical change. It is just as true of the impoverished new middle class—or the even more impoverished would-be new middle class of unemployed ex-students—in the less economically advanced countries today.[34]

These contradictions played out in Egypt, Algeria, Iran, Sudan, and elsewhere, revealing the bankruptcy of Islamist politics. Yet even while Islamists in these countries started to discredit themselves, their counterparts in Lebanon, occupied Palestine, and Iraq began a process of ascendancy. In short, from the 1990s to the early 2010s, a contradictory dynamic of decline and ascendance was at work. This dynamic will likely continue into the future until a real left-wing political alternative is built.

The 2011 uprisings and mass mobilizations that swept the Middle East and North Africa strengthened the existing left and opened up a space from which such a viable new left can be born. These struggles struck a blow to the radical Islamist argument that acts of terror by individuals and small cells are necessary to rid Muslim societies of pro-imperial leaders, and instead put on the map a different model for social change. Egypt and Tunisia showed that nonsectarian mass rallies and demonstrations can succeed in toppling dictators. At the same time, the opportunistic and counterrevolutionary actions of the Muslim Brotherhood since the fall of

Mubarak in Egypt have exposed the limitations of even the moderate wing of political Islam.

In the coming years, a new left will undoubtedly begin to emerge. However, the Islamists will continue to be players on the political stage for some time; it is therefore necessary for progressives to have a method by which to assess these parties and their actions. That is, before we turn to the two wings of imperialism in the United States and their assessment of political Islam, it is necessary and important to outline an alternative anti-imperialist framework.

Political Islam in an Anti-Imperialist Framework

Despite its setbacks in Iraq and Afghanistan and the rise of rivals like China into an increasingly multipolar world, the United States continues to assert its dominance around the globe. It does so economically through institutions like the International Monetary Fund, World Bank, and World Trade Organization, politically through pliant local rulers, and militarily through air wars, drone strikes, and special operations missions. In this context, anti-imperialists must take a principled position against imperialism and support the right of oppressed nations to self-determination.

In concrete terms, this solidarity with anti-imperialist forces means *on some occasions* offering critical support to the parties leading these struggles: the Islamists. When organized against imperialism and oppression, Islamists sometimes deserve the *critical and conditional* support of the left. Hezbollah's resistance to Israel's US-backed invasion of Lebanon in 2006 was one such moment. Such resistance should be defended on the grounds of the right of nations to self-determination. The invasion of Lebanon was an act of imperialist aggression that would have advanced the US/Israeli agenda. Hezbollah, widely supported by Lebanese of all religious backgrounds, dealt a blow to this agenda when it pushed back the Israel Defense Forces militarily. This is a step forward not only because it upholds self-determination but also because any struggle that weakens the Zionist colonial enterprise and by extension the United States—the world's biggest, best-armed, and most violent imperialist power—is a victory for ordinary people in the region and around the world. This does not, however, mean that the left is obliged to support Hezbollah in its wrangling for political power, such as its military operation in Beirut in May 2008. While we should defend Hezbollah's right to hold on to its arms against a US-backed puppet regime and Israel, and its right to contest elections and demand modifications to Lebanon's confessional political system, we are under no obligation to support the particular tactics it employs to realize these goals, and we should not paper over its reactionary views on women, gays and lesbians, and other important questions.

Similarly, Hamas's struggle against Zionism is worthy of support, especially when it has the backing of the Palestinian people. This flows from an understanding that the resistance of a colonized people, no matter what form it takes, should be supported, particularly when left alternatives have discredited themselves. (Popular support for Hamas rose only in conjunction with the betrayals of the secular left.) Furthermore, the Hamas of today is not the same organization as the Hamas of 1987. It has gone through many shifts in response to the day-to-day challenges of fighting Zionism and imperialism. One of these shifts is the downplaying of its Islamist ambitions and a corresponding emphasis on its nationalist politics. Writing in 2000, Khaled Hroub, one of the movement's closest political observers, noted:

> Hamas' doctrinal discourse has diminished in intensity since the mid-1990s. And references to its charter [its 1987 founding document] by its leaders have been made rarely, if at all. The literature, statements, and symbols used by Hamas have come to focus more and more on the idea that the core problem is the multidimensional issue of usurpation of Palestinian land and the basic question is how to end the occupation. The notion of liberating Palestine has assumed greater importance than the general Islamic aspect.[35]

By 2006, with the victory of Hamas in the January elections, this trajectory had reached such a level that Hroub and other commentators genuinely questioned whether the movement was the same as that begun in the late 1980s. This does not mean, however, that Hamas has abandoned its reactionary politics. Although it ran female candidates in the 2006 elections, it still advocates sex segregation as well as archaic notions such as that women's place is in the home. The left should not minimize these differences. In short, a concrete analysis of the politics and strategies of Islamist organizations is necessary before a position of support or denunciation can be pronounced.[36]

Additionally, the left should uphold basic democratic rights and support Hamas's right to take political power after having been elected by the Palestinian people in free and fair elections. Consequently, we should stand opposed to US and Israeli efforts to isolate Hamas and to collectively punish the people of Gaza. Part of the equation is also the consideration that allowing Hamas to rule unhindered would show that it, like other Islamist parties in power, does not really have a solution to the problems faced by the Palestinian people. This vacuum could then potentially be filled by a secular left committed to more effective strategies for liberation that could link the Palestinian struggle with those of Arab workers and the oppressed throughout the region, regardless of religious affiliation.

In US-occupied Iraq, the situation changed over the course of time. During the early stages of the resistance, Shi'a and Sunni were both involved in the struggle, and the possibility of a united national liberation movement had potential. The high point of this united struggle was the solidarity shown by the Shi'a when Sunni fighters were attacked in Fallujah. Until 2005, Muqtada al-Sadr had the support of sections of the Sunni population, and the beginnings of a genuine nonsectarian national liberation struggle existed in Iraq.[37] After that, however, the situation degenerated and sectarianism became rife. All the forces involved in the resistance mercilessly slaughtered and displaced innocent civilians. The Sunni forces also began to collaborate with the United States through the so-called Awakening Councils. In such situations where the resistance has disintegrated into sectarian violence and deal-making with imperialism, it would be wrong to offer support to these forces. While it is important to take a stand in defense of self-determination, this does not translate automatically to support for the forces and groups fighting on the ground at all times.

The same is true of Afghanistan. Leftists must support the right of the Afghan people to self-determination and consequently stand opposed to the US occupation. However, the Taliban, who are leading the struggle against the US/NATO occupation, are neither a genuine national liberation movement nor an anti-imperialist force. Based among the Pashtuns, who constitute about 40 percent of Afghanistan's population, the Taliban is a highly sectarian organization that has little appeal beyond this ethnic group. Its narrow and rigid interpretation of Islam, which favors Pashtun cultural practices, has little to offer the Tajiks, Hazaras, Uzbeks, and other ethnic minorities. In fact, non-Pashtuns seem to prefer the United States to the Taliban.[38] Thus, the prospect of the Taliban's building a genuine national liberation struggle that brings together all the people of Afghanistan is extremely unlikely.

Even among the Pashtuns there has been general discontent toward the Taliban's reactionary politics, so much so that this section of Afghan society also welcomed the United States at the start of the war in 2001. However, the destruction and lawless conditions created by the occupiers and their ally, the Northern Alliance, have pushed Pashtun farmers and displaced rural workers to begin turning toward the Taliban. Today's Taliban has a different rank-and-file makeup from the forces that emerged from the Afghan-Soviet war. Its politics, however, remain reactionary.

The Taliban is also not a principled anti-imperialist force. In addition to its willingness to negotiate with the United States in the 1990s, the Taliban has close ties to Pakistan and at times acts as a conduit of Pakistani influence in Afghanistan. As discussed earlier, Pakistan nurtured and cultivated the Taliban and, even today Pakistan's military intelligence agency, the Inter-Services Intelligence (ISI), maintains strong ties with the Afghan Taliban.[39] In a region destroyed by three decades of war, with an economy dominated by opium production and sales and lacking in industry, the political forces that come into being must inevitably enact the agendas of greater powers. The Northern Alliance is backed by India and the United States, and the Taliban was and continues to be Pakistan's entry into Afghan politics. In short, it does not represent the hopes of the Afghan people for national liberation. For all these reasons, progressives have little reason to offer support, even of a critical kind, to the Taliban.

In general, Islamists might at times fight against imperialism, but they are not principled anti-imperialists. If we look for historical examples, we can find both cases where the Islamists have organized against imperialism and where they have collaborated with imperial powers. For instance, the radical Sunni clergyman Izz ad-Din al-Qassam was a leading figure in the 1936–39 revolt against British control over Palestine, and that rebellion gave momentum to the radical Islamists.[40] The Muslim Brotherhood in Egypt, despite its original aim to be a nonpolitical group, took an anti-imperialist stance and organized against the British. Similarly, in Iran after 1979, Khomeini, at the head of the revolution that deposed the US-backed Shah, dealt a blow to US power in the region. In other words, Islamic fundamentalists sometimes find themselves in situations where they have to organize against imperial powers.

At the same time, however, we also find instances of collaboration and cooperation with colonial powers. In the 1950s, Khomeini, who famously denounced the United States as the "great Satan," took part in

CIA-orchestrated demonstrations against Mohammed Mossadegh; his mentor developed close relations with and took large sums of money from the CIA.[41] When the United States sent troops to Lebanon in 1958, and Britain to Jordan, the Jordanian Muslim Brotherhood joined in on the US/British side to help crush the nationalist uprising in both countries. In short, Islamist groups are often self-serving entities rather than principled anti-imperialists. We should therefore not make the mistake of offering support to all Islamists at all times. Instead, concrete historical analysis and case-by-case assessments are necessary to determine when to offer critical support to the parties of political Islam.

◆ ◆ ◆

In this chapter I have laid out the conditions that have allowed the parties of political Islam to succeed. What we saw is that in contrast to the caricature of Islamists as a medieval-minded clergy railing against the modern world, political Islam is the product of specific historic conditions. These conditions include the failure of secular nationalist movements due to their own internal weaknesses; the inability of Stalinist parties to offer an effective alternative; and economic crises in various countries that could not be resolved through state capitalist methods and that neoliberalism exacerbated. However, it must be emphasized again that imperialist nations, particularly the United States, played a key role in bolstering the parties of political Islam and consequently weakening secular nationalists and the left (as discussed in chapter 4). All of these factors came together at various points to propel Islamism onto the world stage.

Today, the ravages of imperialism and neoliberalism are plain to see. While tens of thousands have lost their lives in the US-led occupations of Iraq and Afghanistan, millions more suffer under the daily depredations of the free market. But there is a major reconfiguration of forces taking place in the region. Secular nationalism, with its considerable mass appeal, was the main driving force of change in the area in the 1950s and 1960s. In the 1970s, the Arab regimes made a concerted effort to stabilize the region, including supporting "Islamist" forces against secular nationalists and the left.

The Arab uprisings of 2011 seems to indicate a break with the status quo of the last two or three decades. The mass movements that have developed across the region are aimed against the dictators who rule with impunity. They also are rebellions against the political and economic system known as neoliberalism. These revolts have raised fundamental questions about the character of the distribution of wealth—that is, who rules and in whose interest. A genuine solution that combines the struggles against the ravages of both capitalism and imperialism in the Middle East and elsewhere only can be forged by rebuilding the left. As the various struggles from Pakistan and Iran to Syria, Tunisia, and Egypt show, the system forces ordinary people to fight back. It is in this context that the existing left can grow and strengthen its bases and that a new left can emerge. Such a left can not only counterpose a different kind of leadership against imperialism but also organize against the priorities of neoliberal capitalism and the local ruling classes that benefit from it. This is the challenge of the new millennium.

Chapter 7

The Foreign Policy Establishment and the "Islamic Threat"

In September 2000, the neoconservative think tank Project for a New American Century released a document outlining its foreign policy vision. It called for the United States to use overwhelming military force to take control of the Persian Gulf region and for "maintaining global US preeminence . . . and shaping the international security order in line with American principles and interests."[1] This goal, the report went on to add, was going to take some time to be realized "absent some catastrophic event—like a new Pearl Harbor."[2] On September 11, 2001, such an event did occur—at a time when the neoconservative wing of the foreign policy establishment held powerful positions in the George W. Bush presidency.

September 11, however, precipitated unanimous agreement in the foreign policy establishment that the War on Terror would henceforth frame US foreign policy. Barely had the ashes settled from the Twin Towers when loud proclamations that "Islamic terrorists" represented existential threats to the United States began to echo in the public sphere. From then on, US policy was geared toward "keeping Americans safe" from Muslim "evildoers." These claims fly in the face of reality, as the previous chapter outlined, since Islamist organizations typically emerge from local conditions and are focused on those conditions. What then lies behind this Islamophobic rhetoric? The agenda behind this focus on the "Islamic threat" is the subject of this chapter.

We begin with the neoconservative vision of the post–Cold War world, because it was this logic that informed the United States' response to 9/11. Even though President Obama dropped the phrase "War on Terror" in an effort to rehabilitate US imperialism after Bush's failures, he nevertheless continued Bush-era policies. We therefore start with the story of the neocons and their rise to power, with an emphasis on locating this strand of thought within the larger foreign policy establishment. Broadly speaking, there are two factions in the policy establishment: the neocons and the "balance-of-forces realist" camp. At times these camps debate, and at others they cooperate. While there are differences in rhetoric and at times strategy, the neocon and liberal/realist factions of the foreign policy establishment are united in their commitment to the project of US imperialism. The overarching threat of "Islamic terrorism" provides a useful cover for their imperial ambitions.

The Neocons

The term "neoconservative" was coined in the early 1970s by Michael Harrington, who is associated with the democratic socialist tradition in the United States, as a way to distance former allies (some liberals, others socialists) who had started to gravitate to the right.[3] These turncoats included figures such as Irving Kristol, Norman Podhoretz, Jeane Kirkpatrick, Michael Novak, Nathan Glazer, and Daniel Patrick Moynihan. Most of the first generation of neocons supported the United States' war with Vietnam and resented the antiwar movement. They saw themselves as liberals who believed in the idea that America was a force for good in the world and that it should maintain global stability and intervene militarily when needed. They stood against the "bad liberals" who championed George McGovern's bid for the presidency in 1972, viewing them as operating with a politics of "appeasement" and liberal guilt.[4] Many opposed Lyndon Johnson's "Great Society" program of domestic reform as well.

The neocons' vision of imperialism is premised on the notion of American exceptionalism: "a pervasive faith in the uniqueness, immutability, and superiority of the country's founding liberal principles, accompanied by a conviction that the United States has a special destiny among nations."[5] This vision of the United States as a unique "beacon for other nations" because of its liberal values is taken for granted within the policy establishment as a whole.[6] However, what is different about the neocons is their singular commitment to unipolarism and militarism. As Danny Cooper writes, the neocons "have been nothing if not consistent in their belief that only overwhelming American military preponderance can prevent the outbreak of great power war . . . [and] that multipolar international orders lead to great power war." In short, what defines the neoconservatives is the notion of a unipolar world dominated by the United States, which they believe is in the interests of all; "American military preponderance is good for America, and good for the world."[7]

It follows, therefore, that they drew different conclusions than the liberals about the United States' role in the world after the defeat in Vietnam. As Gary Dorien notes, the liberal imperialism of the 1940s and '50s "combined a liberal internationalist commitment to the United Nations and international law with a balance of power realism in diplomacy and an ideological abhorrence of Communism."[8] After Vietnam, Cold War liberals backed away from open confrontation and intervention, a posture the neocons saw as weak. For them, any accommodation to the Soviet camp was surrendering to the enemy in the name of realism. Alternatively, they advocated an interventionist strategy with huge increases in military spending.

Several neocons held high positions during the Reagan era, such as Bill Kristol (Irving Kristol's son), Richard Perle, Richard Pipes, and Paul Wolfowitz. They retained the "neo" prefix in order to differentiate themselves from the isolationist (noninterventionist) wing of conservatism. Some even stood to the right of Reagan—such as Podhoretz, editor of the neocon magazine *Commentary*, who argued that liberals were fools and that gay people opposed war because of their lust for "helpless, good-looking boys."[9] Frank Gaffney, who founded the Center for Strategic Policy (CSP) think tank, argued that the Soviet leader Gorbachev had seduced Reagan with false promises.[10]

When the Soviet Union did eventually collapse, the next generation of neocons developed a vision for the post–Cold War world that was premised on the notion of American dominance in a unipolar world. Charles Krauthammer, a nationally syndicated journalist best known for his writing in the *Washington Post*, articulated this position in a 1990 piece titled "The Unipolar Moment" published in the preeminent foreign policy journal *Foreign Affairs*.[11] Krauthammer argued that the end of the Cold War had created a "single pole of world power." This single superpower, the United States, could therefore intervene anywhere it wanted around the world and set the terms of world politics. In order to realize this vision, Krauthammer continued, it was necessary to marginalize the arguments of the realists and the isolationists in the policy establishment, who did not realize how important it was for one hegemonic power to rule in order for there to be global stability.

This article was followed by a report prepared for the Pentagon by Paul Wolfowitz (at the request of Dick Cheney) with the help of Scooter Libby, Richard Perle, Zalmay Khalilzad, and others. The "Defense Planning Guidance" (DPG) report was not intended for public consumption but was leaked to the *New York Times* and the *Washington Post*. The document stated that the United States' first objective should be to "prevent the re-emergence of a new rival."[12] It went on to assert that it must "establish and protect a new order" and that potential competitors should be convinced that "they need not aspire to a greater role or pursue a more aggressive posture to protect their legitimate interests."[13] In short, a *pax Americana* should be established on the military, political, and economic fronts. Even advanced industrialized nations would be discouraged from seeking to "overturn the [United States'] established political and economic order."[14] It followed from this that the United States would act alone if it needed to, in a unilateral manner, with no questions asked. This, the report stated, would guarantee world stability in a way that neither the United Nations nor any other multilateral coalitions could.

In order to maintain world stability, the report continued, the United States was right to wage preemptive war on any aggressor. It named a number of state actors as aggressors, from Iraq and North Korea to India and Japan. Post-Soviet Russia was also viewed as a potentially destabilizing force. Additionally, preemptive strikes were warranted against any threat to US interests. At the time, these ideas were critiqued harshly by the policy establishment; the report was a political embarrassment for the elder Bush. The backlash was so strong that Wolfowitz believed his political career to be over. The document was revised, and a softer version replaced the original. It was not yet the neocons' time—as we will see shortly, the 1990s were to be the era of "humanitarian imperialism," led by Clinton and the liberal imperialists.

What is noteworthy about the document, though, is that the enemies it named were diverse and the list of national interests was broad; these included "access to vital raw materials, primarily Persian Gulf oil; proliferation of weapons of mass destruction and ballistic missiles, threats to US citizens from terrorism or regional or local conflict, and threats to US society from narcotics trafficking."[15] Thus, "terrorism" was named as one among several threats faced by the United States. In fact, Krauthammer's article didn't even mention terrorism,[16] an omission for which he would later atone in an article where he stated that the "new threat [Islamism] is as evil as the old Evil Empire." Several neocons and their sympathizers began to advance this notion that "Islamic terrorism" needed to be viewed as the new post–Cold War enemy, as discussed in chapter 4. Daniel Pipes (first-generation neocon Richard Pipes's son) echoed this point, writing, "Like communism during the Cold War, Islam is a threat to the West." In short, even before the events of 9/11, the neocons were attempting to replace the Soviet Union with a new archnemesis.[17] However, only after 9/11 could this notion come to fruition. Norman Podhoretz, in his 2007 book *World War IV: The Long Struggle against Islamofascism*, compared Islamism to fascism and argued that the struggle against "Islamofascism" was just as important as the previous world wars. In part, this line of argument, with its association between fascism and Islam, came from the neoconservatives' right-wing, Likud-style Zionism, a topic to which we turn next.

The Israel Connection

In a *Wall Street Journal* piece titled "What the Heck Is a 'Neocon'?," leading neocon Max Boot stated unequivocally that "support for Israel" has been and remains a "key tenet of neoconservatism."[18] Many of the first generation of neocons were Jewish and found themselves alienated by the New Left's sympathy for the Palestinian struggle and for Third World causes more broadly. Yet the Jewish experience does not automatically translate into a hard-right Likud-style politics. As Richard Seymour observes, "It is clearly the case that, for many Jewish neoconservatives, their Jewish identity mattered; but there are surely a variety of ways of experiencing life as a Jewish immigrant in the United States, and many more ways of relating to that experience."[19]

Thus, the roots of neocon hard-line Zionism lie less in its Jewish adherents' ethnic identity and more in their politics and in a particular worldview that sees Israel as instrumental in advancing American power.[20] If the United States was going to maintain its dominance in the Middle East, it followed that Israel, the most pro-American country in the region, had to be its key ally. As Dorien notes, most "unipolarist leaders were Jewish neoconservatives who took for granted that a militantly pro-Israel policy was in America's interest. Wolfowitz, Perle, Podhoretz, Krauthammer, [Ben] Wattenberg, [Joshua] Muravchik, both Kristols, Kagan, Boot, and Kaplan fit that description."[21] Yet this position was also held by prominent non-Jews such as Jeane Kirkpatrick, Daniel Patrick Moynihan, James Woolsey, Francis Fukuyama, Zalmay Khalilzad, Linda Chavez, and others.

At any rate, Israel has always been central to neocon thinking—so much so that for years neocons accused "Arabist" State Department officials of promoting "anti-Israel" policies to curry favor with oil-rich Arab dictators.[22] Three of the lobby groups and think tanks associated with neo-conservatism focus solely on the Middle East—the Jewish Institute for National Security Affairs (JINSA), the Washington Institute for Near East Policy (WINEP), and the Middle East Forum (MEF). All three are pro-Zionist institutions that spend time and resources analyzing US strategy in the Middle East and lobbying for Zionist positions. Additionally, neocons have held positions on the boards of other think tanks such as the conservative and pro-Zionist American Enterprise Institute (AEI), with which they are closely associated, as well as the right-wing Hudson Institute. A neocon and senior fellow of the Hudson Institute, the Israeli-born Meyrav Wurmser, established the Middle East Media Research Institute (MEMRI) in 1998. MEMRI mainly seeks out news media articles from Middle East sources that cast the region and its politics in a negative light and translates them for domestic media consumption. (The equivalent of this institute in the Middle East might be one that selectively translated Fox News broadcasts or the rants of televangelists on the Christian Broad-casting Network as the key lens through which to understand the United States.) Another cofounder was a former colonel in the Israeli military in-telligence organization.[23] Before the establishment of Bill Kristol's *Weekly Standard* in 1997 (incidentally located in the same building as the AEI of-fice), the leading neocon publication was *Commentary*, which Podhoretz edited for thirty-five years. The journal was published by the American Jewish Committee, whose stated mission is to "safeguard the welfare and security of Jews in the United States, in Israel and throughout the world."[24]

Concretely speaking, neocon positions on Israel are in line with right-wing Zionist or Likud-style politics, combined with an abhorrence of any negotiations that show compromise and weakness. It follows, therefore, that the neocons were strongly opposed to the Oslo Accords, which were based on the principle of mutual recognition through a process of "land for peace." When Yasser Arafat signed the agreement on the White House lawn in 1993, President Clinton told him that he could proclaim a "state" in the Occupied Territories and become its president. In exchange for US and Israeli recognition of this "state," Arafat was asked to sign away long-standing—and historically just—Palestinian claims on three major issues: the status of Jerusalem, Palestinian refugees and the right of return, and sovereignty over their land. The neocons viewed this as a mistake. Even though Israel had no intention of upholding any of its pledges and the United States had no intention of forcing Israel to comply, the neocons vociferously opposed the Oslo Accords, seeing the deal as an Israeli, and by extension American, retreat. Consistent with their opposition to the deals Reagan struck with the Soviet Union, the neocons argued that Oslo would lead to the dissolution of Israeli power. Frank Gaffney and the CSP stated that the "land for peace" formula was nothing more than a series of "*retreats* by Israel—unilateral, headlong surrenders of strategically vital real estate" to the Arabs who were "committed to its destruction" (emphasis in original).[25]

In 1996, the neocons advised Israeli prime minister Benjamin Netanyahu, with whom they continue to have close ties, that what Israel needed to do to secure itself was to destabilize and overthrow Arab governments. They published a document titled "A Clean Break: A New Strategy for Securing the Realm," arguing that Israel should attack Syrian military targets in Lebanon and even Syria if necessary.[26] At the time, conventional wisdom saw Iraq as a major threat to Israel, and the neocons urged Netanyahu to support the Jordanian Hashemites' challenge to Iraq's borders.

This argument was similar to a position developed in the 1980s by the right-wing Likud party in Israel.[27] The argument went that Israel should fragment, dissolve, or otherwise weaken the neighboring Arab states as a way to shore up its own safety. The logic was that since most of the support for the Palestinian cause came from Arab nations, weakening the latter would help destroy the Palestinian movement. As Noam Chomsky put it, "It is only natural to expect that Israel will seek to destabilize the surrounding states, for essentially the reasons that led South Africa on a similar course in the region. In fact, given continuing military tensions, that might be seen virtually as a security imperative."[28] When Israel invaded Lebanon in 1982, it was pursuing this vision. It would, however, come to realize over the course of years that such a unilateral war-oriented strategy was not going to succeed.

Nevertheless, this thinking continued on both sides of the Atlantic and was the basis, Stephen Sniegoski argues, for the invasion of Iraq in 2003 and the Bush plan to destabilize the Middle East in order to reconstruct it based on the neocons' vision. He writes that

> in contrast to the [United States'] traditional goal of stability [as a way to secure access to oil], the neocons called for destabilizing existing regimes. Of course, the neocons couched their policy in terms of the eventual *restabilization* of the region on a democratic basis. . . . Likudnik strategy saw the benefit of regional destabilization for its own sake—creating as it would an environment of weak, disunified states or statelets involved in internal and external conflicts that could be easily dominated by Israel . . . [and] without outside support, the Palestinians would be forced to accede to whatever type of peaceful solution Israel offered.[29]

Such is the relationship and coincidence of interests between the Likud right in Israel and the neocons in the United States.

Another avenue of cooperation was the development of the notion of the "terrorist threat." Richard Pipes, Podhoretz, Wattenberg, and even the neocon idol Senator Henry "Scoop" Jackson attended an important conference on international terrorism in Israel in 1979. In addition to these figures, several Israeli politicians like Likud party founder Menachem Begin, as well as the elder George Bush and high-level officials from European countries, were in attendance.[30] The conference, held in Jerusalem, was organized by the Jonathan Institute, then headed by Benjamin Netanyahu. Netanyahu founded the institute in 1977 and named it after his younger brother Jonathan, who in Netanyahu's words "fell in the battle against terrorism."[31] In his opening remarks at the conference, Netanyahu's father Benzion sought to project Israel's enemies—Palestinians who had taken up armed struggle for self-determination—as "terrorists" and to rally the rest of the world around the struggle against "terrorism." The terrorist, Benzion continued, "speaks of 'humanitarian' and national causes, he pretends to fight for 'freedom' against oppression, he keeps speaking of 'legitimate rights.'" To counter this, he argued that this terrorist actually has "no moral restraints" and "respects no code of law." Instead, he belongs in the same camp as Nazis; "in his genocidal attitude he takes toward the societies he assails, whether it is Ireland, Lebanon, or Israel, he is an offshoot of Nazi philosophy."[33] The conference was called therefore to "serve as the beginning of a new process—the process of rallying the democracies of the world to struggle against terrorism and the dangers it represents."[34]

One presenter argued that the PLO had served as an intermediary between Moscow and Iran's Ayatollah Khomeini in the plot to overthrow the US-backed Shah.[35] At this stage the emphasis was on the PLO and the conflation of Arabs with terrorism. Only one presenter spoke about "Islamic terrorism,"[36] and overall, Islam was marginal to this conference.

This changed at the second International Conference on Terrorism (ICT), held in 1984 in Washington, DC. During his opening remarks, Netanyahu stated that "modern terrorism has its roots in two movements that have assumed international prominence in the second half of the twentieth century, communist totalitarianism and Islamic (and Arab) radicalism."[37] By this stage, Iran had come to be a thorn in Israel's side with its support for Hezbollah in Lebanon, and Arab radicalism was bracketed while Islamism took center stage. State actors—particularly the Soviet Union and Iran—were seen as giving life to international terrorism. The PLO was not omitted; its "terrorist mini-state in Lebanon" was presented as "a training center and launching group for what had become a kind of terrorist international."[38] Presenters at the conference included neocons such as Moynihan, Kirkpatrick, and Krauthammer, as well as Israeli leaders such as Yitzhak Rabin and American politicians such as George Shultz. A new addition to this conference was a session on "Terrorism and the Islamic World," which included the Orientalists Bernard Lewis, Elie Kedourie, and Panyotidis Vatikiotis.

Lewis argued at the conference that the term "Islamic terrorism" was apt because "Islam is a political religion" and Muhammad, in contrast to other religious leaders, had "founded a state and governed it."[39] In other words, although terrorism carried out by Christians or Jews is not typically referred to as "Christian terrorism" or "Jewish terrorism," linking Islam to the violence of Muslims was deemed appropriate. Lewis explained that it was "inevitable that when the Islamic world confronts the problem of terrorism, that problem, too, assumes a religious, indeed in a sense an Islamic, aspect."[40] Elie Kedourie began his speech by stating that there is "a prevalent—and justifiable—impression that an appreciable part of terrorist activities today originate, and frequently take place, in the world of Islam, and particularly in its Arab portion."[41] He then cherry-picked historical examples from various Muslim kingdoms, starting with the assassination of Ali, going on to the Assassins of the tenth century, and up to Khomeini's Iran, which "exemplifies the idea of a 'terrorist state,'"[42] to knit together a narrative of transhistoric "Islamic terrorism." He ended by raising the alarm that "terrorism in modern Islam is unlikely to prove a flash in the pan."[43]

While the 1984 ICT was held in Washington, DC, signaling that the United States would lead the world in the war on terrorists, its origins in Israel should be kept in mind. Israel was going through a series of changes in the 1980s. In the mid-1970s, the parties of the religious right (the *haredim*) started to play a greater role in domestic politics. These parties were responsible for raising the level of hateful rhetoric against non-Jews. One rabbi stated that the "Arabs are a cancer, cancer, cancer in the midst of us. . . . There is only one solution, no other, no partial solution: the Arabs out! Out! . . . Let me become defense minister for two months and you will not have a single cockroach around here."[44] As Fred Halliday notes, it was in this context that anti-Arab and anti-Muslim rhetoric came together to a much greater extent, especially among the settler community as well as the nationalist and religious parties. However, these sentiments did not prevent the Likud party from using the precursor organization to Hamas, the Mujamma, for its own purposes. When the Israeli state recognized and formally licensed the Mujamma in 1978, the logic was simple—the Islamists' hostility to the secular left made them useful. Some have argued that Israel even funded these forces.[45]

As the 1980s progressed, however, the Iranian revolution and its support of the Shi'a movement in Lebanon, combined with the emergence of Hamas, caused a shift in strategy. As Halliday writes, "By the late 1980s and the early 1990s it did, therefore, appear as if Israel was locked into an overarching battle with the Islamic world."[46] It is from here that the linkages between Islamism and fascism begin to take root, the product of an interchange between Western Orientalists and Likud political thinkers in Israel. These forces worked to convince politicians that "Islamic terrorism" was the next great threat. Daniel Pipes, writing on behalf of the MEF in the 1990s, stated his opposition to Oslo by casting suspicion on the intentions of the Arab leaders and warning of the "threat of militant Islam against America and the West."[47] But despite the efforts of the neocons and Israeli lobbyists, this attitude toward "Islamic terrorism" did not significantly impact the rhetoric or policy of the first Bush and Clinton administrations, as discussed in chapter 4. The 1990s were the era of liberal imperialism, and the neocons would have to wait their turn.

Before we turn to Clinton and humanitarian imperialism, however, it is worth noting that many of the think tanks and lobbying groups cited above are not exclusively neocon hubs. WINEP, for instance, has a "mix of neoconservative and Clintonite views," according to Maria Ryan.[48] WINEP was founded by Martin Indyk, who formerly served as the research director of the pro-Israel lobby group American Israel Public Affairs Committee (AIPAC). James Woolsey, Perle, and Wolfowitz served on its board, and Muravchik and Pipes were adjunct scholars. During the 1990s, though, WINEP was largely supportive of Clinton's policies and many of its leading lights, including Indyk, joined the Clinton administration. Unqualified support for Zionism is a bipartisan requirement in the US policy establishment. Similarly, as of 2007, JINSA's board of fifty-five advisors included only four neocons. As we shall see in the next section, neocons are represented on the boards of various realist/liberal imperialist think tanks as well. In short, the neocons are an integral part of a foreign policy establishment that is pro-Israel and pro–US imperialism. The differences emerge in tactics, strategy, and rhetoric.

Humanitarian Imperialism

Liberal rhetoric has long been deployed in the interest of imperial aims. Richard Seymour, in his book *The Liberal Defence of Murder*, outlines this sordid history, stating that the "tradition of imperial liberalism is almost as old and perplexing as liberalism itself. On the face of it, a doctrine that appears to stress human equality and universalism ought to have nothing to do with a violent system of domination and exploitation. Yet, for many liberals, the virtues of empire were then *very much as they are now* for 'liberal interventionists': it promised pedagogy, cultural therapy, economic development, the rule of law, liberty, and even, sometimes, feminism"[49] (emphasis added).

In a similar vein, Jean Bricmont argues in his book *Humanitarian Imperialism: Using Human Rights to Sell Wars* that the "ideology of our times, at least when it comes to legitimizing war, is no longer Christianity, nor Kipling's 'white man's burden' or the 'civilizing mission' of the French Republic, but is a certain discourse on human rights and democracy, mixed in with a particular representation of the Second World War. This discourse justifies Western interventions in the Third World in the name of the defense of democracy and human rights or against the 'new Hitlers.'"[50] While

Bricmont may be too hasty in dismissing the uses of the "white man's burden" logic, given the revival of Orientalism in the post-9/11 era (as discussed in chapter 3), he is correct to point to democracy and human rights as the key rationales for war. These liberal arguments, however, aren't only the tools of liberal imperialists—they are part of the neocons' arsenal as well. After all, the Bush administration used women's rights as justification for the 2001 war on Afghanistan and named "democracy-building" a goal in Iraq. The difference between the neoconservative and liberal imperialist wings of the policy establishment lies in the latter's recourse to multilateralism and coalition-building when possible (though not always), as well as a willingness to employ diplomacy. As Stephen Walt states:

> The only important intellectual difference between neoconservatives and liberal interventionists is that the former have disdain for international institutions (which they see as constraints on U.S. power), and the latter see them as a useful way to legitimate American dominance. Both groups extol the virtues of democracy, both groups believe that U.S. power—and especially its military power—can be a highly effective tool of statecraft. Both groups are deeply alarmed at the prospect that WMD might be in the hands of anybody but the United States and its closest allies, and both groups think it is America's right and responsibility to fix lots of problems all over the world. Both groups consistently over-estimate how easy it will be to do this, however, which is why each has a propensity to get us involved in conflicts where our vital interests are not engaged and that end up costing a lot more than they initially expect.[51]

He adds humorously that "liberal interventionists are just 'kinder, gentler' neocons, and neocons are just liberal interventionists on steroids."[52] Both strategies, however, have been employed by Republicans and Democrats. George H. W. Bush advocated US global dominance through the use of coalitions and bodies like the UN and eschewed advice from neocon circles, as we saw in chapter 4. It was for the Clinton administration, however, to rework the United States' global image through the use of the language of "humanitarian intervention."

Anthony Lake, Clinton's national security advisor, argued that during the era of "the Cold War we contained a global threat to market democracies." Now, after the collapse of the Soviet threat, it was possible to "consolidate the victory of democracy and open markets."[53] Consequently, the Clinton vision was about promoting democracy through

neoliberal reforms. The world needed to be made safe for neoliberal capitalism—and Clinton took it upon himself to penetrate areas of the world
previously under Soviet control. As Jean-Marc Coicaud puts it, "Clinton
made American economic success and free trade the defining aspect of
his presidency."[54] Where military intervention was needed, Clinton resorted to multilateral institutions like the UN and NATO. The key voices
in his foreign policy team were Lake, Madeleine Albright, Warren
Christopher, and his close friend and advisor Strobe Talbott (of the cen-
trist Brookings Institute). This team advocated the use of military power
to pursue more humanitarian goals than before and underscored the priorities of democracy and human rights. They were also opposed to the
"go it alone" style and advocated that, as much as possible, the United
States should pursue a multilateral strategy.[55] Clinton's "new Wilsonian"
view, which stood in contrast to the elder Bush's balance-of-power realism, was premised on the notion that US policy had entered, as Noam
Chomsky put it, a "noble phase" with a "saintly glow."[56]

The most important think tank associated with the multilateralist
camp of the foreign policy establishment is the Council on Foreign Relations (CFR), which publishes the journal *Foreign Affairs*. Its board of
directors includes Richard Haass (CFR president since 2003), Zbigniew
Brzezinski (former national security advisor to Jimmy Carter), Joseph
Nye (theorist of "soft power"), Madeline Albright, Colin Powell, Richard
Holbrooke, Strobe Talbott, Fouad Ajami (who was part of the Bush inner
circle that framed the response to 9/11),[57] and others such as neocon Elliott Abrams, who is a senior fellow. While CFR veers toward the realist
side, neocon views are represented within it. Similarly, another influential
think tank, the Center for Strategic and International Studies (CSIS), includes realists like Sam Nunn, David Abshire, Richard Armitage, Henry
Kissinger, Brent Scowcroft, and Joseph Nye as well as neocons like Zalmay Khalilzad.

It should therefore come as no surprise that these individuals talk to
one another and vie for influence within the broader political arena.
When they disagree it is typically around strategy or rhetoric, not the
overall aim of maintaining US hegemony. For instance, back in the 1950s
when the Orientalists were arguing that Islam and communism were in-
compatible (as discussed in chapter 4), the newly formed CFR (founded
in 1954) took a position against this thesis. Its Middle East strategist at
the time wrote that "Islam cannot be counted on to serve as such a barrier

[to the USSR]. The theory that communism and Soviet influence could never make inroads in the Moslem world because they are materialistic and atheistic has not been borne out. Religion does have a significant place in Middle Eastern society. It colors both popular and official attitudes. But it does not establish absolute immunity to a political virus such as fascism or communism."[58] In short, CFR offered a realist view of how the United States might maintain its power in the Middle East. This is a difference of strategy, not of goals and outcomes.

The first "humanitarian" mission of the 1990s was Clinton's continuation of George H.W. Bush's Operation Restore Hope in Somalia in 1993. UN troops, under the leadership of the United States, were sent to address the food crisis and feed the hungry—yet the troops arrived months after those most threatened by hunger had already died of starvation. While the United States and United Nations justified the invasion on humanitarian grounds, US interests in Somalia's geostrategic location and oil resources played a more significant role in the Americans' decision to intervene. When eighteen US soldiers were killed in the now-famous Black Hawk Down incident, US troops departed and left the East African nation worse off than when they arrived.[59] This intervention prefigured what was to come. Despite this, liberals provided cover for Clinton's "humanitarianism." Former leftists like Christopher Hitchens, Paul Berman, and Michael Ignatieff cheered on this new imperialism, as did New Left icons like Daniel Cohn-Bendit.

In Iraq the United States (via the UN) imposed a draconian sanctions regime that kept Iraq's economy close to the preindustrial state in which allied bombing had left it in 1991. The Clinton administration repeatedly stated that sanctions were meant to target Saddam Hussein's regime and not the Iraqi people. The reality, however, was that ordinary Iraqis suffered most. More than a million died. When Albright was asked by Lesley Stahl on CBS's *60 Minutes* in 1996 about half a million dead Iraqi children, she replied, "We think the price is worth it."[60] Thus, the humanitarians were quite content to carry out their foreign policy agenda on the dead bodies of children.

Of course, the United States did not intervene in every humanitarian crisis—the most famous case being the Rwandan genocide. Nor would the Clinton administration truly adopt multilateralism. For instance, the United States refused to sign an agreement supported by a majority of the world's countries to ban the use of antipersonnel landmines. Neither did the Clinton administration always seek the consent of the UN Security Council before waging war—the NATO-led war on Serbia in 1999 was carried out without UN authorization. Similarly, Clinton did not go through UN channels before bombing Iraq (with British help) in 1998. Phyllis Bennis shows convincingly that even while Clinton used the rhetoric of "assertive multilateralism," he employed Bush-style unilateralism well before 9/11. She adds that he cynically used the UN to provide "multilateral cover" for US goals, and that Clinton's "humanitarian interventions" were in reality a disguise for "unilateral militarism."[61]

Despite this, the neocons continued to maintain their ideological differences with Clinton, writing several critiques of his foreign policy. In 1996 Bill Kristol and Robert Kagan published an important essay in *Foreign Affairs* titled "Toward a Neo-Reaganite Foreign Policy." Rejecting balance-of-power realism, they argued that "in a world in which peace and American security depend on American power and the will to use it, the main threat the United States faces now and in the future is its own weakness. American hegemony is the only reliable defense against a breakdown of peace and international order. The appropriate goal of American foreign and defense policy, therefore, is to preserve that hegemony as far into the future as possible."[62] This "neo-Reaganite" policy was called "benevolent global hegemony" because it asserted that what was good for the United States was generally good for the world as well. As an aside, we might note that this was not a radically new idea, given the concept of "benevolent supremacy" or Luce's post–World War II–era "American Century" (discussed in chapter 4). What *was* new in the late 1990s was the willingness among the adherents of this policy to use the word "empire" more openly.[63] The rhetorical reticence of the postwar era had finally faded away.

While one might argue that Clinton's vision was not so different from the neocons', it was, at least, packaged in more sophisticated language. As Maria Ryan writes, there was

> significant convergence between the neoconservative objectives and those of the Clinton administration. To be sure, the language some of the neocons used was more explicit. They openly prioritized the credibility of NATO and were frank about why a US and NATO victory was important. Clinton presented a softer image, claiming he was also motivated by humanitarian considerations—and perhaps he was—but even for Clinton humanitarianism alone was not enough to compel intervention.[64]

Toward the end of the 1990s, his administration stated that the United States was an "indispensable nation" and that because of its unmatched power and its values it could "stand taller and see farther" than others. Therefore its dominance of the world was necessarily benign: it was not based on coercion but rather on the attractiveness of American values, commodities, and popular culture.[65] This is what Joseph Nye refers to as "soft power." (Nye served in the Clinton administration and is on the board of the CFR.) While they might quibble over the details, this vision of US dominance is shared by all segments of the policy establishment.

September 11 and the Bush Doctrine

Almost immediately after 9/11, the Bush administration started to look for ways to attack Iraq. As Richard Clarke, then "counterterrorism czar," reveals in his book *Against All Enemies*, President Bush took a few people aside and said to them: "I know you have a lot to do and all . . . but I want you, as soon as you can, to go back over everything, everything. See if Saddam did this. See if he's linked in any way."[66] This effort to target Iraq was part of the larger neocon strategy of destabilizing the Middle East. The Bush Doctrine, as it came to be known, laid out in the National Security Strategy document released in 2002 enshrined neoconservative foreign policy.

The key element of the Bush Doctrine was that it proclaimed the United States' unilateral right to wage preventive war—to attack another sovereign nation not because it directly threatened the United States but because it could *potentially* pose a threat. It gave the president discretion to determine what constituted a threat. Thus, if a nation "harbored terrorists," developed weapons of mass destruction, or otherwise acted in ways that went against the United States' interests, it would be subject to attack and invasion. Another key aspect of the Bush Doctrine was the imperative to put down the rise of any rival that might challenge US hegemony. The NSS document states: "Our forces will be strong enough to dissuade potential adversaries from pursuing a military buildup in hopes of surpassing, or equaling, the power of the United States."[67] This translated into US military presence in the Middle East and Central Asia, considered "hot spots" due to their oil and natural gas resources as well as their closeness to potential rivals like China, India, and Russia. The US wars in Afghanistan and Iraq were designed to accomplish both of the aforementioned aims: to put down potential threats and dissuade potential adversaries. The Bush regime had hoped that after Iraq, it would go on to carry out regime change in Iran and Syria. With the region under its control, the United States could then dictate terms to the other powers that rely on Middle East oil, particularly China.

The leaked Wolfowitz DPG report from the early 1990s—the report so roundly scorned by the policy establishment—was now being put into practice against the backdrop of the tragedy of 9/11. The neocons, as well as others sympathetic to their vision, understood the historic opportunity the 9/11 attacks presented. Condoleezza Rice, Bush's national security adviser and later secretary of state, put it succinctly when she said: "I think this period is analogous to 1945 to 1947 in that the events . . . started shifting the tectonic plates in international politics. And it's important to seize on that and position American interests and institutions before they harden again."[68] Yet capitalizing on this opportunity to realize the neocon vision also meant orchestrating an elaborate public relations campaign designed to elicit public support and stifle criticism. Enter the War on Terror and the language of Islamophobia.

Stephen Sheehi points out that the rhetorical response to 9/11 was worked out by a group of academics, journalists, policy makers, and experts who were invited to strategy sessions at the White House. As Wolfowitz explained, "The US government, especially the Pentagon, is incapable of producing the kinds of ideas and strategy needed to deal with a crisis of the magnitude of 9/11."[69] Among those invited to help in generating the appropriate public response were Bernard Lewis, journalist and former *Newsweek* editor Fareed Zakaria, and Johns Hopkins professor Fouad Ajami, as well as several neocons.

Sheehi points to the different approaches Lewis and Zakaria take. He writes that if "Lewis locates the failures of Islam within the barbarism of the 'Arab mind,' then Zakaria locates the hate for the West in the failure of Arab political culture and economic organization."[70] Zakaria, a student of Samuel Huntington, has argued that the United States should promote free markets and democracy in the Middle East, channeling his mentor's modernization proclivities. He states that Arabs have seen the "reverse of the historical process in the Western world, where liberalism produced democracy and democracy fuels liberalism. The Arab path has produced dictatorship, which has bred terrorism."[71] In this view, the United States therefore had to intervene to carry the "white man's burden" and bring democracy and neoliberalism. This is Clinton-style liberal imperialism. Lewis, on the other hand, has always taken a harder line and in this sense is more closely aligned with the neocons. It is therefore not surprising that the neocons would turn to Lewis to provide the intellectual ballast needed to justify their foreign policy; as Danny Cooper puts it, the neocons "lionize Lewis."[72] Also, according to Bob Woodward, Lewis was "a Cheney favorite," and Cheney used Lewis's academic credentials and credibility repeatedly to justify his own policy positions.[73]

The "clash of civilizations" rhetoric therefore became dominant in the aftermath of 9/11 and was the ideological basis for the wars in Afghanistan and Iraq as well domestic attacks on Muslims and Arabs. For a while it appeared that the neocons were unstoppable—but they overplayed their hand. During its first term, the Bush administration built a "coalition of the willing" to invade Iraq, rejecting criticisms from allies it derogatorily labeled "old Europe." The war on Iraq, however, did not go the way the neocons wanted it to. Instead of greeting US forces as liberators, the Iraqi people resisted and rejected US hegemony. The plan to carry out regime change in Iran and Syria was halted; if anything, Iran was strengthened by the United States' actions. Not only was the neocon vision of a new Middle East in jeopardy, but the United States had alienated its former allies in Europe and strengthened China (as well as Russia and Venezuela). This prompted an about-face in the Bush administration's policies, which moved toward the use of more multilateral tactics. Additionally, the administration moved away from "hard" power (such as the use of coercion and bribery) and toward winning "hearts and minds," as represented in the counterinsurgency strategy championed by its military commander in Afghanistan, General David Petraeus.

The military's 2006 "counterinsurgency manual" laid out how soft power would be used in the battlefield. In the foreword, Petraeus, noting that it had been twenty years since the US military had produced a field manual specifically on counterinsurgency, articulated this new doctrine as follows:

> A counterinsurgency campaign is, as described in this manual, a mix of offensive, defensive, and stability operations conducted along multiple lines of operations. It requires Soldiers and Marines to employ a mix of familiar combat tasks and skills more often associated with nonmilitary agencies. The balance between them depends on the

local situation. Achieving this balance is not easy. It requires leaders at all levels to adjust their approach constantly. They must ensure that their Soldiers and Marines are ready to be greeted with either a handshake or a hand grenade. . . . Soldiers and Marines are expected to be *nation builders as well as warriors*. They must be prepared to help reestablish institutions and local security forces and assist in rebuilding infrastructure and basic services. They must be able to facilitate establishing local governance and the rule of law. The list of such tasks is long; performing them involves extensive coordination and cooperation with many intergovernmental, host-nation, and international agencies.[74] [emphasis added]

In short, it wasn't enough simply to kill and militarily defeat the enemy; soldiers needed to take part in building infrastructure, providing basic services, and being both "nation builders and warriors." To aid this effort, the following year the Pentagon recruited anthropologists through a forty-million-dollar program called the "Human Terrain System." It sent these anthropologists to Iraq and Afghanistan to gather cultural information in order to better prosecute the War on Terror. They stated their goal clearly: "Empathy will become a weapon."[75] Thus, the United States was following in the footsteps long ago blazed by Napoleon in trying to accumulate knowledge to use in controlling colonized populations ideologically.

By the end of Bush's second term, however, the failing occupations in Afghanistan and Iraq—as well as an economic crisis of proportions not seen since the Great Depression—meant that it was time for a changing of the guard. Obama was voted into power by an electorate disgusted by the hubris and arrogance of the Bush regime. The ruling elite also gave him their blessing, hoping to put a friendlier face on US imperialism. The other team of imperialists was ready with a plan to rehabilitate the global image of American empire.

Obama and Liberal Imperialism

In January 2007, a leadership group on US-Muslim relations headed by Madeleine Albright, Richard Armitage (former deputy secretary of state under George W. Bush), several academics like Vali Nasr and Jessica Stern, and Muslim Americans like Daisy Khan and Imam Feisal Abdul Rauf (of Cordoba House fame), produced a document titled "Changing Course: A New Direction for U.S. Relations with the Muslim World." This document received high praise from political figures like Senator Dick Lugar, Congressman Howard Berman, and Leon Panetta (soon to be CIA director and eventually secretary of defense), as well as former generals like Anthony Zinni.[76] In its opening pages, it stated that distrust of the United States in Muslim-majority countries was the product of "policies and actions—not a clash of civilizations." It went on to argue that to defeat "violent extremists," military force was necessary but not sufficient, and that the United States needed to forge "diplomatic, political, economic, and cultural initiatives." The report urged the US leadership to improve "mutual respect and understanding between Americans and Muslims," promote better "governance and improve civic participation," and help "catalyze job-creating growth" in Muslim countries. This was a return to Clintonian liberal imperialism, with its emphasis on diplomacy and markets. The report's call to action stated that it would be vital for the next president to talk about improving relations with Muslim-majority countries in his or her inaugural speech and to reaffirm the United States' "commitment to prohibit all forms of torture."

Who better than Barack Obama to sell this new rhetorical posture? Indeed, in his inaugural address Obama did precisely as the policy group's document suggested. In one of his first speeches, in Cairo, Obama even rejected the "clash of civilizations" argument, emphasizing the shared common history and aspirations of the East and West. Whereas the "clash" discourse sees the West and the world of Islam as mutually exclusive and as polar opposites, Obama emphasized "common principles." He spoke of "civilization's debt to Islam," which "pav[ed] the way for Europe's Renaissance and Enlightenment," and acknowledged Muslims' contributions to the development of science, medicine, navigation, architecture, calligraphy, and music. This was no doubt a remarkable admission for an American president, but one that Obama clearly saw as vital to bolstering the United States' badly damaged image in the "Muslim world."[77] Indeed, this speech marked a significant rhetorical shift from the Bush era.

It was, however, consistent with the line argued by liberal imperialists. As Joseph Nye put it in *Foreign Affairs*:

> The current struggle against Islamist terrorism is much less a clash of civilizations than an ideological struggle within Islam. The United States cannot win unless the Muslim mainstream wins. There is very little likelihood that people like Osama bin Laden can ever be won

over with soft power: hard power is needed to deal with such cases. But there is enormous diversity of opinion in the Muslim world. Many Muslims disagree with American values as well as American policies, but that does not mean that they agree with bin Laden. The United States and its allies cannot defeat Islamist terrorism if the number of people the extremists are recruiting is larger than the number of extremists killed or deterred. Soft power is needed to reduce the extremists' numbers and win the hearts and minds of the mainstream.[78]

The Obama era therefore came to be characterized by a shift to liberal imperialism and *liberal Islamophobia*. The key characteristics of liberal Islamophobia are the rejection of the "clash of civilizations" thesis, the recognition that there are "good Muslims" with whom diplomatic relations can be forged, and a concomitant willingness to work with moderate Islamists. Liberal Islamophobia may be rhetorically gentler than conservative Islamophobia and (as we will see in chapter 10) the language of the "Islamophobic warriors," but it is nonetheless racist and imperialist in that it takes for granted the "white man's burden." It doesn't occur to the likes of Nye, Albright, and Haass that it is for ordinary people in the Middle East to make decisions about their societies. Self-determination does not enter their framework—and "benevolent supremacy" remains unquestioned.

Obama's policy marks a shift to the realist tradition of great power geopolitics. As he himself put it, "The truth is that my foreign policy is actually a return to the traditional bipartisan realistic policy of George Bush's father, of John F. Kennedy, and in some ways of Ronald Reagan."[79] Thus, instead of breaking from the imperial consensus or the policies of Bush's second term, Obama adopted them. Since taking office, as of this writing, he has deployed thirty thousand more troops to Afghanistan, expanded the war into Pakistan (via the "Af-Pak" strategy), tried to bully Iraq into granting an extension of the US occupation (which failed), carried out drone attacks and "black ops" in Yemen and Somalia, and participated in the NATO war on a former ally in Libya, Muammar Gaddafi. This should not come as a surprise, since his inaugural staff included Bush personnel like defense secretary Bob Gates and General David Petraeus, as well as Democratic Party hawks like Hillary Clinton and Joseph Biden. Obama's strategy consisted of a return to multilateralism, using multilateral institutions to incorporate and subordinate international and regional rivals. In his 2010 National Security Strategy document, he argued that the United States should focus its "engagement on strengthening international institutions and galvanizing the collective action that can serve common interests such as combating violent extremism; stopping the spread of nuclear weapons and securing nuclear materials; achieving balanced and sustainable economic growth; and forging cooperative solutions to the threat of climate change, conflict, and pandemic disease."[80] Yet despite this multilateral strategy, the Obama administration still resorted to unilateral actions when needed—the assassination of Osama Bin Laden, for example—as well as to bilateral agreements. Obama's vision was to secure, through this strategy of engagement, a world order under the United States' management and in its interests.

In practice, this didn't go very smoothly. The NATO intervention in Afghanistan began to lose its multilateral character, as various European nations started pulling out their forces in response to domestic opposition. By the end of the first decade of the new millennium, the "hearts and minds" approach and the counterinsurgency strategy had more or less failed. Obama therefore had to return to counterterrorism and say "good-bye to nation building and counter-insurgency operations."[81] The failure of the Bush policies he was pursuing ushered in a new phase in Obama's imperial strategy.

In 2012, Obama's Defense Strategic Guidance document, titled "Sustaining U.S. Global Leadership: Priorities for 21st Century Defense," refocused US foreign policy and its military structure.[82] It made clear that the United States will continue to fight against "violent extremists," even though the assassination of bin Laden has diminished al-Qaeda. As the report states, "its affiliates remain active in Pakistan, Afghanistan, Yemen, Somalia, and elsewhere"; the US military will "monitor" these groups and strike "the most dangerous groups and individuals when necessary."[83] In short, Obama would continue the War on Terror on nonstate actors through surveillance, but also through drone attacks and the use of Special Operations Forces.

The guidance document, however, refocuses attention on the Asia-Pacific area and names China and Iran as state actors that need to be contained. To deter and contain China, the United States will work with its "network of allies and partners."[84] Bypassing its long-term ally Pakistan, the document names India as furthering US aims in Asia. In a similar vein, the document also turns to allies in the Middle East, particularly the Gulf Cooperation Council nations, to "prevent Iran's development of a nuclear weapon capability and counter its destabilizing policies."[85] Needless to say, it affirms the administration's commitment to "Israel's security and a comprehensive Middle East peace." Finally, it turns to its European allies and NATO to take on a greater share of the burden of maintaining global security, so that the United States may not only move some its of forces from Europe but also downsize its military.

The Obama administration has learned that interventions such as those in Iraq and Afghanistan are the wrong ways to project US power. As Obama notes in his preface to the guidance document, we will re-member "the lessons of history and avoid repeating the mistakes of the past when our military was left ill prepared for the future. As we end today's wars and reshape our Armed Forces, we will ensure that our mil-itary is agile, flexible, and ready for the full range of contingencies."[86] The document continues, "U.S. forces will no longer be sized to conduct large-scale, prolonged stability operations."[87] Instead, the political class seems to have drawn the lesson that the way to achieve its objectives is through missions like the NATO intervention into Libya, which involved air power and relied on local allies on the ground. In sum, the new phase of Obama's imperial posture involves reestablishing US hegemony in Asia (preventing the rise of China) and in the Middle East (containing Iran) through multilateral alliances and the use of air strikes, drone attacks, and counterterrorism and special operations forces as well as cyber warfare. Despite the right's charge that Obama is a "secret Muslim agent" working on behalf of foreign governments, he is in reality a liberal imperialist at the helm of a nation that is trying to reassert its domination in an in-creasingly multipolar world.

◆ ◆ ◆

In this chapter I looked at US foreign policy since the end of the Cold War and traced the evolution of the "Islamic threat." As we saw, even though the language of "Islamic terrorism" was in development through a collaborative engagement between the neocons (and Lewis) and their Likud counterparts in Israel since the late 1970s, it was not until the events of 9/11 that this rhetoric became the United States' dominant means of justifying its imperialism. The implosion of the Bush regime then saw the baton handed over to the liberal imperialists, who instituted a rhetorical shift and continued the multilateral strategies adopted in Bush's second term to project and maintain US hegemony. Correspondingly, conservative Islamophobia gave way to liberal Islamophobia. This did not, however, change the realities of people's lives in the "Muslim world," which in some ways got worse under Obama. This is true, too, of the domestic environment for Muslims in the United States, a topic I turn to in the next chapter.

Section 3

Islamophobia
and Domestic Politics

Chapter 8

Legalizing Racism: Muslims and the Attack on Civil Liberties

A nation at war typically turns against those it sees as domestic representatives of the "foreign enemy." This is particularly true of the United States. During World War I, Germans endured raids on their communities. Several states banned the teaching of the German language on the grounds that it promoted un-American values. Even humble, everyday sauerkraut was relabeled "liberty cabbage."[1] In the 1940s, after the attack on Pearl Harbor, 110,000 people of Japanese descent were rounded up and put into concentration camps. Young and old were incarcerated simply for having a Japanese ancestor and forced into harsh conditions in makeshift camps, often without cooking or even plumbing facilities. Of those incarcerated, nearly three-quarters were US citizens.[2] Of course, national origin and ethnicity have never been the only sources of demonization. In the context of the Cold War, McCarthyism ushered in an era of attacks on the left and on dissenting ideologies. Not only were members of the Communist Party victims of this "red scare," but the New Left of the 1960s, including members of the anti–Vietnam War movement, the civil rights movement, and others, were subject to state surveillance and intimidation.

Today, the events of 9/11 have been used to ratchet up attacks on Muslim citizens and residents. Along the way, the right to dissent has also been targeted. As journalist Stephan Salisbury writes in *Mohamed's Ghosts*, "Almost always the surveillance and information gathering start with a swarthy group of strangers—American blacks, Italian immigrants, Jews, Arabs. Ethnicity and race are infused with a 'foreign ideology'—anarchism, socialism, Communism, black nationalism, 'jihadism.' Fear fertilizes the public soil, governmental power drives the plow."[3] He adds that what starts with "swarthy strangers" then goes on to encompass all those who disagree with the government's agenda. For instance, the surveillance program of the New York Police Department, discussed later in the chapter, targets not just Muslim Americans but liberal political groups as well.[4] Similarly, the Federal Bureau of Investigation (FBI) has used *agents provocateurs* to entrap activists in the Occupy Wall Street movement.[5]

The executive branch of the US government is entrusted with the task of policing the domestic enemy through its law enforcement apparatus. This includes a wide range of institutions such as the FBI, the Department of Homeland Security (DHS), the National Counterterrorism Center (NCTC), the Department of Justice (DOJ), various city police departments, and the court system. Since 9/11, the legal apparatus has been configured to serve the goals of the War on Terror, a process that has led to systematic violations of the rights of Muslims. The result has been a nightmare for Muslims, particularly for Arabs and South Asians, in the United States. Almost every Muslim family knows someone who has been caught up in this dragnet. At the beginning of the decade, Brooklyn was home to about a quarter-million people of Pakistani origin. By 2003, as many as fifty to sixty thousand of them were reported to have left; they had been jailed or deported, or had fled the witch-hunt mentality pervading the city.[6]

This chapter provides an overview of the ways in which the law enforcement community has targeted Muslims (both citizens and immigrants) since 2001. It is beyond the scope of this chapter to detail every way in which the law has been bent to allow for surveillance, arrests, indefinite detention, torture, and deportation. Instead, it offers a broad snapshot of how the law enforcement apparatus has participated in the construction and persecution of the "Islamic terrorist" within the United States. While the foreign policy establishment oversees the war on the enemy abroad, the law enforcement apparatus targets the enemy at home. The net result is a spectacle of terrorism that is constantly kept alive in the American imagination.

Terrorizing Arabs and Muslims

While racism against Arabs and Muslims has a long history in the United States, legalized persecution against them took institutional form in the early 1970s. The overarching context was the Arab-Israeli conflict, the growth of the PLO, and the use of armed struggle in the pursuit of national liberation. As we saw in previous chapters, the association of the enemies of Israel with "terrorism" began around this time. One of the first legal manifestations of this logic in the United States occurred after an infamous incident at the 1972 Munich Olympics in which a group of Palestinians took Israeli athletes hostage and murdered them. In response, the Nixon administration launched "Operation Boulder," giving law enforcement agencies "carte blanche authorization to investigate individuals of Arabic-speaking origin, whether citizen or not, allegedly to determine their possible and/or potential relationship with 'terrorist' activities related to the Arab-Israeli conflict."[7] Thus, a violent act committed in Munich by a handful of Palestinians became the basis on which all Arabs were designated as suspicious and therefore worthy of investigation.

Elaine Hagopian writes that Zionist intelligence sources were associated with the operation. So it is not surprising that Arabs were targeted, despite the fact that it was the Jewish Defense League (JDL) that had committed known and verified acts of terrorism in the United States. In fact, according to a Rand Corporation study, JDL was one of the most active terrorist groups (as classified by the FBI) for more than a decade.[8] Yet it was Arabs who were automatically suspected of "terrorist" activities.

After the Iran hostage crisis, President Carter took similar measures against Iranians in the United States. Such activities to combat "terrorism" continued under Reagan. The elder Bush launched a surveillance program against Arab Americans in 1991, in the context of the first Gulf War. The FBI interrogated Muslim leaders as well as activists, including antiwar demonstrators. The DOJ required Arab residents and immigrants to submit to fingerprinting, and the Federal Aviation Administration devised a system of racial profiling.[9] The two International Counterterrorism conferences that took place in 1979 and 1984, discussed in the previous chapter, no doubt contributed to a climate in which Arabs were increasingly being profiled as terrorists in the 1980s and leading up to the 1990s.

Under Bill Clinton in 1996, Congress passed the Antiterrorism and Effective Death Penalty Act (AEDPA), which, among other things, made it legal to deport immigrants—or, in the lurid language of AEDPA, "alien terrorists"—based on secret evidence. In 1995, when white right-wing Christian terrorist Timothy McVeigh bombed a federal building in Oklahoma City, killing 168 people, the existing "terrorism" hysteria generated after the 1993 WTC attempted bombing ensured that Arabs and Muslims were immediately blamed. Steve Emerson, an Islamophobic warrior (more on him in chapter 10), told CBS News that the bombing had been "done with the intent to inflict as many casualties as possible," which he claimed was a "Middle Eastern trait."[10] In short, even before the events of 9/11, the groundwork had been laid for the legalized targeting of Muslims and Arabs. As critical race theorist Ian F. Haney Lopez explains, the legal system is not a neutral body that operates above and outside of society. Instead, "the law serves not only to reflect but to solidify social prejudice, making law a prime instrument in the construction and reinforcement of racial subordination."[11]

The events of 9/11 brought the legal apparatus into conjunction with the foreign policy establishment. Now, the terrorist enemy would be fought both abroad and at home. Immediately after the attacks, about 1,200 Muslim citizens and noncitizens, most of them Arab and South Asian, were rounded up, summarily arrested, and questioned by the FBI, the Immigration and Naturalization Service (INS, now known as ICE, Immigration and Customs Enforcement), and various state and local law enforcement agencies. They were detained for varying periods of time, often in solitary confinement, and with a shroud of secrecy surrounding the whole affair. Not one of these people was found to be a "terrorist" or to have any link whatsoever to the attacks on September 11th.[12] A few months later, the DOJ announced that it had made a list of about eight thousand men between the ages of eighteen and thirty-three from specific (but unnamed) countries who had entered the United States after January 2000 who were to be "interviewed" by law enforcement personnel. Of this list, fewer than twenty were arrested on immigration charges and three on criminal charges, but none were shown to have any links to terrorism.[13] Even as George W. Bush repeatedly assured the world that the United States was not at war with Islam or with Muslims, regular Muslims were being rounded up and terrorized (in both senses of the term) through the logic of guilt by association.

Another program initiated in 2002, the National Security Entry-Exit Registration System (NSEERS), which had its origins in the 1996 AEDPA terrorism bill and was amended by the USA PATRIOT Act, required male immigrants sixteen and older from twenty-five countries to report to INS offices in order to be "fingerprinted, photographed, interviewed, and have their financial information copied, or to register when they enter the country, then re-register after thirty days," as legal scholar Nancy Murray writes.[14] (The countries were named this time, and included Muslim-majority and Middle Eastern countries as well as North Korea.) By fall 2003, more than eighty-three thousand immigrant residents had registered under the program. As their reward for coming forward, 13,799 found themselves facing deportation proceedings. As for whether "terrorists" were apprehended by this program, eleven people were found to have "links" to terrorism. The program yielded not a single terrorism conviction.[15] It was eventually suspended in 2011, but its effects linger.

In 2003, another thousand people were arrested as part of a program to catch "absconders" from Middle Eastern nations who had overstayed their visas and who might have knowledge of "terrorist activity."[16] Many of these people were put "on planes to destinations where they knew no one. They left behind jobs, homes, and families, including American-born children."[17] Such actions are nothing if not the wholesale demonization of Muslims, who are now "guilty until proven innocent." Their consequences reach far beyond the Arab and South Asian Muslim communities. Non-Muslim peace activists and antiwar organizers soon became targets of surveillance and interrogation as well.

Such policing of dissenting views is not new; in the 1960s, the FBI launched its counterintelligence program, known as COINTELPRO, to track, infiltrate, threaten, discredit, and harass members of the New Left, in particular the Black Power movement. As lawyer Steve Downs writes, "The FBI planted false reports in the media, smeared reputations through forged letters and rumors, used *agents provocateurs* to disrupt organizations and create false arrests, engaged in violence, and in many other ways attacked the ability of targeted organizations to function and achieve their political goals . . . to 'protect national security, prevent violence, and maintain the existing social and political order.'" The program was roundly criticized in the 1970s and was suspended; attorney general Edward H. Levi declared that "such activity was intolerable in our society."[18] Yet in the rush of post–9/11 fear, systematic violations of civil liberties have been deemed not only tolerable but necessary to "keep the nation secure."

As a result, the FBI can now gather information about "concentrated ethnic communities," on the grounds that such information can aid in the analysis of "potential threats and vulnerabilities" and assist in "domain awareness."[19] Put simply, the FBI is legally permitted to racially profile the Muslim community, though it does not use that term. Federal law bans profiling on the basis of race or ethnicity, but it does not explicitly ban profiling on the basis of religion or national origin. Assuming that a devout Muslim from a Middle East country is linked to terrorism is perfectly legal.[20] These culturally racist practices are justified through pseudoscientific theories of "radicalization" that will be discussed later in the chapter. In a nutshell, what we see here is one of the myths discussed in chapter 3—"Islam is inherently violent"—being operationalized by the FBI and other law enforcement agencies in their day-to-day activities.

Surveillance, Detention, and Deportation

In August 2011, the Associated Press began releasing a series of reports documenting the NYPD's surveillance of Arab and Muslim communities in the northeastern United States. With training from the CIA, the NYPD spied on mosques (often using informers called "mosque crawlers"), community centers, Muslim-owned businesses, religious bookstores, and a host of other "hot spots."[21] The NYPD's "demographics unit" went undercover into minority neighborhoods in the tristate area (New York, New Jersey, and Connecticut) to obtain information as part of what it called a "human mapping program."[22]

The reports received significant mainstream media attention and drew sharp criticism. The presidents of many of the targeted universities released statements condemning the NYPD's espionage. Yale University president Richard Levin wrote that "police surveillance based on religion, nationality, or peacefully expressed political opinions is antithetical to the values of Yale, the academic community, and the United States."[23] Newark mayor Corey Booker similarly stated that profiling based on religion was "a clear infringement on the core liberties of our citizenry."[24]

These revelations marked the first mainstream public discussion, a full decade after the events of 9/11, of the systematic violations of the civil liberties of Muslims and Arabs. The reports offered many Americans their first glimpse into the nightmare endured by Muslim citizens and immigrants. But the NYPD surveillance program is merely the tip of the iceberg. Not only are such surveillance programs widespread in the law enforcement community, but worse offenses against human rights are still under wraps. The media have paid little attention to prisoners abused through indefinite detention without the right to trial, solitary confinement, and torture. While the torture of Muslim prisoners in places like

Abu Ghraib and Guantanamo Bay did receive front-page attention after the release of scandalous photos, mainstream discussion continues to reflect a naïve faith that justice prevails in the "land of the free." Jeanne Theoharis, however, in a piece titled "Guantánamo at Home," writes that the "problem of torture and other human rights violations in America's 'war on terror' has been framed as a problem that happens largely beyond our shores. The underlying assumption is that if Guantánamo detainees were to be tried on United States soil and in federal courts (as many groups demand), such egregious abuses would not occur."[25] In fact, as Theoharis argues, this assumption is false.

A 2011 report appropriately titled *Under the Radar: Muslims Deported, Detained, and Denied on Unsubstantiated Terrorism Allegations*, released by the Center for Human Rights and Global Justice at New York University Law School, documents the ways in which the law has been used to "cast Muslims as dangerous threats to national security."[26] The report argues that "religious, cultural, and political affiliations and lawful activities of Muslims are being construed as dangerous terrorism-related factors to justify detention, deportation, and denial of immigration benefits."[27] One way in which this has happened is that Muslims have been presented as terrorists in cases that are actually about immigration violations. Charges brought against Muslim immigrants "are almost always ordinary immigration violations," the report states, yet the government has routinely insinuated connections to terrorism without providing any proof of these allegations.[28]

The story of Foad Farahi illustrates this trend. Farahi, an imam with Iranian ancestry, came to the United States in 1994 with a student visa and later applied for political asylum. After 9/11, the FBI approached him numerous times, asking him to become an informant and to spy on his community. He consistently refused. At his asylum hearing, law enforcement agents met him in court and told him that they had evidence demonstrating that he had supported a terrorist group. They gave him a choice: drop his case and leave the United States voluntarily or be charged as a terrorist. Farahi first opted for voluntary departure, no doubt frightened at the prospects of being "disappeared" like so many other Muslim men. Later, when he realized that the state had no case against him, he decided to fight. Despite repeated requests, the state refused to share information about the terrorism allegations with Farahi or his lawyer so that they might mount a defense. Eventually, Farahi's voluntary departure order was overturned and his asylum case was to be reopened.[29] Others who were not as brave as Farahi—or, perhaps, who had more to lose—have succumbed to this pressure. The law enforcement community commonly uses threats based on little or no evidence to coerce people to cooperate in the War on Terror and become snitches—or face the state's reprisal.

Another nightmare that Muslim citizens and immigrants have had to endure is arrest and detention for long periods of time. The law has been bent to allow such detentions in the name of national security. *Under the Radar* highlights a trend where Muslim immigrants are painted as threats and detained for minor immigration violations that do not normally warrant detention. Even those who have not broken the law sometimes find themselves in detention centers. In her book *Patriot Acts*, journalist Alia Malek tells the story of a teenager who was detained for being a terrorist:

> On March 24, 2005, Adama Bah, a sixteen-year-old Muslim girl, awoke at dawn to discover nearly a dozen armed FBI agents inside her family's apartment in East Harlem. They arrested her and her father, Mamadou Bah, and transported them to separate detention facilities. A government document leaked to the press claimed that Adama was a potential suicide bomber but *failed to provide any evidence* to support this claim. Released after six weeks in detention, Adama was forced to live under partial house arrest with an ankle bracelet, a government-enforced curfew, and a court-issued gag order that prohibited from speaking about her case. In August of 2006, Adama's father was deported back to Guinea, Africa. Adama, who had traveled to the United States with her parents from Guinea as a child, also found herself facing deportation. She would spend the next few years fighting for asylum and struggling to support her family in the United States and Guinea.[30] [emphasis added]

Bah is not the only teenager to have experienced such trauma. In his powerful book *How Does It Feel to Be a Problem?: Being Young and Arab in America*, Moustafa Bayoumi tells the story of another teenager who was ripped from her life in Brooklyn and placed in detention. To protect her identity, Bayoumi refers to her as "Rasha." One night the FBI came to Rasha's home and placed her and her entire family in detention centers. Her family had an appeal pending about their immigration status, but they were locked up anyway. Bayoumi describes her months-long experience in the detention facility:

> For a while she stopped eating. She would lie on her bed sometimes for two or three days continuously, finally lugging herself out of bed

one day when the cell door opened so she could join the others and eat. *Like lab rats,* she thought. She slowly snapped out of her depression, but she couldn't stop feeling angry. She tried to transform her anger into a life lesson, to believe that God was trying to show her the nature of her humanity. But she felt wronged. Never in her life had she thought that she would end up in jail unless she had committed a crime. So why was she here? For what? Because she had overstayed her visa and was now undocumented? She didn't commit a crime, and she was being punished for some else's acts. For someone else's crime. She hadn't been convicted. She had been abducted.

This wasn't justice. It was revenge.[31]

Ultimately, Rasha's family was released. This has been the story of thousands of men and women—young and old, citizen and noncitizen—who have been arrested, detained, and deported in the name of the War on Terror. The government has justified this treatment, even of those who have done nothing wrong, by stating that "preemptive prosecution" is essential to keep America safe. Preemptive prosecution is the domestic legal variant of the doctrine of "preemptive war," discussed in the previous chapter. If the rationale for preemptive war is to prevent the rise of a future rival to the United States on the global stage, preemptive prosecution is about apprehending "potential" terrorists.

Preemptive Prosecution

Preemptive prosecution involves targeting innocent people who haven't actually done anything wrong. It includes a range of tactics such as the use of *agents provocateurs* to incite people to do things they otherwise would not to the charge of "material support" for terrorists, which can be applied to something as innocuous as giving money to a charitable foundation. The logic underlying these cases is that Muslims are naturally "predisposed" to commit violent acts and should therefore be put away. Downs explains that "to prove predisposition, the government claims that routine, normal behavior of the defendants—dress, religious observances, Islamic financial transactions, literature, etc.—indicates a 'predisposition' to commit terrorism, based on the false stereotype that *all* Muslims are predisposed to commit terrorism. If they are sufficiently 'Muslim,' they are sufficiently 'predisposed.'"[32]

This bizarre logic is reminiscent of Stephen Spielberg's dystopian film

Minority Report, in which a "precrime" unit reads people's minds in order to arrest them before they actually commit a crime on the grounds that they are "predisposed" to do so. In the movie, the unit is shut down. In real life, though, scores of people are facing an average of twenty years in prison for crimes that they did not commit; no one was killed, and no property was destroyed.[33] Here I discuss a few cases of preemptive prosecution.

"Material Support" for Terrorists

The charge of "material support" for terrorism has been used against people for a wide range of reasons, from donating to charitable organizations to participating in antiwar protests. Charity is one of the five pillars of Islam, a religious obligation for all Muslims, yet after 9/11 the Bush administration shut down virtually all Muslim charitable organizations operating in the United States and froze their assets, allegedly to prevent the flow of money to "terrorists." In doing so, it equated this fundamental aspect of the Islamic faith with aiding the "enemies" of the United States. Muslims who made contributions to charitable organizations that then donated money to groups the US government designated "foreign terrorist organizations" (FTOs) were tried in court for providing material support to terrorists. As Michael Ratner of the Center for Constitutional Rights explains, even limited contact, such as providing blankets to a hospital associated with an FTO or teaching nonviolent forms of conflict resolution to an FTO, is seen as material support.[34]

The largest Muslim charitable organization in the United States, the Holy Land Foundation, was alleged to be associated with Hamas and shut down by executive order shortly after 9/11. During the ensuing trial, it was well established that the Holy Land Foundation's leaders had not performed, supported, or encouraged any form of violence, and furthermore, that the money sent abroad was used to provide basic needs and services for the very poor, such as for Palestinians suffering under the humanitarian crisis in Gaza. The government did not establish any direct funding ties to "terrorism." Instead, the case rested on the argument that the foundation had sent money to *zakat* (charity for the poor) committees controlled by Hamas. The defense argued that these charitable committees were the only means through which aid could get to the people who needed it— and that UN agencies and USAID had also used the same committees. The reason that Hamas controlled these committees, they explained, was that Hamas is the elected government of Palestine. Even so, through racist fearmongering, the prosecution managed to secure harsh convictions. Two of the defendants are serving sixty-five-year prison terms.[35]

Material support charges have been used to target a wide variety of people. While Muslims have been the key targets, non-Muslims have also been subject to similar treatment. In 2010, the FBI raided the homes and offices of antiwar activists (including Caucasian US citizens) in Illinois, Minnesota, and North Carolina. They were given grand jury subpoenas on the grounds that they provided material support for terrorism. The state not only equated their peace activism with providing material support to terrorists but also infiltrated various left groups. FBI agents became active in the groups, formed friendships, and recorded private conversations.[36]

In yet another tragic case, Fahad Hashmi, a US citizen who grew up in Queens, New York, was arrested in 2006 and charged with providing material support to terrorists. Hashmi's crime was that he had allowed an acquaintance to stay in his London apartment, a man named Junaid Babar, who was carrying items that would later be delivered to al-Qaeda. And what, one might wonder, were these weapons of mass destruction? They were raincoats, ponchos, and waterproof socks. By the government's logic, Hashmi should have smelled a rat, knowing how deadly waterproof garments are and how decisively they would tip the balance of power in the direction of al-Qaeda. For this crime, he was put into prison for four years, three of them spent in solitary confinement.

The news media covered this story as though a "web of terror" had been discovered in New York City, hardly deviating from the official script. New York police chief Raymond Kelly claimed, "This arrest reinforces the fact that a terrorist may have roots in Queens and still betray us."[37] Hashmi, who was Jeanne Theoharis's student at Brooklyn College, was at the London School of Economics pursing a master's degree when he was arrested. Theoharis describes Hashmi as a "devout Muslim and outspoken political activist" whose "spunk and stubborn willingness to question authority" she admired. A promising student and a young man of conviction, Hashmi should have had a bright future ahead of him. Instead, Theoharis describes his appalling treatment at the Metropolitan Correctional Center in lower Manhattan, where he was put under Special Administrative Measures (SAMs) forbidding contact with the external world:

> Fahad was allowed no contact with anyone outside his lawyer and, in
> very limited fashion, his parents—no calls, letters, or talking through

the walls, because his cell was electronically monitored. He had to shower and relieve himself within view of the camera. He was allowed to write only one letter a week to a single member of his family, using no more than three pieces of paper. One parent was allowed to visit every two weeks, but often would be turned away at the door for bureaucratic reasons. Fahad was forbidden any contact—directly or through his lawyers—with the news media. He could read only portions of newspapers approved by his jailers—and not until 30 days after publication. Allowed only one hour out of his cell a day, he had no access to fresh air but was forced to exercise in a solitary cage.[38]

After four years of such treatment, the state managed to break Hashmi's spirit. Activists mobilized to support Hashmi, but the prosecution made sure that they would not be allowed into the courtroom, and won a motion to have Fahad judged by an anonymous jury with extra security. Such measures ensured that the jury would likely be prejudiced before the trial even started. Weighing these factors, Hashmi accepted a plea bargain on one count of conspiracy to provide material support to terrorism. Indeed, he inadvertently conspired to keep members of al-Qaeda dry: for that, his life had to be destroyed. He is serving fifteen years in jail and is still under solitary confinement and SAMs in a super-max prison in Colorado at the time of this writing.

The acquaintance who delivered the rain gear to al-Qaeda, Babar, was released on bail in 2008, and in 2010 his sentence was commuted to "time served." The judge noted that he "began cooperating even before his arrest."[39] This has led to speculation that Babar had become an *agent provocateur* for the government before he visited Hashmi's apartment, and that he may even have been sent to "get" Hashmi because of his politics and criticism of US policy.

Agents Provocateurs and Entrapment

The US government's increased use of *agents provocateurs* has resulted in numerous cases of entrapment, where individuals have been enticed to carry out terror plots that would not otherwise have occurred. Since 9/11, informants in mosques and in Muslim communities have led to the prosecution of more than two hundred people.[40] The Center for Human Rights and Global Justice report *Targeted and Entrapped* outlines various problems with the use of such informers, not the least of which is that they are recruited through threats, as mentioned above, as well as bribes—such as reduced criminal charges or a change in immigration status, creating what the report calls "a dangerous incentive structure."[41] Its authors found that in the cases they studied, the "government's informants introduced and aggressively pushed ideas about violent jihad and moreover, actually *encouraged* the defendants to believe that it was their duty to take action against the United States." The informants also goaded the defendants to acquire violent videos and weapons which were later used to convict them, and even went so far as to pick the locations that were to be attacked. In short, without the active leadership of the *agents provocateurs*, the "foiled terror plots" would never have existed.

The Newburgh Four case illustrates how entrapment works. This is the story of four African American men from poor families, two of whom had psychological issues, and all of whom had trouble with the law at various points. When David Williams was approached by an FBI informant, his younger brother had just been diagnosed with liver cancer. The family desperately needed money, and the FBI informant, Shahed Hussain, promised that and more. David's aunt Alicia McWilliams, who became an activist around his case, says that David "watched his brother almost die and be revived five times. He knew [his brother] Lord needed a liver. The whole experience took him for a loop." The informant capitalized on this vulnerability and incited David and three others to carry out a plan to bomb synagogues in the Bronx. Hussain not only picked the sites and drove the four men there, he provided them with bombs—and even badgered one man who said he refused to kill women and children, eventually convincing him to go forward with the plan. Without Hussain, the "terror plot" would not have existed. As Ted Conover, a resident of the targeted Bronx community, asks: "Why does the government's anti-terror net catch such unconvincing villains: black men near mosques who, in exchange for promises of money, sign on to knuckleheaded schemes that would never exist if it weren't for the informants being handsomely paid to incite them?"[42]

Conover, a distinguished writer at NYU's Arthur L. Carter Journalism Institute, observes that this was a perfect public relations moment for the law enforcement community. He writes that

> the arrest of the Newburgh Four was choreographed to perfection. A police helicopter shot live video as Hussain drove them down the Saw Mill River Parkway. After he and the four others left fake bombs at the Riverdale Temple and Riverdale Jewish Center, located about a block from each other, a massive police presence revealed itself: a

special semi-rig sealed off one end of the street and an armored truck the other; and a slew of plainclothes officers descended on the suspects, guns drawn, breaking their SUV's windows and pulling the men out. Within an hour, Mayor Michael Bloomberg, Police Chief Ray Kelly, and local elected and police officials were on the scene and in front of the television cameras, praising the capture of the dangerous criminals and the aversion of what, in the mayor's words, "could have been a terrible event in our city."[43]

Thus is the specter of "Islamic terrorism" kept alive.

The Terrorism Spectacle

In the fictional world of the television show *24*, government agent Jack Bauer (played by Kiefer Sutherland) swoops in to rescue innocent civilians from diabolical and devastating terror plots. The show received high ratings and ran for eight seasons, becoming the longest-running espionage drama on US television.[44] Despite the show's occasional attempts to portray "good" Muslims, as well as bad American leaders, its central premise strengthened the notion that terror plots are ubiquitous and that counterterrorism agents like Bauer are necessary to keep Americans safe. This fictional world is bolstered by reality in cases like that of the Newburgh Four, where slavish news media coverage only reinforces viewers' fear and paranoia about the ubiquity of "Islamic terrorism."

Downs refers to this manipulation of public opinion as a "cynical grand opera" whose mechanics he describes as follows:

> The drama often begins when the FBI sends dozens of agents to arrest the defendants, search the mosque, and interview hundreds of frightened friends and neighbors in a manner designed to intimidate the community. . . . At the trial, the government often makes an absurd display of security in order to intimidate the jury and media into believing the defendants are really dangerous. A massive police presence surrounds the court, with snipers posted on rooftops. (Whom are they supposed to shoot?) The government often requests anonymous juries and witnesses, and it calls phony experts, who are essentially government mouthpieces, to testify about a fantasy "terrorist network" that might involve the defendant. The government feeds "secret" evidence, obtained from illegal electronic surveillance, to the judge in order to affect the court's rulings and to prevent the defense from seeing or objecting to the material, and uses material obtained from these secret sources to as-

sault the defendant's character, even when the material is irrelevant to the charges. In this way, the government creates an atmosphere of hysteria and confusion to cover the lack of any substantive evidence that a real crime was committed.[45]

Rarely do journalists from the mainstream media question this "grand opera," and hence the illusion is maintained that the law enforcement community is "keeping America safe" from the barbarian hordes of "Islamic terrorists." But even with the help of this elaborate charade and an entire justice system bent to serve the needs of the War on Terror, the government has managed to secure only about twenty indictments per year for violent terrorist plots, according to a report from the Triangle Center on Terrorism and Homeland Security.[46] It is not clear from this report how many are products of entrapment or other preemptive prosecution tactics. What is clear, though, is that there is a huge gap between the threat as constructed and the reality of "Islamic terrorism." Of the fourteen thousand Americans murdered in 2011, *not one death* was the product of Muslim "terror plots."[47]

A comprehensive study of Muslim Americans who planned attacks either domestically or internationally or who joined groups on the government's list of "terrorist" organizations between September 2001 and May 2011 identified a total of 172 terror suspects or perpetrators.[48] Of these, only eleven people actually carried out attacks inside the United States; they were responsible for the deaths of thirty-three others over the course of a decade. What of the rest? Of the 172 cases listed, twenty-nine were still in trial as of the publication of the study. Sixty-three of the cases involved an undercover informer, and the report states that in these cases the entrapment defense had not worked. Sixty-four of the people included in the report had attended "terrorist training camps" in Afghanistan, Pakistan, or Somalia, though it clarifies that most "had no on-the-ground training."[49] And of these sixty-four, only thirty returned to the United States. Finally, the report states that "no Muslim-Americans were indicted for knowingly aiding or abetting the 9/11 attacks."[50] In all, eleven people on this list killed thirty-three people between 2001 and 2011. To put this in perspective, during this same period, there were *one hundred and fifty thousand* murders in the United States.

One might argue that the reason there have been so few fatalities from "Islamic terrorism" is that the law enforcement community has done such an excellent job. As we saw earlier, and as this report verifies, a significant number of "Muslim terrorists" either were entrapped or had simply attended a training camp. Furthermore, in international arenas outside the jurisdiction of US law enforcement, the figures are similar to those stated above. In 2010, the last year for which figures are available, according to the State Department's *Country Reports on Terrorism*,[51] the number of American civilians killed worldwide from terrorism-related acts was fifteen; all but two of these were in Afghanistan under US/NATO occupation.[52] In fact, more Americans died from lightning strikes and dog bites in 2010 than from terrorism.[53] More significantly, a Harvard Medical School study found that forty-five thousand Americans die each year due largely to the fact that they don't have health insurance.[54] Fifteen times the number of Americans who were killed on 9/11 die *each year* because they don't have health insurance, yet there is no war on the for-profit health care industry, much less an effort to save the lives of these people by providing them free and quality health care.

Seen in perspective, the domestic War on Terror is not really about keeping Americans safe as much as it is about creating a spectacle of fear. During the Cold War, schools routinely conducted "duck and cover" drills in which students and teachers hid under tables, supposedly to protect them from a blast in the event of a nuclear attack by the Soviet Union. Whatever the marginal benefits of ducking under a table, the ability to survive a nuclear bomb depends on one's distance from the blast, not on the furniture. The real goal of such activities was to keep the threat of attack alive and to foster fear and paranoia. In the War on Terror era, color-coded "terror threat levels" (ultimately phased out in 2011) and "if you see something, say something" signs in airports and subway stations have served a similar purpose by generating the spectacle of terrorism. And mainstream media coverage of "foiled terror plots" orchestrated by the law enforcement community only serves to reinforce this atmosphere.

Despite the spectacle and the institutionalized nature of racist law enforcement practices, there are insiders who find these practices problematic. When the Justice Department asked local law enforcement agencies to round up and interview immigrant men, police chiefs in Detroit, Portland, and Tucson refused to participate, stating that they had strict guidelines against such racial profiling. They also argued that these men were being targeted not because they were suspected of doing anything wrong but because of their country of origin.[55] In order for fear to be kept alive, such resistance, scant as it may be, has to be stamped out. One way is through the advancement of pseudoscientific theories that claim to predict human behavior. The theories of radicalization employed by the law enforcement community after 9/11 are based on the notion that it is possible to understand the process by which people turn to violence "using Islam as an ideological or religious justification."[56] More importantly, radicalization models claim to be able to predict future behavior, thereby operationalizing and justifying racial profiling and preemptive prosecution.

Theories of Radicalization

In 2007, the NYPD produced a document titled *Radicalization in the West: The Homegrown Threat*, in which it argues that there are four stages of radicalization: pre-radicalization, self-identification, indoctrination, and jihadization.[57] According to this model, all young Muslim males from middle-class and immigrant families fall into the pre-radicalization stage. In short, simply being a member of this group places one on a conveyor belt aimed toward "radicalization." Now if, by some chance, a member of this group should give up smoking, drinking, and gambling and start to grow a beard and wear traditional Islamic clothing, he is on the fast track toward acquiring "Jihadi-Salafist ideology," which puts him squarely in the next stage: "self-identification." Another characteristic of "self-identification" is political awareness and community activism. By the third stage, "indoctrination," the NYPD tells us, the person has withdrawn from the mosque and has become politicized around a set of new beliefs leading to the fourth stage, "jihadization," which is when he becomes ready to plan a terrorist attack. Signs of reaching this fourth stage include conducting research on the Internet, performing reconnaissance activity, and acquiring materials. While the report states that there is no profile for a potential terrorist, the thrust of its analysis is precisely about creating such a profile and predicting the activity of potential terrorists. Based on data from a grand total of ten cases, the report states that there is "remarkable consistency in the behaviors and trajectory of each of the plots across the stages" and that "this consistency provides a tool for predictability."[58] It is theories of this kind that are used to justify the kind of human mapping program discussed earlier, where infiltrators are sent to bookstores, community centers, mosques, and other "hot spots" where Muslim citizens and immigrants spend their time.

One does not need a Ph.D. in sociology or psychology to see that this is an inherently racist behavioral model fraught with double standards. For instance, the same kind of surveillance does not take place in white Christian communities, even though white supremacist terrorist organizations have long existed in the United States. A DHS report released in 2009 cautioned against violence by white supremacist groups: "The threat posed by lone wolves and small terrorist cells is more pronounced than in past years. In addition, the historical election of an African American president and the prospect of policy changes are proving to be a driving force for rightwing extremist recruitment and radicalization."[59] The report also names the recession and economic insecurity as factors that spur the growth of domestic terrorism. One of the key differences between the DHS report and the aforementioned NYPD report is that race, gender, and religion are incidental to the DHS's analysis. While it speaks about the anti-black, anti-immigrant, xenophobic, and pro-gun politics of white supremacist groups, it fails to make the leap to the conclusion that there is a four-step process of radicalization that begins with a person simply being a white Christian male. Naturally, there is no program to infiltrate white Christian communities to see how these dangerous men eat, worship, play, or shop.

But even beyond declining to profile all white Christian men, the civil liberties of far-right-wing groups are respected by the law enforcement community. There is no preemptive prosecution of these groups, which span a wide ideological range that includes white supremacists, anti-government fanatics, and various Christian fundamentalist tendencies, even though many such groups form "militias" and hold regular paramilitary training camps. As Downs notes, "Nobody bothers them because indoctrination and weapons training is constitutionally protected free speech and exercise of the Second Amendment right to bear arms. The criminal line is crossed only when such groups conspire to commit a specific crime. However, preemptive prosecution makes an exception for Muslims."[60] In short, while white supremacists are allowed to train with guns at sites all over the United States, if a regular Muslim American so much as acquires a weapon, he or she is deemed suspicious. As *Targeted and Entrapped* notes, the "evidence" that is routinely used in court cases to prove radicalization and a predisposition to commit violence by Muslims includes items such as violent videos, radical religious speeches, or weapons.[61]

The double standards and institutionalized nature of racism toward Muslims could not be more obvious. Yet, for the skeptical reader, I will adduce evidence from a report titled *Rethinking Radicalization* put out by NYU Law School's Brennan Center for Justice. The report draws from "studies by psychologists, social scientists, the security services of the United Kingdom, and security experts" to show that human behavior is complex and that it cannot be reduced to a four-step program or a "religious conveyor belt" theory.[62] An in-depth study by MI5, the British secret service agency, found that there is no "single pathway to extremism" and that the trajectories that lead people to embrace violence are complex.[63] A US Department of Defense study released in 2010 stated that "identifying potentially dangerous people before they act is difficult. Examinations after the fact show that people who commit violence usually have one or more risk factors for violence. Few people in the population who have risk factors, however, actually [commit violent acts]."[64] An academic study sponsored by DHS concluded that "there is no one path, no 'trajectory profile' to political radicalization. Rather there are many different paths. . . . Some of these paths do not include radical ideas or activism on the way to radical action, so the radicalization progression cannot be understood as an invariable set of steps or 'stages' from sympathy to radicalism."[65]

The Brennan report argues that there are differences within the security and law enforcement community on the question of radicalization. The NYPD (as well other local law enforcement agencies) and the FBI advocate stage-based models for radicalization which put Islam at the "front and center of their analysis."[66] On the other hand, the DHS and NCTC have shied away from this stagist approach, emphasizing the complexity of the process. They have also suggested that while Islam can be used to justify acts of terrorism, radicalization is not caused by Islam. While all sides within the national security establishment agree with the theory of radicalization and the need to apprehend "Muslim terrorists," they disagree about practical implementation. Here we see a similar dichotomy between the conservative wing of the law enforcement apparatus and what we might call a "realist" wing, similar to that which exists in the foreign policy establishment. That such parallel views should exist within the law enforcement community is hardly surprising, given the interconnections between the political establishment, the military, and the legal system. Personnel often move from one realm to the other, carrying with them their backgrounds and points of view. For instance, about a third of the FBI's counterterrorism staff has past military service in the Middle East.[67]

◆ ◆ ◆

In the new order of the War on Terror, law enforcement agencies have been adapted to target the "Islamic terrorists" in our midst. During the NATO intervention into Libya in 2011, the FBI drew up lists of Libyan residents in the United States to be interviewed—demonstrating again the links between domestic counterterrorism in the United States and military interventions abroad.[68] When the United States goes to war against a foreign enemy, it inevitably makes war on the perceived enemy within, which includes not only members of particular ethnic or national groups but also dissenters of all races. The end goal is to win consent for an imperial agenda through a process that orchestrates fear of the enemy within and preempts criticisms of empire-building. As we will see in the following chapter, the public campaign around "homegrown terrorism" was ratcheted up even further during the Obama presidency.

Chapter 9

Green Scare: The Making
of the Domestic Muslim Enemy

When a petite, blond, green-eyed woman from Philadelphia was
arrested on terrorism-related charges in 2010, the media went
wild trying to explain and understand what had happened—
Colleen LaRose, dubbed "Jihad Jane," looked nothing like what they expect terrorism suspects to look like. The subsequent media frenzy
involved plenty of hand-wringing and deep soul-searching to explain
why such an all-American woman might convert to Islam and become
involved in "terror plots." CNN concluded that "the indictment of Jihad
Jane shatters any thought that we can spot a terrorist just by appearance."[1]
The underlying logic here is that brown men can indeed be correctly
identified by appearance as terrorists—although terrorists, who seem to
be everywhere, come in all shapes, sizes and colors.

What this event also illuminates is that by the end of the first decade
after 9/11, there was a shift in the language of Islamophobia that emphasized the enemy within. Whereas the Islamophobia of the immediate post-9/11 period focused largely on the enemy "out there," against
which the United States supposedly had to go to war from Afghanistan
to Iraq to protect itself, now the enemy was inside the country's borders.
The tone of the earlier period, set by George Bush, was "we're fighting
them there so we don't have to fight them here."[2] In a West Point speech
in 2002 he stated, "We must take the battle to the enemy, disrupt his
plans and confront the worst threats."[3] The "terrorists" in our midst
were those sent from the outside who "hate our freedoms." Thus even
though, as we have seen, thousands of innocent Arabs and Muslims

were racially profiled in the aftermath of 9/11, the emphasis wasn't on "homegrown terrorism."

This shift occurred around 2009, when there was a spike in the number of Muslim Americans identified as "homegrown terrorists." That year, forty-eight Muslim Americans (defined as those who have stayed in the United States for a long period) were included in terrorism statistics, in contrast to two in 2008.[4] This spike came in part from the inclusion of seventeen Somali Americans who allegedly joined al-Shabaab in Somalia.[5] These figures precipitated a discourse around "homegrown terrorism."

The backlash against Islam and its practice in the United States was not yet as harsh as it was in Europe. Building on the centuries-long history of racism against Muslims discussed in chapter 1, European conservatives seized the opening created by 9/11 and went on the offensive, arguing that Muslims were not properly "integrated" into society and therefore susceptible to Islamist propaganda. They began introducing measures to ostracize Muslims and ban veils, minarets, and other symbols of Islam. Liberals and social democrats echoed these arguments, stressing the limits of multiculturalism and the need to preserve European Enlightenment ideals.[6]

This dimension of Islamophobia blossomed in the United States only at the end of the decade, when mosques and Islamic community centers came under attack from California to New York. A network of right-wing Islamophobes had been attempting to unleash anti-Muslim racism almost since 9/11 through a series of campaigns against Arab professors, Muslim community centers, and schools, but their breakthrough into the public sphere happened only after liberal Islamophobes cleared the way. Building on the media furor around "homegrown terrorism," President Obama unveiled his "Af-Pak strategy" and announced plans to send more troops to Afghanistan and increase drone strikes on Pakistan. Liberal imperialists and the mainstream media raised the alarm about "terrorists in our midst," providing the far-right "Islamophobic warriors" with the opening they had been waiting for. In the summer of 2010, they were successful in making the "Ground Zero Mosque" controversy (discussed in detail below) large enough to whip up fear and hatred against Muslim Americans and their cultural and religious symbols. An anti-Sharia campaign followed, leading about two dozen states to consider banning its use in the justice system. By the end of the decade, the turn inward was complete, with the birth of a new "green scare" akin to the red scare of the Cold War.

This chapter lays out the anatomy of this green scare.

Manufacturing the Green Scare

In 2009, several US citizens or legal residents were arrested for alleged connections to "terrorist" activity. In the latter part of the year these became high-profile cases that drew sustained media attention.[7] Following hard upon this media frenzy, in December 2009 the Obama administration announced plans to escalate the war in Afghanistan by sending in more troops and by stepping up drone attacks on Pakistan, in what came to be known as the "Af-Pak strategy." Almost a full year into his presidency, the "peace president" had failed to fulfill his campaign promises to shut down Guantanamo Bay and undo the violations of civil liberties unleashed by Bush. The "homegrown terrorist" threat being whipped up by the media served well to continue the status quo.

The first prominent case was that of Najibullah Zazi, an Afghan citizen and legal US resident who was arrested in September 2009 on charges of conspiracy to use weapons of mass destruction. This was followed by David Coleman Headley, a US citizen arrested in October for planning to attack a Danish newspaper. In December, revelations surfaced that Headley might have conspired with operatives of Lashkar-e-Taiba, a Pakistani group, in the 2008 Mumbai attacks. In March 2010 he pled guilty to all charges in an Indian court.

On November 5, Major Nidal Malik Hasan killed thirteen people and wounded thirty at Fort Hood outside Killeen, Texas. The ensuing media circus focused on Hasan's religion and continued the trend of conflating Islam and violence.[8] Later that month, the federal government indicted eight people in Minnesota for allegedly recruiting approximately two dozen Somali Americans (citizens and legal residents) to fight with an insurgent group in Somalia. That December, five young men from northern Virginia were arrested in Sargodha, Pakistan, accused of traveling there to fight alongside Taliban militants in Afghanistan.

Though none of the "homegrown terrorism" cases mentioned above lacked for sensational media treatment, the case of "Jihad Jane" caused the biggest uproar. While the Virginia case prompted speculation in the press about why five "normal" young men might be moved to fight with the Taliban, it was accepted that this was a possibility for young Muslim men. LaRose's gender, ethnicity, and "Main Street" Pennsylvania background meant that *anyone* could be a terrorist. Like the McCarthy-era red scare that imagined Communist spies lurking in every neighborhood, school, and workplace, the "green scare" encouraged Americans to view not only Muslims but anyone who converted to Islam as a threat.

Coming as they did in quick succession, these cases spurred the rapid development of a new media lexicon around "homegrown terrorism." The *Washington Post* was typical: "The arrests came at a time of growing concern about homegrown terrorism after the recent shootings at the Fort Hood, Tex., military base [by Hasan] and charges filed this week against a Chicago man [Headley] accused of playing a role in last year's terrorist attacks in Mumbai."[9] Even though scores of Muslim Americans had been arrested in the past, often with little or no basis, this consistent attention cast Muslim citizens and legal residents as enemies of the state, marking a new turn in the rhetoric of the War on Terror. The groundwork was being laid for the new green scare.

The most virulent expression of this green scare was articulated by NYU professor Tunku Varadarajan. In a November 2009 *Forbes* article titled "Going Muslim," Varadarajan argued that what precipitated the tragedy at Fort Hood was not the racist harassment that Hasan faced in the army or the emotionally debilitating pressure of his job as an overworked army psychiatrist, but rather a condition that he suggests is inherent to all Muslims: the tendency toward violence.[10] He argued that Hasan didn't "go postal"—that is, break down and become violent (the term became popular after a 1986 shooting by a postal worker). Rather, Varadarajan argued, Hasan was simply enacting, in a cold and calculated manner, the teachings of Islam. He was "going Muslim." As Varadarajan put it, "This phrase ['going Muslim'] would describe the turn of events where a seemingly integrated Muslim-American—a friendly donut vendor in New York, say, or an officer in the U.S. Army at Fort Hood—discards his apparent integration into American society and elects to vindicate his religion in an act of messianic violence against his fellow Americans."

In short, for Varadarajan all Muslim Americans are "imminently violent," and while they appear to be integrated into American society, they are in fact ticking time bombs who will inevitably explode into violent, murderous rage. The logic of biological racism is intertwined here with the logic of cultural racism. The homegrown terrorist, identified as brown, male, and Muslim, is inherently violent despite all semblances to the contrary. What makes "those people," including the occasional white person like LaRose, threats is their religion; they are culturally programmed by Islam to carry out murder and mayhem, like jihadist Manchurian candidates. In making this argument, Varadarajan was simply echoing the logic of "preemptive prosecution" and theories of radicalization long employed by the law enforcement apparatus. The cases of Hasan and Zazi (the "friendly donut vendor") and the overall hysteria around "homegrown" terrorism created a space for the articulation of such arguments in the mainstream.

Rather than push back against this racism, President Obama—who has several Muslim relatives, has spent time living in Indonesia (the country with the largest Muslim population in the world), and presumably should know better—used these high-profile cases in a speech unveiling his strategy to escalate the war in Afghanistan. One might speculate that a White House eager to prime public opinion for a troop surge of thirty thousand may even have encouraged a pliant media to devote attention to "homegrown terrorism." Obama said in a speech at West Point: "I am convinced that our security is at stake in Afghanistan and Pakistan. This is the epicenter of violent extremism practiced by al-Qaeda. It is from here that we were attacked on 9/11, and it is from here that new attacks are being plotted as I speak. This is no idle danger; no hypothetical threat. In the last few months alone, we have apprehended extremists within our borders who were sent here from the border region of Afghanistan and Pakistan to commit new acts of terror."[11] Obama's speech capitalizes on the climate of fear whipped up by the continuous and sustained coverage of the Zazi, Headley, and Virginia cases, all of which were related to Afghanistan and Pakistan. Obama's reference to "extremists within our borders" thus added to the hype about the grave danger that terrorism and "violent extremism" allegedly pose to US citizens, a threat dire enough to justify sending thirty thousand more troops to Afghanistan.

The reality, however, flies in the face of this rhetoric, as the last chapter showed. Interestingly, even the Rand Corporation, a right-wing institution, admitted that the danger posed to Americans by "terrorism" is limited. In the *Los Angeles Times*, Gregory Treverton noted that in "the five years after 2001, the number of Americans killed per year in terrorist attacks worldwide was never more than a hundred, and the toll some years was barely in double figures. Compare that with an average of 63 by tornadoes, 692 in bicycle accidents and 41,616 in motor-vehicle-related accidents."[12] Indeed.

In 2009, the State Department reported that the number of Americans killed that year around the world due to terrorism was a grand total of nine. Fourteen people were injured, and four were kidnapped.[13] To put those numbers in perspective, the Bureau of Labor Statistics counted 4,340 deaths due to workplace events or exposure in 2009.[14] Deaths from car accidents numbered 30,797.[15] Yet no one declared war on corporations or auto manufacturers. What's more, a State Department terrorism report released in April 2009 states that "al-Qaeda . . . and associated networks continued to lose ground, both structurally and in the court of world public opinion." Nevertheless, the report asserted that these organizations "remained the greatest terrorist threat to the United States and its partners."[16] All this reveals not only the disconnect between rhetoric and reality but also the mechanics involved in mobilizing a politics of fear. It is worth emphasizing that the threat from terrorism is a *manufactured crisis*, one that is useful to justify war and continued violations of civil liberties domestically. The green scare is just as useful today as the red scare was during the Cold War.

The essentialism involved in painting all Muslims with the brush of violent jihad fits neatly into the Orientalist "clash of civilizations" rhetoric. This presented something of a problem for the Obama administration, which at the time was making a concerted effort to eschew that argument in favor of a "counterinsurgency" strategy, as discussed in chapter 7. The realist think tank CSIS released a report outlining Zazi's and Headley's cases and argued that while the United States needs to clamp down on "Internet radicalization," it must balance this with efforts to "puncture" the "clash of civilizations" narrative—not because it is inherently objectionable but because al-Qaeda uses the same argument in its recruitment efforts![17] This balance requires some rhetorical finesse—a specialty of the liberal imperialists in the Obama administration, who were indeed able to pull it off.

Thus, the report approvingly notes that "White House officials already have discarded phrases like 'war on radical Islam.'" Yet, the authors add, such rhetorical gestures are insufficient given the reality of war. The key challenge is "how to balance the need to combat global terrorism" (read: expand the empire) "with the drawbacks of large-scale, direct military intervention" (read: large-scale casualties and the problems of occupation). This was the challenge inherited by the Obama administration. Despite self-consciously dropping the use of phrases like "War on Terror" and mitigating some of the worst Islamophobic rhetoric of the Bush administration, the challenges of empire and, in the following years, the failure of the counterinsurgency strategy would eventually lead the Obama administration back into the arms of counterterrorism and its corresponding rhetoric.

The "Ground Zero Mosque" Controversy

The immediate consequence of the "homegrown terrorist" hysteria was that the far-right-wing Islamophobes (more on them in the following chapter) who had long hoped to capture the national debate were able to do so. They took center stage in the wake of a controversy they generated around the construction of an Islamic community center in downtown Manhattan. In 2009, Imam Feisal Abdul Rauf, who had served as a cleric in downtown Manhattan for more than a quarter century, proposed the construction of a center modeled on the 92nd Street Y and the Jewish Community Center in Manhattan. The goal of the proposed center was to promote greater understanding of the Muslim community. Its name, Córdoba House, refers to the city of Córdoba, Spain, a leading cultural center of the Muslim empire that ruled the Iberian Peninsula (see chapter 1). Córdoba represented not only a high point of intellectual development but also a period of peaceful coexistence among Muslims, Christians, and Jews.

Imam Rauf, who positions himself as a "moderate Muslim," envisioned a community center with recreation facilities like a swimming pool, basketball court, gym, culinary school, art studios, a child care center, and badly needed prayer space for the neighborhood Muslim community. His plan was to enable people of all faiths to interact. Rauf is an establishment figure who has conducted trainings for the FBI and the State Department since 9/11; we met him in chapter 7 in relation to the 2007 policy group's advice on improving US relations with the "Muslim world."

The Obama era, it was believed, would be a time when "good Muslims" could reshape the political agenda. When the *New York Times* ran a front-page story on Cordoba House in December 2009, the overall tone was positive, even though it noted with some alarm what it might mean for a Muslim community center to be built so close to Ground Zero. Rauf told the *Times*, "We want to push back against the extremists."[18] A mother of a 9/11 victim also publicly backed the Islamic center.[19] New York mayor Michael Bloomberg supported the project, as did city officials. Even right-wing Fox News anchor Laura Ingraham seemed unperturbed: in an interview with Cordoba House cofounder Daisy Khan in December 2009, Ingraham supported the project. Even while arguing that Muslim-majority countries from Saudi Arabia to Lebanon are intolerant toward Christians, she told Khan, "I can't find many people who really have a problem with it. . . . I like what you're trying to do."[20]

On May 6, 2010, the New York City Community Board voted *unanimously* to approve the project. As *Salon* reporter Justin Elliott has documented, the Cordoba House project did not become controversial until May 2010.[21] In response to the community board's decision, Pamela Geller, a right-wing blogger, posted an entry titled "Monster Mosque Pushes Ahead in Shadow of World Trade Center Islamic Death and Destruction." In it, she wrote, "This is Islamic domination and expansionism. The location is no accident. Just as Al-Aqsa was built on top of the Temple in Jerusalem." The next day, her group Stop Islamization of America (SIOA) launched "Campaign Offensive: Stop the 911 Mosque!"[22] While this wasn't the first time the organized Islamophobes had blogged about the community center, their moment had finally arrived in the aftermath of the "homegrown terrorism" hysteria, which created space for the hard right to fan the flames of racism.

Stop Islamization of America, whose name is based on the notion that Muslims are conspiring to take over the United States, called a protest for May 29 against what Geller called the "911 Monster Mosque." Geller is a fan of far-right Dutch politician Geert Wilders (the feeling is mutual, given his glowing blurb for the book she coauthored on the Obama presidency) and an admirer of open fascists and street gangs such as the English Defense League that routinely attack Muslims and immigrants. She once claimed that Black South Africans are launching a "genocide" against whites.[23] A staunch Zionist, she wrote a column in an Israeli newspaper in which she referred to the term "Palestinian" as "fallacious" and exhorted Israelis to "stand loud and proud. Give up nothing. Turn over not a pebble. For every rocket fired, drop a MOAB. Take back Gaza. Secure Judea and Samaria."[24]

Subsequently, the *New York Post* began running articles that extensively quoted Geller and her vitriolic rhetoric. One article falsely claimed that Cordoba House's opening date was set for September 11, 2011. This was the moment, Elliot suggests, when this story spread like wildfire, gaining media attention not only on Fox News and other conservative outlets but also in the mainstream media. However, even at this stage, the community center was still far from becoming a symbol of Muslim "insensitivity." When Mark Williams, a Tea Party leader, attacked Imam Rauf, New York City politicians came out against Williams and asserted their support for the center.[25] Williams's blog posts were despicable. He wrote: "The animals of allah for whom any day is a great day for a massacre are drooling over the positive response that they are getting from New York City officials over a proposal to build a 13 story monument to the 9/11 Muslims who hijacked those 4 airliners. The monument would consist of a Mosque for the worship of the terrorists' monkey-god and a 'cultural center' to propagandize for the extermination of all things not approved by their cult."[26]

The far right continued its well-funded campaign against the Islamic community center. The conservative blog *Pajamas Media*, which received $3.5 million from the notorious Islamophobe and right-wing Zionist Aubrey Chernick, used its platform to oppose the community center.[27] Neocon Frank Gaffney wrote in June that the "Ground Zero mosque is designed to be a permanent, in-our-face beachhead for Shariah, a platform for inspiring the triumphalist ambitions of the faithful."[28] Newt Gingrich echoed this point on Fox News, stating that the center represented Muslim "triumphalism."[29] The talking points were well orchestrated; neocon Daniel Pipes used the same wording, stating that the building "reeks of Islamic triumphalism."[30] But this line of attack was not restricted to the right-wing media world of Fox News, the *Washington Times*, and the *New York Post*.

When Newt Gingrich and Sarah Palin added their voices, the "debate" spread to the mainstream. Gingrich ranted that "Nazis don't have the right to put up a sign next to the Holocaust Museum in Washington. We would never accept the Japanese putting up a site next to Pearl Harbor. There is no reason to accept a mosque next to the World Trade Center."[31] In short, political figures used their credibility to legitimize the rants of the far right.

After May, more and more voices critical of the project started to find a home in the mainstream media. The pro-Israel Anti-Defamation League weighed in, saying that it was insensitive to build the center "in the shadow" of the World Trade Center because it would cause pain to the victims of 9/11.[32] Rudy Giuliani called the mosque a "desecration."[33] To be sure, some of the mainstream media defended Muslims, the center, and by extension, the United States' image as a tolerant multiracial society. Mayor Bloomberg defended it in a speech delivered with the Statue of Liberty in the background.[34] Mainstream liberal figures like Keith Olbermann, Jon Stewart, and Stephen Colbert also took a tough line against the bigots and exposed the racism at the heart of their project.

The *New York Times* featured a front-page story titled "When an Arab Enclave Thrived Downtown,"that advanced the proposition that Arabs (and Muslims) are an integral part of American society.[35] *Time* did a cover story that asked, "Is America Islamophobic?"[36] Under this question on the cover is the symbol of Islam, the crescent and star, filled in with the US flag. Yet this coverage was contradictory. While *Time* defended Muslims against racist attacks, its article stopped short of showing the connections between Islamophobia and the War on Terror. Moreover, *Time's* cover just a few weeks prior to this issue featured an Afghan woman whose nose had been cut off, with the title "What Happens If We Leave Afghanistan"— both reinforcing the connection between Islam and violence against women and recycling the old "white man's burden" argument.[37]

The far right's effort to brand the center as the "victory mosque" was successful because it built on the media hysteria whipped up in the previous months by the Obama administration. The frenzy around "homegrown terrorism" opened the door, and it was just a matter of time before the far right came waltzing (or perhaps goose-stepping) in. These forces, along with sectors of the Republican Party, were so successful in setting the terms of the debate that anywhere between 54 and 68 percent of Americans expressed opposition to the project at its proposed location.[38]

This opposition arose in no small part due to the role played by Democratic Party politicians, whose positions on the community center ranged from neutral to downright hostile. House speaker Nancy Pelosi's response was to ask who was funding the opposition. The following day she added that the location of the project was a "local decision" and that freedom of religion was a constitutional right.[39] This rather tepid defense paled in comparison to the rhetoric used by the other side.

Pelosi's counterpart in the Senate, majority leader Harry Reid, decided to speak out against the project, stating that while the First Amendment protects freedom of religion, he believed that the "mosque should be built someplace else."[40] Jeff Greene of Florida, running in the Senate primary, said that "common sense and respect for those who lost their lives and loved ones gives sensible reason to build the mosque someplace else."[41] Then came liberal Democrat Howard Dean, who argued that this was "a real affront to people who lost their lives" in the 9/11 attacks. In an interview with a New York radio station, he said he would like to see the center built in another, less controversial location.[42]

As this lopsided debate unfolded, President Obama qualified his earlier statements in support of the project by saying that while he affirms the religious rights of all people, he was not in saying this commenting "on the wisdom of making a decision to put a mosque there."[43] Obama was quickly adapting to right-wing pressure; when Gainesville, Florida, minister Terry Jones announced his plan to burn the Koran on September 11, Obama did not argue that such an act was offensive, that it constituted an attack on religious freedom, or that it was reminiscent of Ku Klux Klan cross burnings in the South, but that it threatened "national security" and would put US soldiers in Iraq and Afghanistan "in harm's way": "This could increase the recruitment of individuals who'd be willing to blow themselves up in American cities or European cities."[44] Obama's summoning the specter of suicide bombers in America's cities only further stirred the pot of Islamophobic hatred.

Polls in mid-2010 showed that close to 20 percent of Americans believed that Obama was a "secret Muslim" and that this made him an unfit president. Rather than challenge the racist assumptions of his accusers, Obama chose instead to emphasize his Christian credentials. This posture only gave credence to the notion that there is something wrong with being Muslim. In short, with a few exceptions (such as Keith Ellison, the first Muslim to be elected to Congress), the liberal imperialists in the Democratic Party pandered to the far right on this question. It is therefore not surprising that the right was able to set the terms of the discussion.

The Rise of the Islamophobic Network

The Cordoba House controversy was, of course, not the far right's first attack on Muslims. As Max Blumenthal notes, the "Ground Zero mosque" controversy is "the fruit of an organized, long-term campaign by a tight confederation of right-wing activists and operatives who first focused on Islamophobia soon after the September 11th attacks, but only attained critical mass during the Obama era."[45] He explains that the efforts began in the early 2000s, when a coalition of Jewish groups ranging from the Anti-Defamation League (ADL) and the American Jewish

Committee (AJC) to AIPAC came together to address what they saw as a sudden increase in pro-Palestinian activism on college campuses. The key targets on campuses were Middle East scholars whose work challenged the right-wing narrative of Middle East politics generally and of the Arab-Israeli conflict in particular.

Martin Kramer's *Ivory Towers on Sand: The Failures of Middle Eastern Studies in America* (published in 2001) provided the intellectual ballast necessary to make the argument that Middle East scholars were un-American because of their criticisms of Israel and of US foreign policy.[46] Kramer, who studied under Bernard Lewis, produced a book that fueled an effort to target and stifle critical thought. As Joel Beinin notes, "Kramer and his ilk were emboldened by their links to officials in the upper-mid levels of the Bush administration," and particularly to the neo-cons who shared their worldview.[47] He adds that the "neo-cons have much more powerful political connections than those that the AJC, the ADL and AIPAC were able to mobilize." But this unity was not coincidental. Rather, if Lewis, Zakaria, and others were the intellectual core brought together to formulate the propaganda war after 9/11 (as discussed in chapter 7), Kramer, Daniel Pipes, David Horowitz, and others served as the activists out in the world policing critical thought. Their job was to ensure that the War on Terror brand remained uncontested and that their propaganda was not punctured by scholars with the knowledge and ability to expose the lies. Bush even nominated Pipes to a seat on the board of directors of the federally funded United States Institute of Peace, which was supposed to produce knowledge to aid in conflict resolution. Pipes's nomination was scuttled, but this move represents the neocons' penchant for thought control.

Pipes went on to found the website *Campus Watch,* which asserts that Middle East scholars are un-American. In terms that barely disguise its racism, the website explains why this might be so; one page, since removed, stated that "Middle East studies in the United States has become the preserve of Middle East Arabs" who "have brought their views with them."[48] The next logical step was to target Arabs. Indeed, Campus Watch's first prominent attack occurred against Professor Joseph Massad of Columbia University. The David Project, a Hillel-funded group founded explicitly to influence campus debates on Israel, produced a documentary film titled *Columbia Unbecoming* which claimed that Jewish students were being intimidated by Arab professors and that Columbia's campus climate was rife with anti-Semitism. David Horowitz contributed to this attack by calling Massad "dangerous" in his book *The Professors: The 101 Most Dangerous Academics in America*. Funds poured in from a network of sources (discussed in greater depth in the next chapter), and pressure on the Columbia administration intensified. Democratic congressman Anthony Weiner added fuel to the fire by calling for Massad to be dismissed. In the end, however, Columbia students and faculty launched a campaign in defense of Massad that defeated the Islamophobes. Massad not only earned tenure but won the prestigious Lionel Trilling Award for excellence in scholarship.

Undaunted by this defeat, the David Project turned its attention to the Islamic Society of Boston, which had been trying to build a center to serve the Muslim population in Roxbury. The David Project unleashed a campaign of lawsuits and propaganda, claiming that the center was receiving money from sources such as the Muslim Brotherhood and the Wahhabis in Saudi Arabia. The right-wing media jumped into action, from Murdoch's *Boston Herald* to the local Fox affiliates. The *Boston Globe* also echoed this argument in a series of reports that advanced the notion that the center could become a place to train underground terror cells.[49]

Yet again, however, the Islamophobic network failed. This time it was defeated by an interfaith effort launched by liberal Jews, who successfully pushed back against the fearmongering. In 2008, the community center was built; none of the David Project's dire predictions were ever realized. However, as Blumenthal notes, the "local crusade established an effective blueprint for generating hysteria against the establishment of Islamic centers and mosques across the country, while galvanizing a cast of characters who would form an anti-Muslim network which would gain attention and success in the years to come."[50]

Indeed, their first success was a campaign against Debbie Almontaser, who was to serve as the principal of Khalil Gibran International Academy. The academy, a secular public elementary school with an English-Arabic curriculum, was proposed for construction in Brooklyn as one of sixty-seven bilingual schools in the New York City system. Almontaser, a long-time educator of Yemeni descent, was accused of being a jihadist and a 9/11 denier by Stop the Madrassa, a coalition launched by the Islamophobia network. Pamela Geller, who was just cutting her teeth as an Islamophobic warrior, blogged that Almontaser "opposed the war on terror," was associated with the Council on American-Islamic Relations (CAIR), and had even had the audacity to accept an award from this "radical" group. If that was not enough, she went on to accuse Almontaser of "whitewash[ing] the genocide against the Jews."[51] Daniel Pipes, who also took part in the campaigns against Massad and the Boston Islamic center, claimed the school should be stopped because "Arabic-language instruction is inevitably laden with Pan-Arabist and Islamist baggage."[52] The campaign reached fever pitch when the Islamophobes found a picture of a T-shirt with the slogan "Intifada NYC" produced by the group Arab Women Active in the Arts and Media (AWAAM), a local Arab feminist organization. The weak connection between AWAAM and Almontaser is that they share an office with the Yemeni-American association on whose board Almontaser sits. This was all the Islamophobes needed to brand Almontaser as a jihadist.

The *New York Post* carried a story that stated that the T-shirt was "apparently a call for a Gaza-style uprising in the Big Apple."[53] Almontaser's efforts to explain the meaning and significance of the term *intifada* were countered with an ADL spokesperson who called AWAAM "an active supporter of the terrorist groups Hezbollah and Hamas." The usual suspects all chimed in and the pressure mounted. After enduring an intense campaign of personal harassment and intimidation, Almontaser was forced to resign when her former supporter Mayor Bloomberg caved. The Khalil Gibran International Academy was eventually established, Almontaser sued the city, and the Islamophobic network learned valuable lessons on how to wage a successful campaign and apply pressure on elected officials. It wasn't long before another opportunity fell into their laps in the form of the Cordoba House project—though even here their victory was only partial. They did manage to sway public opinion. Attacks on mosques and community centers across the country escalated, and Cordoba House's founders changed its name to the more neutral "Park51." However, plans to construct the center continued and it eventually opened in 2012.

◆ ◆ ◆

This chapter focused on the turn inward from the Muslim enemy "out there" to the "terrorists" in our midst. While the Islamophobic warriors played a key part in intensifying the attacks on Muslims, they could not have succeeded had the liberal Islamophobes not paved the way. Obama's strategy of escalating the war on Afghanistan relied on the mainstream media to generate hysteria about "homegrown terrorists." Once the curtain was raised, the Islamophobic warriors (who were waiting eagerly in the wings, rehearsing and fine-tuning their attack campaign strategies) seized the moment with the "Ground Zero Mosque" controversy. In the following chapter I examine this Islamophobic network in greater detail, outlining their funding sources and their connections to think tanks and the foreign policy establishment.

Chapter 10

Islamophobia
and the New McCarthyism

While it was the "Ground Zero mosque" controversy that brought the most rabid Islamophobes into the limelight, they have the Norwegian right-wing terrorist Anders Behring Breivik to thank for making them hard to ignore. Breivik, who killed seventy-seven people in a bombing and mass shooting in 2011, cited several prominent Islamophobes in his manifesto. Robert Spencer (cofounder with Geller of SIOA) led the pack, receiving 162 mentions in the hate-filled diatribe.[1] In this context, a series of articles and reports appeared in 2011 that sought to shed light on the organized nature of the Islamophobic network, its sources of funding, and its international scope. For instance, David Yerushalmi was featured in a lengthy *New York Times* report as the mastermind behind a crusade to ban the use of Sharia law in US courts.[2] Steven Emerson, Frank Gaffney, and Bill French were discussed in an investigative report on the Islamophobes' sources of funds.[3] And the Center for American Progress put out a detailed report titled *Fear, Inc.: The Roots of the Islamophobic Network in America*,[4] which was covered by sectors of the mainstream media.

This was indeed a welcome development in that these and other reports helped to shed much-needed light on the network of hard-core Islamophobes. However, they didn't go far enough. For instance, *Fear Inc.* constantly and repeatedly emphasizes the point that the Islamophobic network consists of a small, tight-knit group of individuals who have influence beyond their numbers. Even while the report is quite thorough in terms of showing the connections between the extremists and the neocons, as well as other political figures, conservative foundations, and the mainstream media, it nevertheless insists that the Islamophobes are a fringe group outside of mainstream politics. At the end of the day, even while these and other reports have been useful in terms of exposing the machinations of the hardcore Islamophobes, they fall short because they fail to demonstrate the institutionalized nature of anti-Muslim racism.

This chapter sets out to situate the right-wing fanatics within the broader context in which they operate. Following David Caute, I will argue that the extremists function to create a climate of fear that bolsters the aims of empire. In his book *The Great Fear*, Caute showed that Mc-Carthyism wasn't simply about one out-of-control senator, but a political system (including both Democrats and Republicans) that allowed a figure like Joseph McCarthy to set the political agenda. McCarthy was a useful tool in prosecuting the Cold War—particularly in creating a climate of fear where dissent could be punished and neutralized. The right-wing Islamophobic warriors play a similar role during the era of the War on Terror. They are not "alien outsiders" but emerge from within the political establishment, the security apparatus, the academy, the think tank milieu, and the mainstream media. Thus, far from "infiltrating" an otherwise good system, the new McCarthyites are a product of, and fit comfortably within, the structures of American empire; their role is to push the envelope.

The New McCarthyites

There are four interconnected groups of people who have come together to project the image of a vicious and menacing "Muslim enemy" and to generate fear and hatred. They include members of the neocon camp who have devoted themselves to ferreting out the "Islamic terrorist"; Zionists whose goal of policing criticism of Israel dovetails neatly with the logic of Islamophobia; the Christian Right, which has joined the ranks of the Islamophobic warriors; and a group of former Muslims (and Christians) from the Middle East and South Asia who have profited from Islam-bashing.

The Neocons and Zionists

Frank Gaffney and Daniel Pipes are two leading neocons who have focused on the politics of Islamophobia. Gaffney, as stated earlier, was a Reagan-era deputy assistant defense secretary who served under Richard

Perle from 1983 to 1987. For Gaffney, it was an easy shift from cold warrior to Islamophobic warrior. He is a senior adviser to the group Americans for Victory Over Terrorism (AVOT), which is a subsidiary of Project for the New American Century (PNAC).[5] AVOT, headed by conservative William Bennett, states on its website that it is "dedicated to victory in the War on Terrorism" through "the shaping of public opinion, the encouragement of a foreign policy based on the founding principles of America, increased research about Islam and Islamism and a steadfast commitment to attacking those who would blame America first."[6]

This statement captures the strategy adopted by the neocons to "win" the War on Terror. A crucial part of this strategy is the battle for public opinion. Within the journals of the foreign policy establishment, the neocons have forcefully put forward their vision and polemicized against other foreign policy paradigms such as those of the realists (see chapter 7). The pivotal 1996 Kristol-Kagan piece about "benevolent global hegemony"[7] not only argued against realism and stressed that American domination of the world would be benevolent and in the interests of all nations, but also underscored the point that the American public would have to be won over to this idea; they had to be "educated" and "inspired" to accept their special responsibilities as citizens of empire.[8] This meant not only serving in the military but also developing an ideological "sense of mission" in imperialist interventions, based on a faith in "American greatness."[9]

What better way to promote this ideology than to create an overarching enemy, the Muslim "evildoers"—and later the "Islamofascists"—against whom America, the great and good, should make war? September 11 provided the neocons with the enemy they needed to promote their vision. As Cooper states, the neoconservatives are "most comfortable when they have . . . an ideological competitor against which they can define themselves."[10] While neocons like Podhoretz celebrated the collapse of the Soviet Union, Cooper notes that, lacking a new rival, he was "clearly lost."[11] This sentiment applies across the board. Dorien, interviewing prominent neocons for his book *Imperial Designs*, similarly observes that "most were anxious to find a substitute for the energizing and unifying role that the cold war played for them."[12] This new enemy has taken the form of Islam. As the AVOT statement makes clear, it is not simply the violent section of the Islamist movement that they wish to "research," but "Islam and Islamism" as a whole. It shouldn't be surprising, then, that simply being a

Muslim makes you worthy of suspicion, according to this logic. Drawing a page from the McCarthyist playbook, Gaffney was one of many who claimed that Obama might be a "secret Muslim."[13] The implication, of course, is that being a Muslim is sufficient cause for not trusting him.

The last aspect of AVOT's strategy involves silencing dissenting views. As its website proudly declares, AVOT has a "steadfast commitment to attacking those who would blame America first." This is an open declaration of war on Muslims and the left. Its targets are people in Muslim-majority countries, particularly Arabs, and the left in the West, particularly the American left. Neocons have vigorously argued that the United States has been a force for good in the Middle East and that people in that region therefore have only themselves to blame for the state of their countries. This argument is peddled not just by the likes of Pipes and Lewis but also by mainstream figures like Fareed Zakaria and Thomas Friedman.[14] Ayaan Hirsi Ali, a close associate of the neocons, gives legitimacy to this argument through her status as a "native informer." Ali, who blames Islam for her difficult childhood in Somalia (and pretty much everything else), asks: "Why are Muslims so hypersensitive to criticism and why don't they do anything with it except to respond by denying it or playing the victim?"[15] In short, Muslims who attempt to place legitimate blame at the doorstep of the United States are playing the victim. Irshad Manji, another ideological collaborator with empire, puts it more condescendingly when she tells her "fellow Muslims" to "grow up," insisting forcefully that the United States has been a champion of human rights and that "neither Israel or America lies at the root of Muslim misery."[16]

The attack on the left, particularly the academic left, has been led by the groups discussed in the last chapter, such as the David Project and Campus Watch. Kramer's book *Ivory Towers on Sand* was followed by *Unholy Alliance: Radical Islam and the American Left* (2004), by the ex-leftist David Horowitz, and Andrew McCarthy's *The Grand Jihad: How Islam and the Left Sabotage America* (2010). Building on Kramer's early polemic that Middle East studies departments are wrong about US policy, these books attempt to cast the net more widely, condemning the left as a whole and constructing a conspiratorial alliance between Islamists and the left. As we saw in chapter 7, the origins of this argument go back to the 1980s and the influential conferences organized by the Zionist Jonathan Institute.

Breivik carried this argument to its logical conclusion when he assassinated teenagers at a camp run by the social-democratic Norwegian

Labor Party. Although the neocons disavowed Breivik's actions, the explicit goal of their ideological attacks is to both silence dissenting views and intimidate activists. This process of intimidation is carried out through smear campaigns and harassment on the part of the Islamophobes, but it is also carried out by the legal apparatus. As chapter 8 argued, the law enforcement community has targeted not only Muslims and Muslim activists but progressive groups as well. These practices, initiated during Bush's regime, were extended and strengthened by the Obama administration. This should not surprise us. After all, the Smith Act, which was used to persecute the left during the Cold War, was passed under Democratic president Franklin Delano Roosevelt.

In addition to AVOT, Gaffney's Center for Security Policy (CSP) has been instrumental in promoting anti-Muslim propaganda. As the authors of *Fear Inc.* write, CSP is "a key source for right-wing politicians, pundits, and grassroots organizations, providing them with a steady stream of reports mischaracterizing Islam and warning of the dangers of Islam and American Muslims."[17] In addition to CSP, the other leading sources of anti-Muslim racism are Pipes's Middle East Forum, Robert Spencer's Jihad Watch, Pamela Geller and Robert Spencer's Stop Islamization of America, Steven Emerson's Investigative Project on Terrorism, and David Yerushalmi's Society of Americans for National Existence. Together, these groups have peddled the notion that that there is a conspiracy by Muslims to take over the United States and that Islamists have "infiltrated" all levels of society. They make no distinction between regular Muslims and Islamists, contending that Muslim Americans have ties to terrorist organizations and want to replace the US constitution with Sharia law. Their defense of America is as dogged as their commitment to defend Israel against Muslims and Arabs.

While these arguments managed to enter the public sphere in a significant way only after the events of 9/11, they have a longer history. In 1994, PBS aired Steven Emerson's film *Jihad in America*, which argued that secret terrorist groups operating in the United States posed a grave threat to national security. Emerson made his name as a journalist working for *US News and World Report*, where he rose to become a senior editor in the area of national security issues, and went on to write about terrorism for CNN. Not only did *Jihad* run on PBS, it also won the prestigious George Polk Award for best television documentary. Emerson then formed the Investigative Project on Terrorism in 1995 in order to more consistently spew out conspiracy theories about the "Islamic threat." His books include *American Jihad: The Terrorists Living among Us* (2002) and *Jihad Incorporated: A Guide to Militant Islam in the US* (2006). For this clique, there are no "good Muslims." When Republican governor Chris Christie appointed a Muslim to a New Jersey state judgeship, Emerson accused Christie of "having a strange relationship with radical Islam."[18] Not to be outdone, blogger Debbie Schlussel ranted that Christie was a "halal pig" and that Judge Sohail Mohammad was a Hamas supporter.[19]

The legal apparatus has been an important arena for the right-wing Islamophobes. David Yerushalmi works as the legal counsel for CSP. He was also actively involved in the Cordoba House controversy as legal counsel for SIOA. In June 2011, Yerushalmi wrote a widely cited report in Daniel Pipes's Middle East Forum journal *Middle East Quarterly* that claimed that 80 percent of US mosques promote or support violence.[20] Perhaps his most important contribution to the Islamophobia network, however, is that he laid the legal basis for the anti-Sharia campaign. Yerushalmi coauthored with Frank Gaffney a CSP report titled *Shariah: The Threat to America*[21] that promted approximately two dozen states to consider banning use of Sharia. While Yerushalmi has played an important role in the anti-Sharia wave, as chapter 8 shows, the legal apparatus is not hostile to such positions. Yerushalmi is not so much an outsider trying to corrupt an otherwise just system as an insider and a new McCarthyite pushing the system further to the right.

David Gaubatz helped Yerushalmi gather early information by heading up his "Mapping Shari'a in America: Knowing the Enemy" campaign.[22] Prior to his life as an Islamophobic warrior, Gaubatz worked in the Middle East for the US Air Force's Office of Special Investigations. He built his career after 9/11 by arguing that Muslim civil rights groups such as CAIR are actually front groups for terrorist organizations. He is coauthor of *Muslim Mafia: Inside the Secret Underworld That's Conspiring to Islamize America* (2009), which has been used by right-wing politicians to target CAIR and other groups.

David Horowitz has added his shrill voice to this crusade by going after the Muslim Student Association (MSA), a campus group with dozens of chapters in universities across the country. Horowitz claims that the MSA is "lying about its core mission—which is to advance the Islamic jihad against the Jews and Christians of the Middle East, and ultimately against the United States. . . . Unfortunately the lies of the MSA (like its sister organizations CAIR and the Muslim American Society) are successful in snookering the willing accomplices of the political left and the unwitting accomplices of the inattentive middle to support and protect them."[23] In short, the logic of these far-right-wing Islamophobes is that there are no "good Muslims" and that Muslim organizations, despite their stated intentions, are really front groups for the Muslim Brotherhood or the Wahhabis, who intend to attack Jews and Christians. While this rhetoric is extreme, these views are just one step removed from the FBI and NYPD "radicalization" theories discussed in chapter 8. The propaganda video *The Third Jihad*, which was shown to New York City police officers as part of their training, demonstrates this overlap between the new McCarthyites and the security establishment. The list of interviewees for this pseudodocumentary includes not just right-wing Islamophobes but also figures such as New York City police commissioner Ray Kelly, former New York City mayor Rudolph Giuliani, former CIA director James Woolsey, former head of Homeland Security Tom Ridge, Connecticut senator Joe Lieberman, and others.[24] In their division of labor, the role for people like Horowitz is to win over public opinion through propaganda. Horowitz organized "Islamofascism Awareness Week," which brought prominent anti-Muslim zealots to college campuses in 2007. His Freedom Center is affiliated with Robert Spencer's Jihad Watch, and Spencer's articles on jihad appear regularly in Horowitz's *Front Page* magazine.

Fear Inc. shows the interconnections between various Islamophobic warriors and the extent to which they coordinate their activities. The Islamophobia campaign has brought neocons together with other kindred spirits such as right-wing Zionists, the Christian far right, and conservative Muslims and ex-Muslims. In short, as we will see shortly, right-wingers of all stripes have united under the rubric of anti-Muslim racism. In order to carry out their attacks on Muslims, both ideological and physical, they have received substantial resources from right-wing organizations. Seven foundations contributed close to forty-three million dollars to these new McCarthyites between 2001 and 2009. The main funders are the Donors Capital Fund, the Richard Mellon Scaife Foundation, the Lynde and Harry Bradley Foundation, the Newton D. and Rochelle F. Becker Foundations and Charitable Trust, the Russell Berrie Foundation, the Anchorage Charitable Fund, the William Rosenwald Family Fund, and the Fairbrook Foundation.[25]

Two of these foundations (Becker and Berrie) are explicitly committed to promoting what they see as the interests of the Jewish community (specifically Zionism), and a third, the Fairbrook Foundation, is even more extreme in its Zionist orientation. Run by Aubrey and Joyce Chernick, it "has provided funding to groups ranging from the ADL and CAMERA, a right-wing, pro-Israel, media-watchdog outfit, to violent Israeli settlers living on Palestinian lands and figures like the pseudo-academic author Robert Spencer," according to Max Blumenthal's investigative journalism.[26] Chernick also contributes to WINEP and the Hudson Institute. It is important to note that these right-wing foundations and groups do not represent the views of the majority of Jewish Americans, even though they may claim to do so. An August 2011 Gallup poll asked respondents in various religious groups if they thought that American Muslims are sympathetic to al-Qaeda. Seventy percent of Jewish Americans said no; the only groups with higher "no" percentages were Muslims and atheists.[27] Clearly this is about politics, not religion. Conservatives of all stripes see Islamophobia as instrumental to advancing their individual agendas.

The Christian Far Right

The Christian Right is an integral part of the Islamophobia bandwagon and ardently supports Israel. For the Christian evangelical movement, Israel is of crucial importance; evangelicals believe that Jews will go back to Israel before the return of Christ. And while they also believe that Jews will be converted to Christianity, they firmly support a Jewish state in Palestine.[28] Thus, the Christian Right has lined up with Zionists in demonizing Palestinians. At least since the 1980s, the Christian Right has been an important base for the Republican Party. In fact, the Christian Right and the GOP have become some of the most extreme Zionists (even if they believe that Jews can't get into heaven). This marks a shift from the 1970s and earlier, when Israel had a "social democratic" world image and liberal Democrats were the most ardent supporters of Zionism. The events of 9/11 further solidified the Christian Right–neocon–Zionist alliance. The alignment of US and Israeli policy meant, as Hagopian writes, "defining Arab/Muslim states and/or movements within them as terrorist or supporters of terrorism."[29] For the evangelicals, "the attacks on Israel by Palestinian suicide bombers are an important test in the global fight against Islamic terrorism."[30]

Thus, evangelicals like John Hagee, Pat Robertson, Jerry Falwell, Franklin Graham, and Ralph Reed have added to the Islam-bashing. Graham has called Islam "a very evil and wicked religion." For Graham, "true Islam" advocates the beating of wives and the murder of adulterous children and therefore "cannot be practiced" in the United States.[31] In addition to these established figures, other imitators, such as the newly infamous Florida pastor Terry Jones, who rose to international prominence by announcing that he would burn a copy of the Koran, have capitalized on this hatemongering.[32] There are numerous connections between the religious right and the rest of the Islamophobic network, including groups such as Christians United for Israel. Also closely associated with the religious right is the Tea Party movement. State and local groups, particularly in Tennessee, California, and Florida, have enthusiastically climbed onto the Islamophobia gravy train.[33] In Murfreesboro, Tennessee, the Tea Party bigots and the religious right ganged up to stop the construction of an Islamic center, even going so far as to set a fire at the construction site. They were assisted by groups like ACT! for America, founded by Brigitte Gabriel (a Lebanese Christian), whose members have been involved in rallies not only in Tennessee but also in Florida and other states.

People like Gabriel play an important role in the Islamophobic network—they legitimize the racist attacks on Muslims and Arabs through their personal testimony. Gabriel travels the country giving talks about how horrible Muslims really are, based on her supposed experience growing up in Lebanon. At a counterterrorism event at Duke University in 2004, she explained the differences between Arabs (and Muslims) and Israelis as follows: "It's barbarism versus civilization. It's democracy versus dictatorship. It's goodness versus evil."[34] Tellingly, her first book was titled *Because They Hate: A Survivor of Islamic Terror Warns America* (2006).

Ex-Muslims

A whole slew of people, mostly "ex-Muslims," have played this role of legitimation. One such ideologue, Nonie Darwish, is the director of Former Muslims United, cofounded by Wafa Sultan, Walid Shoebat, and Ibn Warraq. Darwish is of Egyptian origin and was raised in Gaza. She believes that Islam "will destroy itself because it's not a true religion."[35] Her books *Now They Call Me Infidel: Why I Renounced Jihad for America* (2006), *Israel and the War on Terror* (2007), and *Cruel and Unusual Punishment: The*

Terrifying Global Implications of Islamic Law (2009) have been endorsed and supported by Pipes, Spencer, and Horowitz.

Darwish and Shoebat, along with Walid Phares, a professor at the National Defense University and a Fox News contributor, regularly give lectures to the law enforcement community on "terrorism."[36] Phares leads seminars for government employees and addresses law enforcement and homeland security conferences. He offers courses on terrorism for the Centre for Counterintelligence and Security Studies (CI CENTRE), one of several far-right-wing operations that populate the antiterrorism training industry. As Thom Cincotta writes, this antiterrorism training industry consists of "a panoply of companies that offer instruction in surveillance tactics, cyber-security, bomb detection, school safety, and critical infrastructure."[37] A subset of this industry consists of groups that offer courses to law enforcement agencies on "jihad" and the threat it poses to national security. Phares fills the minds of his audience with his conspiracy theories about a jihadist strategy to infiltrate key institutions in the United States such as the defense sector, the academy, and community organizations. His books include *Future Jihad: Terrorist Strategies against America* (2005), *The War of Ideas: Jihadism against Democracy* (2007), and *The Confrontation: Winning the War against Future Jihad* (2008).

Shoebat similarly tells his audiences that CAIR and the Islamic Society of North America are "the terrorist arms of the lawmaker: Sharia, Koran and Hadith."[38] Shoebat is even more extreme than his fellow ex-Muslims. His newfound Christian beliefs hold that during the "end times" of biblical prophecy, Muslims will fight alongside Satan on earth.[39] Despite these outlandish claims (or perhaps because of them), he is enthusiastically promoted by his colleagues in the Islamophobic network. Gaffney gushed, "In the twenty-five years I have been in Washington I have never heard anything so extraordinary and the truth told so eloquently by someone like this."[40] In 2011, he was paid five thousand dollars by the Department of Homeland Security to spout his nonsense at a South Dakota law enforcement conference.[41]

"Education" and Media Propaganda

The promotion of such extremists as "educators" to the law enforcement community prompted Cincotta and Political Research Associates to issue a report on three counterterrorism training organizations: the International Counter-Terrorism Officers Association, Security Solutions International, and the CI CENTRE. These groups employ right-wing Islamophobes and regularly organize conferences for law enforcement personnel. In this environment the right-wing Islamophobes don't stick out like sore thumbs; in fact, they fit quite comfortably within the established legal and political structures and often share a stage with mainstream figures from the security establishment. Thus, CI CENTRE's 2010 "Spy Cruise," an intelligence-themed conference held on a cruise ship, listed former CIA directors Porter Goss and Michael Hayden as speakers. (Goss's speech had the telling title "Radical Fundamentalism and (Judeo-Christian) Western Civilization are Irreconcilable.")[42] When the FBI uses the work of Robert Spencer and the Orientalist Raphael Patai in its trainings, it does so because that work fits with its existing ideological framework, or—to be precise—with the views of conservative sections of the FBI and the security apparatus (see figure on p 191). *Wired* found and exposed a PowerPoint presentation by the FBI's Law Enforcement Communications Unit that drew from the Islamophobic warriors' highly distorted view of Islam.[43] In response to this and perhaps other revelations, the Obama administration called for a reexamination of the counterterrorism material used by his agencies.[44] Indeed, there are differences among various branches of government about how to view "Islamic terrorism," as the previous chapters illustrated.

In addition to this "educational" role within the security apparatus, the Islamophobic network broadcasts its views to the public. It does so not only through the right-wing media, such as the Christian Broadcasting Network, Fox News, and the rest of the Murdoch empire, but also in the mainstream media, where its extremist views go mostly unchallenged. Apart from a few reports such as those by Anderson Cooper of CNN, who did an exposé on Walid Shoebat,[45] and a few stories on NPR, this disturbing trend has been largely ignored. In fact, people like Emerson have easy and ready access to the mainstream media. Leading newspapers have quoted him as a "terrorism expert," his columns have appeared in the *Wall Street Journal*, and NBC employed him as a terrorism analyst—featuring him fifty times in just the first two months after 9/11.[46] Similarly, Pipes, between September 2001 and September 2002, appeared 110 times on television and did 450 radio interviews.[47]

One example illustrates how Islamophobic propaganda is amplified in the mainstream media. The new McCarthyites have long claimed that

80 percent of mosques are controlled by jihadists. In 2004, Republican congressman Peter King stated on the Fox News network's *Sean Hannity Show* that "eighty to eighty-five percent of mosques in this country are controlled by Islamic fundamentalists." He backed up his claim by citing the research of Emerson and Pipes.[48] This nonsense was repeated again and again by the Islamophobes, even in the mainstream media. In 2010, Pamela Geller stated that "four out of five mosques preach hate" on CNN.[49] In March 2011, King held his "green scare" hearings on the supposed radicalization in American Muslim communities. A few months later, in June 2011, Yerushalmi made the same claim in the spurious report mentioned above. Gaffney immediately endorsed the findings in his column in the *Washington Times*.[50] The upshot of this propaganda is that few in the media challenged the King hearings, giving credence to the notion that Muslims are in fact being "radicalized" and need to be questioned and monitored in ways similar to the "reds" in the Cold War era.

The overall dynamic is one in which the right-wing media are the hubs of Islamophobic propaganda, which then spills over into the mainstream media either directly, via the Islamophobic warriors, or through sympathetic politicians like King, Newt Gingrich, Michele Bachmann, Allen West, and others. As we saw in the last chapter, during the misnamed "Ground Zero mosque" controversy, the Democrats only added fuel to the fire and helped to bring Islamophobic rhetoric into the mainstream, albeit in less crass ways. Several mainstream figures have also played this role, and to them we turn next.

Mainstream and Liberal Enablers

The more sophisticated counterparts to Gabriel, Shoebat, and Phares are people like Ayaan Hirsi Ali, Fouad Ajami, Azar Nafisi, Irshad Manji, Kanan Makiya, and Ibn Warraq. These individuals have much more access to the mainstream media because their language is more "reasonable" and they are promoted by powerful political figures. Hamid Dabashi, in his book *Brown Skin, White Masks*, argues that these people, to whom he refers as "native informers," reinforce anti-Muslim and anti-Arab racism through their dismal accounts of their countries of origin. He states that in the "immediate aftermath of 9/11, comprador intellectuals [native informers willing to aid the US, particularly of Iranian, Arab, and Pakistani origin] were actively sought out by the militant ideologues of the US empire. Their task was to feign authority, authenticity, and native knowledge by informing the American public of the atrocities taking place in the region of their birth, thereby justifying the imperial designs of the United States as a liberation."[51] He adds that this logic "has been at times explicit, as in the writings of Fouad Ajami and Kanan Makiya during the build up to the invasion of Iraq; at times implicit, as in the cases of Nafisi and Hirsi Ali."[52]

Ayaan Hirsi Ali had a short career in Dutch politics before accepting a position at the neocon-dominated American Enterprise Institute think tank. Ali, who is originally from Somalia, was forced to resign her seat in Parliament after it was revealed that she lied in her application for political asylum in the Netherlands.[53] The neocons welcomed her with open arms, and her book *Infidel* became a *New York Times* bestseller for a few weeks. After her journey across the Atlantic, she penned *Nomad: From Islam to America; A Personal Journey through the Clash of Civilizations* (2011), recycling the tired myths of the supposed clash of values between Islam and the West.

Azar Nafisi similarly journeyed from Iran to the United States, where she became a protégée of Bernard Lewis, a colleague of Fouad Ajami at Johns Hopkins, and an employee of Paul Wolfowitz.[54] Her memoir *Reading Lolita in Tehran* is the story of how she saved seven students in Tehran by inviting them to her house to teach them about Nabokov's *Lolita* and other literary classics of the Western canon. In so doing, Nafisi succeeds in rewriting Iran's history and turning its people into caricatures. As Dabashi writes, the "entirety of Iran as a nation, a culture, a society, a reality fades out behind the tale of a self-indulgent diva very pleased with her heroic deeds and quixotic victories."[55] The book was on the *New York Times* bestseller list for more than a hundred weeks. It was translated into dozens of languages and has been widely adopted into course syllabi on campuses across the United States.

Ali, Nafisi, and Manji (a Canadian of Egyptian and South Asian descent) have contributed most to the argument that the United States should defend human rights and women's rights in the "Muslim world." To quote Dabashi again:

> Next to national-security interests, human rights and women's rights in particular are now routinely cited as principal objectives of American imperial interventions. The role of Hirsi Ali, Nafisi, Irshad Manji, and their ilk is to speak on behalf of such insights as integral to the humanitarian mission at the heart of American imperialism. Offering,

in English for the American and European market, a fierce critique of women's rights in Iran (Nafisi) or genital mutilation in Africa (Hirsi Ali) or gay and lesbian rights in Islam across the board (Irshad Manji) places the authority to right those wrongs in the hands of foreign readers and their elected officials, rather than the societies affected.[56]

Rather than stand in solidarity with men and women in Muslim-majority countries who are fighting for rights of various kinds, Nafisi and company attempt to invoke the rhetoric of the white man's burden.

The discourse of human rights has been central to the neocon propaganda war. It is therefore important to recognize that such liberal rhetoric isn't simply the bastion of the liberal imperialists but is at the heart of neoconservatism as well. What is different in the rhetoric of the liberal imperialists is that it attempts to separate Islam from Islamism as seen in the work of the late Christopher Hitchens, Paul Berman, Martin Amis, Nick Cohen, Bernard-Henri Lévy, and Andrew Anthony.[57] Arun Kundnani writes that these

> new liberals (correctly) put aside these arguments about the nature of Islam and the patterns of Islamic history [as articulated by Lewis and the Orientalists] and, instead, focus their attention on Islamism, a modern political movement, which they (incorrectly) take to be analogous to Stalinism or fascism. Islamism is regarded as an appropriation of modern European totalitarianism that is basically alien to "traditional Islam." The distinction between Islam and Islamism is important, for it insulates this discourse from straightforward charges of Islamophobia—its target, after all, is a twentieth-century political ideology with European roots, not an oriental religion.[58]

Hitchens, once a regular columnist for the *Nation*, became in his later years an outspoken liberal Islamophobe. In his book *God Is Not Great*, he takes aim at all religions, arguing, much like Voltaire, that religion "poisons everything" and is responsible for creating tyrannical regimes in both ancient and modern times. His criticisms, however, are selective: he indicts Saddam Hussein for using Islam for political gain but has nothing to say about the born-again George W. Bush and his recourse to religion to justify his policy objectives. Hitchens audaciously goes on to blame Islam for the horrible state of Iraq after the US-led invasion and occupation. In the final analysis, despite his equal-opportunity critique of the world's major religions, his book serves to prop up US foreign policy. This is hardly surprising given that he "gravitated towards the neoconservatives, [was] feature[d] frequently on right-wing talk-shows, and [was] regularly seen with David Horowitz," as Richard Seymour has observed.[59]

In contrast, other liberal imperialists like Michael Ignatieff and Paul Berman are more hesitant to be openly associated with the neoconservatives.[60] Berman, who is part of what he calls the "anti-totalitarian" left, supported the 2003 war on Iraq because "al-Qaeda . . . and Saddam's Baath Party are two of the tendencies within a much larger phenomenon, which is a Muslim totalitarianism."[61] As Kundnani notes, Hitchens shared with Berman the view that "as soon as the West had won its historic battle against communism, a new totalitarianism—Islamism—emerged as a political force. The West, it is argued, is morally obliged to expunge this totalitarian threat both in the Islamic world and among its own Muslim communities."[62] Thus, although the liberal imperialists use more subtle language, they ultimately end up making a similar argument to the neocons (see, for instance, Podhoretz's *World War 4: The Long Struggle against Islamofascism*) and the Islamophobic warriors. Daniel Pipes has similarly argued that "what Nazism or fascism was to World War II and Marxist/Leninism was to the Cold War, militant Islam is to this war [the War on Terror]."[63]

Systemic Racism

A wide range of people and groups have participated in constructing a diabolical "Islamic threat." What we have seen in this chapter is that the new McCarthyites aren't aberrations in an otherwise fair and neutral system, despite their rabidly racist views; their role is to push the envelope. To recap, the first group of new McCarthyites discussed in this chapter was a segment of neocons who have devoted themselves to anti-Muslim advocacy through various groups and organizations. However, given that they are part of the foreign policy establishment or from the military, the CIA, the Department of Defense, or other branches of the security apparatus, their ideology is echoed and endorsed by others who share their views but may not explicitly identify as neocons. Other Islamophobic warriors include right-wingers of various stripes—Zionists, Christian fundamentalists, and right-wing ex-Muslims and Christians from the Middle East and South Asia. Their arguments are made more palatable by the liberal Islamophobes who populate the academy, the mainstream media, and various think tanks.

The chart on page 191 attempts to capture these sources of Islamophobia and their impact on public discourse. The reader will notice that there is no separate box for the Islamophobes. This is because, as was shown above, they are part of the establishment and exist within foreign policy think tanks, universities and colleges, the political class, and the security apparatus (defined as the branches of government that prosecute the War on Terror abroad and as well as at home). Think tanks have played an increasingly important role in shaping foreign policy as we saw in chapter 7. As Lawrence Davidson argues in his book *Foreign Policy: Privatizing America's National Interest*, the best-funded think tanks play a decisive role in shaping foreign policy and setting the terms of public discussion through their members' frequent appearances as "experts" in the mainstream media. Academics are another source of ideas often connected to think tanks and to politicians. Political figures from both the Republican and Democratic parties have tied their policy aims to the rhetoric of Islamophobia, and many Republicans have used anti-Muslim racism to further their electoral campaigns. Finally, the security establishment has individuals who pursue their own visions for national and domestic security and are often sought out by the media as "experts." *Wired*'s investigative reporting found that the "U.S. military taught its future leaders that a 'total war' against the world's 1.4 billion Muslims would be necessary to protect America from Islamic terrorists."[64] Among the various options put forward were to wipe out whole cities (as was done with Hiroshima) and to target the "civilian population wherever necessary." While the Pentagon has since suspended such training, the officer responsible for giving these lectures maintains his position within the military: the "commanders, lieutenant colonels, captains and colonels" who took his course and listened to his rants have since been promoted to higher-level assignments.[65] Finally, it must be noted that all of these groups interact with one another. For instance, the CSP report *Shariah: The Threat to America* features articles by Gaffney, Yerushalmi, McCarthy, and other Islamophobes, but also by military generals (William Boykin, Edward Soyster), FBI and CIA people (John Guandolo, James Woolsey), and others from the security establishment who share their views.[66] The lines between various boxes are intended to show these connections.

From this analysis it can be discerned that the McCarthyism of the twenty-first century isn't the product of just one individual: it is the collective effort of right-wingers in the academy, the think-tank milieu, the political sphere, and the security establishment. But the green scare, just like its twentieth-century counterpart, is supported and endorsed by liberals in every sphere who share with conservatives a common commitment to US imperialism. It is, however, worth noting that Islamophobia is less potent as an agent of fear than its red counterpart. During the Cold War, the Soviet Union was indisputably a powerful nuclear armed threat to the United States. The same cannot be said of radical Islamist groups, as even members of the security establishment freely admit. The "green scare" can be effective only up to a point; it must constantly be rehashed in public memory through media spectacles in order to keep the fear alive. Both conservatives and liberals participate in these efforts.

At times, however, these two wings of Islamophobia do come into conflict. As we saw above, the Pentagon stopped its rabid Islamophobic training; the Obama administration called for an investigation into counterterrorism training. These conflicts are due to differences in strategy. For instance, when Florida pastor Terry Jones threatened to burn the Koran on the ninth anniversary of the 9/11 attacks, the Obama administration had to rein him in. This had less to do with Obama's commitment to fighting Islamophobia and more to do with his administration's emphasis on winning hearts and minds in the "Muslim world." After re-

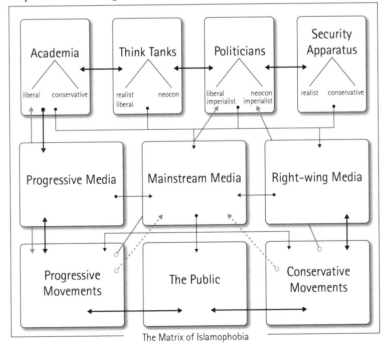

The Matrix of Islamophobia

inforcing the notion that the United States was a nation built on religious tolerance, Obama said of Jones, in a television interview, that "I just want him to understand that this stunt that he is pulling could greatly endanger our young men and women in uniform who are in Iraq, who are in Afghanistan."[67] The turn to counterinsurgency meant that obvious provocations of this kind had to be managed even while the logic of empire was reinforced.

Yet what pushed the likes of Terry Jones back was not the actions of liberal imperialists but ordinary people in Florida who organized and demonstrated against his bigotry. Grassroots groups such as the Gainesville International Socialist Organization, Students for Justice in Palestine, Stand Up Florida, Amnesty International, and Gainesville Students for a Democratic Society mobilized against Jones and brought out hundreds on September 11, 2010, to stop the Koran-burning outside Jones's church. They were successful; no Korans were burned that day.[68] The box in the chart that represents social movements is placed next to the box marked "the public," because it is from the ranks of ordinary people that activists emerge to challenge racism in all its forms. Progressive movements have the ability to reshape the discussion and push back against racism, influencing what political figures say and even pushing them to the left. Liberal and radical students and faculty have long been a part of such movements, and their participation often spills over into their research and teaching. It is through such grassroots activism that racism can be successfully fought and an entire society transformed.

Conclusion

Fighting Islamophobia

I n this book we have journeyed from the seventh century to the twenty-first and found that the relationship between the "East" and "West" has not been characterized by a transhistoric "clash of civilizations." We also saw that the image of the menacing "Muslim threat" has been mobilized largely by ruling elites to serve a political agenda, whether the domination of Europe by the papacy in the eleventh century or US expansionism today. An external enemy is usually paired with an internal one against whom palpable fear and hatred are generated. It follows that Islamophobia is about politics and not religion; it is therefore in the realm of politics that Islamophobia must be fought.

The Democratic Party is not an ally in this fight. Some on the left, and many Muslims, believed that the Obama presidency would mitigate and undo the virulent Islamophobia unleashed during the Bush years. Not only had tens of thousands of Muslim Americans been detained or deported in the years following 9/11, but hundreds of thousands were "interviewed" and thereby deemed suspicious by the newly formed Department of Homeland Security. There was much hope during the 2008 elections that all of this would change with a new Democratic president. A poll conducted by the Council on American-Islamic Relations found that 89 percent of Muslim Americans voted for Obama; only 2 percent voted for the Republican, John McCain. More than two-thirds declared themselves to be Democrats, 29 percent said they were independents, and only 4 percent identified as Republican.[1] But their hopes would be dashed. Signs of betrayal were already evident on the campaign trail.

When he was "accused" of being a Muslim, Obama denied the charge and affirmed his Christian beliefs. He also assiduously avoided the Muslim community. Before a scheduled speech in Detroit, two women wearing hijabs were asked to move from behind the podium so that they wouldn't be in the same frame with candidate Obama.

If the right was flaying Obama for being a "secret Muslim," liberals too were party to this line of attack. For instance, Edward Luttwak, a fellow at the realist/liberal imperialist think tank CSIS, wrote an op-ed piece in the *New York Times* that was "anti-Muslim, and altogether Islamophobic to an unprecedented and scandalous degree," writes Hamid Dabashi.[2] The essence of Luttwak's argument was that Obama is a Muslim (because his father was Muslim) and that because he had adopted Christianity, Muslims were bound by their religion to execute him. In the face of such drivel in the supposedly liberal media, it is understandable why Muslim Americans believed that they should not critique Obama during the campaign but instead should simply vote for him and wait.

They waited in vain. After Obama won the election, he continued Bush's second-term foreign policy agenda. While he retreated rhetorically from the use of harsh Islamophobic language, in practice he sent thirty thousand more troops to Afghanistan, expanded the war to Pakistan, and tried to alter the Status of Forces Agreement in Iraq so as to not only extend the US occupation but also grant immunity to US troops from Iraqi prosecution. Not only did he carry out far more drone attacks on Afghanistan and Pakistan than his predecessor, he also integrated them into his strategies for Yemen and Somalia. He made a show of demonstrating his loyalty to Israel and failed, like every previous president, to prevent Israeli attacks on Palestinians.

In the context of the Arab uprisings of 2011, the Obama administration at first supported its dictatorial allies (such as Egypt's Hosni Mubarak, a personal friend of the Clinton family).[3] When it became clear that they were going to be swept from power, Obama embraced the Arab Spring, at least in public, while at the same time supporting counterrevolutionary forces around the region. The United States continued to fund the Egyptian military, the key source of counterrevolution in that country. Elsewhere the Obama White House stayed silent—such as when Saudi Arabia not only repressed its Shi'a rebellion but also sent troops to Bahrain to crush the uprising in that country. Had Obama wanted to intervene on the side of the prodemocracy demonstrators in Bahrain, he could have used the Fifth Fleet, which is stationed there. Instead, he opted to support pro-Western forces in Libya and Syria as a means of replacing inconsistent allies and deflating movements demanding real democracy and social change.

Domestically, Obama has attacked Muslims and Arabs by continuing Bush's policies of torture, extraordinary rendition, and preemptive prosecution. American Muslims continue to be harassed and persecuted by the state. The drama of "homegrown terrorism" was only heightened under Obama in 2009, paving the way for the far-right-wing Islamophobic warriors. Obama has even gone further than Bush in several ways. He has secured for the president the power to execute US citizens suspected of ties to terrorism without so much as a trial or the apparently unnecessary burden of proof; the cleric and US citizen Anwar al-Awlaki was summarily executed in 2011. He also signed the National Defense Authorization Act, which, among other things, allows the military to detain "terror suspects" who are US citizens indefinitely without charge. Although this is both unconstitutional and illegal, according to the American Civil Liberties Union,[4] and even though this process has torn Muslim families apart, Obama adopted Bush's policies and codified them into law.

Instead of pushing back against preemptive prosecution and the racist practice of targeting Muslims before they actually do anything, Obama strengthened it. Giving credence to existing radicalization programs in the law enforcement community, he unveiled his "counter-radicalization" strategy in 2011. In the opening statement of his strategy document, Obama argued that "most recently, al-Qa'ida and its affiliates have attempted to recruit and radicalize people here in the United States, as we have seen in several plots and attacks, including the deadly attack two years ago on our service members at Fort Hood." After spending much time in 2009 emphasizing the threat of terrorists inside US borders, as discussed in chapter 9, Obama put forward a plan to police "homegrown terrorism" by eliciting the help of the Muslim community. Yet liberal Islamophobia does not target all Muslims. It acknowledges that there are "good Muslims"—those who cooperate with the goals of empire. Thus, Obama stated that Muslims are "best positioned to take the lead because they know their communities best." Heaping praise on Muslim Americans who have worked with the law enforcement community, he called for more such work. The document solicits the support of teachers, coaches, and community members, who are to be turned into a McCarthy-type informant system.[5]

Adhering to the precepts of liberal Islamophobia, the report goes on to state that "we must counter al-Qa'ida's propaganda that the United States is somehow at war with Islam" and instead affirm that "Islam is part of America, a country that cherishes the active participation of all its citizens, regardless of background and belief. We live what al-Qa'ida violently rejects—religious freedom and pluralism." Obama added that "our rich diversity of backgrounds and faiths makes us stronger." This is the modus operandi of liberal Islamophobia: to roundly reject Islam-bashing—and then proceed to institute proposals that target Muslims. When representative Peter King held his McCarthy-style hearings in March 2011 to determine the extent of Muslim radicalization in the United States, he was rightly criticized by liberals. However, that August, when Obama institutionalized this process through his "counter-radicalization" strategy, there was nary a peep of protest.

In reality, al-Qaeda is an insignificant force, and its ability to recruit in the United States is highly limited. Even members of the security apparatus admit as much. A month before the release of the "counter-radicalization" document, the *Washington Post* reported that it was widely believed in the CIA, as well by counterterrorism officials, that al-Qaeda was all but finished.[6] A *Foreign Affairs* article by John Mueller titled "The Truth about al-Qaeda" arrived at the same conclusion.[7] Yet, despite the lack of any credible evidence to suggest that al-Qaeda remained a threat to national security, the Obama administration launched a plan to increase racial profiling of Muslim Americans. Why? There are a number of reasons, but one is certainly that the "counterinsurgency" strategy— that is, the attempt to "win hearts and minds"—was largely failing abroad. Obama therefore had to turn back to counterterrorism and resuscitate the "Islamic terrorist" enemy, albeit in liberal guise.

It is worth emphasizing that what makes this particularly insidious is that Obama is able to do so while convincing the public of his antiracist credentials. Furthermore, this focus on Muslims as terrorists deflects attention away from the right-wing Christian terrorists who continue to attack abortion clinics. The Obama document, which was released shortly after far-right Christian terrorist Anders Behring Breivik carried out a tragic attack in Norway, gestured toward including white supremacists under the umbrella of terrorists. However, it insisted that "al-Qa'ida and its affiliates and adherents represent the preeminent terrorist threat to our country."[8] The primary focus of the "counter-radicalization" strategy remained the Muslim community. It should therefore come as no surprise that law enforcement officials continued to spy on and infiltrate Muslim communities during the Obama era. As Abdul Malik Mujahid, a leader of the Muslim Peace Coalition, puts it, "The Muslim community in the United States has been living in a virtual internment camp ever since 9/11. Since then, more than 700,000 Muslims have been interviewed by the FBI. That means nearly 50 percent of all Muslim households have been touched by this 'investigation.' Practically all mosques have been 'checked for nuclear bombs' or other fear-provoking reasons. That's the level of trust we 'enjoy' in the Muslim community."[9]

Reda Shata learned firsthand why it doesn't pay to associate with the law enforcement establishment. He worked with the FBI and the police, inviting officers to his mosque for breakfast and even dining with Mayor Bloomberg. He personified everything that American imperialism has defined as a "good Muslim." Yet an undercover police officer and an informant were assigned to spy on him and to keep tabs on his mosque. When he learned that he was viewed as a suspect by the very people he had invited into his mosque, Shata said: "This is very sad. . . . What is your feeling if you see this about people you trusted?" Indeed. The CBS report in which his story appears goes on to note that "the dichotomy between simultaneously being partner and suspect is common among some of New York's Muslims. Some of the same mosques that city leaders visited to hail their strong alliances with the Muslim community have also been placed under NYPD surveillance—in some cases infiltrated by undercover police officers and informants."[10] The Obama administration has contributed federal funds for the NYPD spying program.[11]

After years of betrayals under a Democratic president, sectors of the Muslim community started to push back. For instance, in the lead-up to the 2012 elections, a growing minority of Muslim Americans spoke out against sitting at the back of the bus. In Florida, when the chair of the Democratic National Committee, Debbie Wasserman Schultz, declined an invitation to attend an event hosted by a Muslim organization, she was called out. Lambasting both the Republicans and Democrats, activist Muhammad Malik said, "I don't think it's an issue of a few bad apples—as long as Islamophobia is cozy within our political and social institutions, threats to full participation, dignity, and civil rights will remain alive and well."[12] Poll numbers showed declining confidence in Obama; in 2011, seven out of ten Muslim Americans viewed Obama favorably, compared with nine out of ten in 2008.[13] Among Muslim religious leaders, fifteen clerics in New York City boycotted the supposedly tolerant Bloomberg's annual interfaith breakfast in 2011 and sent a letter of protest signed also by rabbis, nuns, and pastors.[14] A hundred imams in the New York area issued a statement in support of the antiwar movement's April 2011 demonstration. This support was mobilized by activists in the United National Antiwar Coalition, with the help of the Muslim Peace Coalition.

When the Islamophobic warriors went on a rampage against mosques and proposed Islamic community centers across the country, small coalitions of progressive activists came together to fight back. In New York City, several left groups pulled together coalitions to plan actions against the right-wing attack on the proposed Islamic community center. On September 11, 2010, progressives far outnumbered the bigots in two parallel demonstrations in downtown Manhattan. Thousands of New Yorkers of all shades and sizes marched to oppose Islamophobia, chanting, "*Asalamu alaikum*, Muslims are welcome here." The zealots, who were largely bused in from outside the city, retreated. Park51 opened in 2012. Such efforts have been reproduced around the United States, sometimes resulting in victories, other times in defeats. CAIR chapters have mobilized against anti-Muslim bigotry and provided much-needed legal defense for besieged community members. The families of those targeted have been a constant source of resistance against anti-Muslim racism. Along with progressive lawyers, they have fought to win justice for their family members and to raise public consciousness and awareness. By the end of the first decade after 9/11, these families were coming together from across the country at various conferences to begin mounting a collective fight against preemptive persecution and prisoner abuse. After the NYPD's "human mapping program" became public, DRUM (Desis Rising Up and Moving), a South Asian immigrant rights organization that has been active around anti-Muslim racism, called demonstrations and press conferences. Activists in the Occupy Wall Street movement then took up this issue, helping to organize rallies to call for the resignation of NYPD commissioner Ray Kelly. At these rallies, activists explicitly connected the NYPD's targeting of the black and Latino communities and the savage repression of OWS protestors with its racial profiling of Arabs and Muslims.

It is through grassroots efforts like these that Islamophobia can be fought. In the context of these struggles, it is becoming clear that it is important to connect local issues to the broader context. As the Occupy

Wall Street movement has argued, the "99 percent" is up against a tiny minority at the top of society that benefits not only from an unjust economic system but also from an unjust political system. As Mujahid puts it: "First, Islamophobia, war, and terrorism are all connected phenomena. So we need to fight against war and Islamophobia, as well as terrorism. Second, hate and poverty are not only problems the Muslim community faces. Other communities face similar problems. We can and must unite with as [many] broad forces as we can to mount a resistance."[15]

Indeed, Muslims, Arabs, and others who "look Muslim" aren't the only people who stand to benefit from a successful struggle against Islamophobia. Such a struggle is also in the interests of the vast majority of Americans, who have had trillions of dollars stolen from their health care, education, infrastructure, and public transportation and funneled into the machinery of death. Working-class Americans of all races have nothing to gain from the spoils of empire—and everything to lose. The multiracial demonstrations against the attacks on mosques from Staten Island to Murfreesboro to Gainesville show that such solidarity is possible. The only way to challenge the climate of fear and hate is to confront bigotry wherever it raises its head, and simultaneously to build an alternative to the mainstream parties that not only have failed to stand up against racism but have actively fueled it. Only a politics that links the attacks on civil liberties with US imperialist policy can show that anti-Muslim bigotry is about creating a political climate in which the United States can invade other countries at will and suppress dissent at home.

At the end of the day, the vast majority of ordinary people around the world are forced to live under a profoundly unjust and unequal system. The year 2011 showed that this system and its warped priorities will not go unchallenged. The uprisings in Tunisia and Egypt spread not only to other countries in the region but also to Europe and the United States. Protestors learned strategy and tactics from one another as public spaces became key focal points for the movements. From Tahrir Square in Egypt to Pearl Square in Bahrain, the Puerta del Sol in Madrid, Syntagma Square in Athens, and Zuccotti Park in New York City, protest moments self-consciously honored one another through solidarity greetings and the imitation of tactics. Despite local differences, all of the movements were directed against the regime of the 1 percent. Instead of feeling pity for their Arab brothers and sisters, people in the West took inspiration from the successes of their counterparts in Tunisia and Egypt. In place of the "white man's burden," a politics of international solidarity began to come into being.

The last time that people from around the world stood up together was almost half a century ago. The national liberation struggles that swept the world from India to Algeria in the postwar period rattled the centers of imperialism, even as struggles were beginning to emerge inside Europe and the United States. Today we are entering a similar era. This is an era of revolution that brings with it the potential to create a brand-new society free of racism and war: a new world where every individual, regardless of race, ethnicity, nationality, or religion will be treated with respect; a world where the ideology of Islamophobia will be dumped into the dustbin of history, and that will be the end of that.

List of Acronyms

ADL	Anti-Defamation League
AEDPA	Antiterrorism and Effective Death Penalty Act
AEI	American Enterprise Institute
AIPAC	American Israel Public Affairs Committee
AJC	American Jewish Committee
AKP	Justice and Development Party (Turkey)
AQAP	Al-Qaeda in the Arabian Peninsula
AVOT	Americans for Victory Over Terrorism
AWAAM	Arab Women Active in the Arts and Media
CAIR	Center for American-Islamic Relations
CAMERA	Committee for Accuracy in Middle East Reporting in America
CFR	Council on Foreign Relations
CIA	Central Intelligence Agency (US)
CI CENTRE	Centre for Counterintelligence and Security Studies
COINTELPRO	Counter Intelligence Program
CP	Communist Party
CSIS	Center for Strategic and International Studies
CSP	Center for Security Policy
DHS	Department of Homeland Security (US)

DOJ	Department of Justice (US)
DPG	Defense Planning Guidance
DRUM	Desis Rising Up and Moving
FBI	Federal Bureau of Investigation (US)
FIS	Front Islamique du Salut (Algeria)
FLN	National Liberation Front (Algeria)
FTO	Foreign terrorist organization
ICE	Immigration and Customs Enforcement (US)
ICT	International Conference on Terrorism (US)
IMF	International Monetary Fund
INS	Immigration and Naturalization Service (now ICE)
ISI	Inter-Services Intelligence (Pakistan)
JDL	Jewish Defense League
JI	Jamaat-e-Islami party (Pakistan)
JINSA	Jewish Institute for National Security Affairs
MB	Muslim Brotherhood
MEF	Middle East Forum
MEMRI	Middle East Media Research Institute
MSA	Muslim Student Association
NATO	North Atlantic Treaty Organization
NCTC	National Counterterrorism Center (US)
NSEERS	National Security Entry-Exit Registration System
NYPD	New York Police Department
OWS	Occupy Wall Street
PLO	Palestine Liberation Organization
PNAC	Project for the New American Century
SAMs	Special administrative measures
SIOA	Stop Islamization of America
UN	United Nations
USAID	United States Agency for International Development
WINEP	Washington Institute for Near East Policy
WTC	World Trade Center

Notes

Introduction

1. Bernard Lewis, "The Roots of Muslim Rage," *Atlantic Monthly*, September 1990.

1. Images of Islam in Europe

1. Norman Daniel, *Islam and the West: The Making of an Image* (One World: Oxford, 1960), reprint, 1993, 14–15.
2. See R. W. Southern, *Western Views of Islam in the Middle Ages* (Cambridge, MA: Harvard University Press, 1962), 16–19.
3. Maxime Rodinson, *Europe and the Mystique of Islam* (London: I. B. Tauris, 2002), 5.
4. Jason Webster (author of *Andalus: Unlocking the Secrets of Moorish Spain*, New York: Doubleday, 2004), quoted in the documentary film *An Islamic History of Europe* (London: BBC Four, 2009), directed by Rageh Omaar. Available at http://www.youtube.com/watch?v=x0IaCK-7z5o.
5. Southern, *Western Views of Islam*, 21.
6. Iman Feisal Abdul Rauf, interview by Joseph Ward III, *Intersections International*, July 16, 2010, available at http://www.intersectionsinternational.org/files/ImamFeisalAbdulRauf_InterviewTranscript.pdf.
7. George Saliba, *Islamic Science and the Making of the European Renaissance* (Cambridge, MA: MIT Press, 2007).
8. Zachary Lockman, *Contending Visions of the Middle East: The History and Politics of Orientalism* (Cambridge: Cambridge University Press, 2004),31.
9. Rodinson, *Europe and the Mystique of Islam,* 14–15.
10. John Esposito, *The Islamic Threat: Myth or Reality?*, 3rd ed. (New York: Oxford University Press, 1999), 39.
11. Ibid., 39.
12. Quoted in Neil Faulkner, "A Marxist History of the World, Part 31: Crusade and Jihad," *Counterfire*, April 11, 2011, available at http://www.counterfire.org/index.php/articles/a-marxist-history-of-the-world/11777-a-marxist-history-of-the-world-31-crusade-and-jihad.

13. Southern, *Western Views of Islam*, 5.

14. Ibid., 5.

15. Daniel, *Islam and the West*, 100.

16. Ibid., 35.

17. Rodinson, *Europe and the Mystique of Islam*, 21–22.

18. Ibid., 29.

19. Ibid., 24–27.

20. Quoted in Esposito, *Islamic Threat*, 41.

21. Rodinson, *Europe and the Mystique of Islam*, 36.

22. Lockman, *Contending Visions*, 41.

23. Ibid., 42.

24. Rodinson, *Europe and the Mystique of Islam*, 37.

25. Lockman, *Contending Visions*, 45–6.

26. Ibid., 47.

27. Edward Said, *Orientalism* (New York: Vintage, 1978), 118.

28. Rodinson, *Europe and the Mystique of Islam*, 59.

29. Ibid., 46–47.

30. Daniel, *Islam and the West*, 312.

31. Emmanuel Chukwudi Eze, *Race and the Enlightenment: A Reader* (Oxford: Blackwell Publishers, 1997), 5.

32. Rodinson, *Europe and the Mystique of Islam*, 48–49.

2. Colonialism and Orientalism

1. Rodinson, *Europe and the Mystique of Islam*, 9–10.

2. Arthur Goldschmidt Jr. and Lawrence Davidson, *A Concise History of the Middle East*, 9th ed. (Boulder, CO: Westview, 2010), 162.

3. Said, *Orientalism*, 82.

4. Ibid., 83–84.

5. Ibid., 87.

6. Hans Koning, *The Conquest of America: How the Indian Nations Lost Their Continent* (New York: Cornerstone Press, 1993), 27.

7. George Fredrickson, *Racism: A Short History* (Princeton, NJ: Princeton University Press, 2002), 40–47.

8. Ibid.; see chapter 2.

9. See also Eric Williams, *Capitalism and Slavery* (London: David and Charles, 1964), 7–20, and Robin Blackburn, *The Making of New World Slavery* (New York: Verso, 1997), 12–15.

10. Rodinson, *Europe and the Mystique of Islam*, 65.

11. Quoted in Melani McAlister, *Epic Encounters: Culture, Media and US Interests in the Middle East since 1945* (Berkeley: University of California Press, 2005), 9.

12. Lockman, *Contending Visions*, 58.

13. Rodinson, *Europe and the Mystique of Islam*, 62.

14. Ibid., 60.

15. Quoted in Lockman, *Contending Visions*, 94.

16. David Spurr, *The Rhetoric of Empire* (Durham, NC: Duke University Press, 1993), 113.

17. Quoted in Lockman, *Contending Visions*, 78.

18. Quoted in Richard Seymour, *The Liberal Defence of Murder* (New York: Verso, 2008), 99.

19. Raphael Patai, *The Arab Mind* (New York: Hatherleigh Press, 2002).

20. Quoted in Esposito, *Islamic Threat*, 230.

21. Douglas Little, *American Orientalism: The United States and the Middle East since 1945* (Chapel Hill: University of North Carolina Press, 2002), 11.

22. Ibid., 12.

23. Ibid., 13.

24. Mark Twain, quoted in ibid., 13.

25. McAlister, *Epic Encounters*, 14–20.

26. Little, *American Orientalism*, 13.

27. Said, *Orientalism*, 294–95.

28. Lockman, *Contending Visions*, 102.

29. Said, *Orientalism*, 297.

30. Ibid., 296.

31. Lockman, *Contending Visions*, 129–30.

32. Sidney Lens, *The Forging of the American Empire: From the Revolution to Vietnam; A History of US Imperialism* (Chicago: Pluto Press and Haymarket Books, 2003), 179.

33. John Foster Dulles, quoted in McAlister, *Epic Encounters*, 45.

34. Henry Luce, quoted in ibid., 47.

35. Ibid., 55.

36. Lens, *Forging of the American Empire*, 367–68.

37. Daniel Lerner, *The Passing of Traditional Society: Modernizing the Middle East* (New York: Free Press, 1965).

38. Everett Rogers, *Diffusion of Innovations*, 5th ed. (New York: Free Press, 2003).

3. The Persistence of Orientalist Myths

1. John McCain, town hall meeting, Lakehall, MN, October 10, 2008. Footage from Associated Press available from Youtube at http://www.youtube.com/watch?v=jrnRU3ocIH4. Accessed August 24, 2011.

2. Associated Press, "Obama Says He's Christian, Not Muslim," *The Boston Channel*, October 2008. Available at http://www.thebostonchannel.com/r/15101761/detail.html, accessed September 9, 2011.

3. *Wikipedia*, s.v. "List of Countries by Muslim Population," last modified September 9, 2011, accessed September 9, 2011.

4. Maxime Rodinson, *The Arabs* (Chicago: University of Chicago Press, 1979).

5. Said, *Orientalism*, 296.

6. Peter Morey and Amina Yaqin, *Framing Muslims* (Cambridge, MA: Harvard University Press, 2011); Stephen Sheehi, *Islamophobia: The Ideological Campaign against Muslims* (Atlanta: Clarity Press, 2011); Jack Shaheen, *Reel Bad Arabs: How Hollywood Vilifies a People*, 2nd ed. (New York: Olive Branch Press, 2009).

7. Quoted in Lockman, *Contending Visions*, 69.

8. See for instance Barbara Hodgson, *Dreaming of East: Western Women and the Exotic Allure of the Orient* (Vancouver: Greystone Books, 2005); Reina Lewis, *Rethinking Orientalism: Women, Travel, and the Ottoman Harem* (New Brunswick, NJ: Rutgers University Press, 2004); Reina Lewis and Nancy Micklewright, eds., *Gender, Modernity and Liberty: Middle Eastern and Western Women's Writings: A Critical Sourcebook* (London: I. B. Tauris, 2006); and Sara Mills, *Discourses of Difference: An Analysis of Women's Travel Writing and Colonialism* (New York: Routledge, 1991), all of which have analyzed European women's contributions to discourse on the "East" in the eighteenth and nineteenth centuries. What these authors show is that while some of the dominant myths about

Muslim women are echoed here, there are also other accounts that contest the notion of Muslim women as horribly oppressed.

9. Leila Ahmed, *Women and Gender in Islam* (New Haven, CT: Yale University Press, 1992), 152–153.

10. Quoted in Bill Sammon, "Bush Urges Afghans to Help Oust Taliban," *Washington Times*, September 26, 2001, accessed October 26, 2009.

11. Laura Bush, quoted in Sharon Smith, "Using Women's Rights to Sell Washington's War," *International Socialist Review* 21, January–February 2002, available at http://www.isreview.org/issues/21/afghan_women.shtml, accessed April 10, 2012.

12. Malalai Joya, *A Woman among Warlords* (New York: Scribner, 2009).

13. Deepa Kumar, "Heroes, Victims, and Veils: Women's Liberation and the Rhetoric of Empire Post-9/11," *Forum on Public Policy* 4, no. 2 (2008): 23–32.

14. N. C. Aizenman, "Nicaragua's Total Ban on Abortion Spurs Critics," *Washington Post*, November 28, 2006, available at http://www.washingtonpost.com/wp-dyn/content/article/2006/11/27/AR2006112701577.html, accessed October 28, 2009. See also Michelle Ralston and Elizabeth Podrebarach, "Abortion Laws around the World," Pew Forum on Religion & Public Life, September 30, 2008, available at www.pewforum.org/Abortion/Abortion-Laws-Around-the-World.aspx.

15. Dilip Hiro, *Holy Wars: The Rise of Islamic Fundamentalism* (New York: Routledge, 1989).

16. Maxime Rodinson, *Muhammad* (New York: New Press, 2002).

17. Asma Barlas, *"Believing Women" in Islam: Unreading Patriarchal Interpretations of the Qur'an* (Austin: University of Texas Press, 2002).

18. See Montgomery Watt, *Muhammad at Medina* (Oxford: Clarendon Press, 1956), cited in Ahmed, *Women and Gender in Islam,* 43.

19. Rodinson, *Muhammad*, 230.

20. Ahmed, *Women and Gender in Islam*, 62.

21. The Egyptian civilization (3100–333 BCE) ended with the Greek conquest of Egypt.

22. Quoted in Ahmed, *Women and Gender in Islam*, 29.

23. Pope Benedict XVI, "Faith, Reason, and the Univeristy: Memories and Reflections," delivered September 12, 2006 in Regensburg, Germany, transcript available at http://news.bbc.co.uk/2/shared/bsp/hi/pdfs/15_09_06_pope.pdf, accessed April 10, 2012.

24. Quoted in Mahmood Mamdani, *Good Muslim, Bad Muslim* (New York: Doubleday, 2005), 45.

25. Quoted in Maxime Rodinson, *Marxism and the Muslim World* (New York: Monthly Review Press, 1981), 50.

26. Lockman, *Contending Visions*, 79–80.

27. Earl of Cromer, quoted in Said, *Orientalism*, 38.

28. Richard Seymour, "The Changing Face of Racism," *International Socialism Journal* 126 (April 2010), available at http://www.isj.org.uk/?id=638, accessed April 9, 2012.

29. Karim H. Karim, *Islamic Peril: Media and Global Violence*, 2nd ed. (New York: Black Rose Books, 2003).

30. Talal Asad, *On Suicide Bombing* (New York: Columbia University Press, 2007).

31. Rudolph Guiliani, remarks delivered at Republican presidential debate, May 3, 2007, in Simi Valley, CA, transcript available at http://2008election.procon.org/pdf/Rep20070503.pdf, accessed September 9, 2011.

32. See in particular Stephen Jay Gould's excellent *The Mismeasure of Man*, revised and expanded edition (New York: W. W. Norton, 1996).

33. Tariq Ali, *The Clash of Fundamentalisms: Crusades, Jihad, and Modernity* (New York: Verso, 2002), 54.

34. Saliba, *Islamic Science.*

35. Pope Benedict XVI, "Faith, Reason, and the University."

36. Anthony DiMaggio, "Fort Hood Fallout: Cultural Racism and Deteriorating Public Discourse on Islam," *ZNet*, December 3, 2009, accessed January 18, 2010.

37. Tunku Varadarajan, "Going Muslim," *Forbes*, November 9, 2009, available at http://www.forbes.com/2009/11/08/fort-hood-nidal-malik-hasan-muslims-opinions-columnists-tunku-varadarajan.html, accessed January 18, 2010.

38. Amitabh Pal, "*Islam" Means Peace: Understanding the Muslim Principle of Nonviolence Today* (Westport, CT: Praeger, 2011).

39. Lockman, *Contending Visions*, 19

40. Ali, *Clash of Fundamentalisms*, 40.

41. Colin Wells, quoted in John Feffer, *Crusade 2.0: The West's Resurgent War on Islam* (San Francisco: City Lights Books, 2012), 36.

42. Andrew Curry, "The First Holy War," *U.S. News and World Report*, August 23, 2005.

43. Quoted in Said, *Orientalism*, 32–33.

44. Quoted in Little, *American Orientalism*, 15.

45. See Paul D'Amato's critique of Niall Ferguson's book *Empire*: "When Britannia Waived the Rules," *International Socialist Review* 32, November–December 2003, available at http://www.isreview.org/issues/32/ferguson.shtml, accessed April 9, 2012.

46. After a week in Afghanistan, leader Medea Benjamin reversed Code Pink's antiwar position. See Aunohita Mojumdar, "Code Pink Rethinks Its Call for Afghanistan Pullout," *Christian Science Monitor,* October 6, 2009, http://www.csmonitor.com/World/Asia-South-Central/2009/1006/p06s10-wosc.html, accessed April 10, 2012.

47. Lens, *Forging of the American Empire;* William Blum, *Rogue State* (Monroe, Maine: Common Courage Press, 2000); Stephen Kinzer, *Overthrow: America's Century of Regime Change from Hawaii to Iraq* (New York: Times Books, 2006).

48. Quoted in Little, *American Orientalism*, 28.

49. Ibid., 27–28.

50. Ervand Abrahamian, *A History of Modern Iran* (Cambridge: Cambridge University Press, 2008).

51. Goldschmidt and Davidson, *Concise History*, 190–93 and 198–201.

52. Bernard Lewis, interview by David Horowitz, "A Mass Expression of Outrage against Injustice," *Jerusalem Post*, February 25, 2011, available at http://www.jpost.com/Opinion/Columnists/Article.aspx?id=209770, accessed April 9, 2012.

53. Ibid.

4. Allies and Enemies: The United States and Political Islam

1. *New York Times*, "US Warship Becomes Arab Court in Miniature for Ibn Saud's Voyage," February 21, 1945.

2. Little, *American Orientalism*, 194–95.

3. Quoted in ibid., 27.

4. Ibid., 195–96.

5. Dwight D. Eisenhower, "The Eisenhower Doctrine on the Middle East: A Message to Congress," *Department of State Bulletin* 36, no. 917 (January 21, 1957): 83–87. Available at http://www.fordham.edu/halsall/mod/1957eisenhowerdoctrine.html, accessed September 22, 2011.

6. Quoted in Robert Dreyfuss, *Devil's Game: How the United States Helped Unleash Fun-*

damentalist Islam (New York: Henry Holt, 2005), 121.

7.   Rachel Bronson, *Thicker than Oil: America's Uneasy Partnership with Saudi Arabia* (Oxford: Oxford University Press, 2006), 74.

8.   Dreyfuss, *Devil's Game*, 72–73.

9.   Ibid., 76–85.

10. Joyce Battle, *US Propaganda in the Middle East: The Early Cold War Version*, National Security Archive Briefing Book 78 (Washington, DC: National Security Archive, 2002). Available at http://www.gwu.edu/~nsarchiv/NSAEBB/NSAEBB78/essay.htm, accessed September 15, 2011.

11. Ibid., 20.

12. See chapter 4 of Dreyfuss, *Devil's Game*.

13. Ibid., 97–104.

14. Ibid., 125.

15. Walter Laqueur, *Communism and Nationalism in the Middle East* (New York: Praeger, 1956), 6.

16. Fawaz Gerges, *America and Political Islam: Clash of Cultures or Clash of Interests?* (Cambridge: Cambridge University Press, 1999), 40.

17. Ibid., 41.

18. Ibid., 42.

19. Madawi Al-Rasheed, *A History of Saudi Arabia* (New York: Cambridge University Press, 2002).

20. See Gilles Kepel, *Jihad: The Trail of Political Islam* (Cambridge, MA: Harvard University Press, 2003), chapter 3; also Bronson, *Thicker than Oil,* and As'ad AbuKhalil, *The Battle for Saudi Arabia: Royalty, Fundamentalism, and Global Power* (New York: Seven Stories Press, 2003).

21. See chapter 7 of Dreyfuss, *Devil's Game*.

22. Ibid., 172.

23. Ronald Reagan, "Remarks at the Annual Dinner of the Conservative Political Action Conference," speech delivered March 1, 1985, *Public Papers of the Presidents of the United States: Ronald Reagan, 1985,* Bk 1 (Washington, DC: United States Government Printing Office, 1988), 228.

24. Dreyfuss, *Devil's Game*, 113–16.

25. For more about the dynamics of the Iranian revolution, see Nikki Keddie, *Modern Iran: Roots and Results of Revolution* (New Haven, CT: Yale University Press, 2003); Maryam Poya, "Iran 1979: Long Live Revolution . . . Long Live Islam?" in Colin Barker, ed., *Revolutionary Rehearsals* (London: Bookmarks, 1987); and Saman Sepehri, "The Iranian Revolution," *International Socialist Review* 9, August-September 2000.

26. Gerges, *America and Political Islam*, 43.

27. Ibid., 66.

28. Saadia Toor, *The State of Islam: Culture and Cold War Politics in Pakistan* (London: Pluto Press, 2011).

29. Dreyfuss, *Devil's Game*, 244.

30. Robert M. Gates, *From the Shadows: The Ultimate Insider's Story of Five Presidents and How They Won the Cold War* (New York: Simon and Schuster, 1996).

31. Zbigniew Brzezinski, interview by A. G. Frank, *Nouvel Observateur,* January 15-21, 1998.

32. The last description—"definitely dictator material"—was not typically a pejorative in the eyes of the CIA. Tim Weiner, *Blank Check: The Pentagon's Black Budget* (New York: Warner Books, 1990), 32.

33. Reagan, "Remarks," 228.

34. Steve Coll, "Anatomy of a Victory: CIA's Covert Afghan War," *Washington Post*, July 19, 1992.

35. Mamdani, *Good Muslim*, 128, 135

36. John Cooley, *Unholy Wars: Afghanistan, America and International Terrorism* (London: Pluto Press, 2002), 70.

37. Ibid., 70–72.

38. Ibid., 71–73.

39. Mamdani, *Good Muslim*, 130

40. Gerges, *America and Political Islam*, 111.

41. Kepel, *Jihad*, 10.

42. Gerges, *America and Political Islam*, 122–23.

43. Ahmed Rashid, *Taliban: Militant Islam, Oil and Fundamentalism in Central Asia* (New Haven, CT: Yale University Press, 2000).

44. Little, *American Orientalism*, 42.

45. On the portrayal of Arabs in Hollywood, see Shaheen, *Reel Bad Arabs*.

46. Fred Halliday, *Islam and the Myth of Confrontation* (New York: I. B. Tauris, 2003),188.

47. Israel Ministry of Foreign Affairs, "Benjamin Netanyahu," August 10, 2005, available at http://www.mfa.gov.il/MFA/MFAArchive/2000_2009/2003/2/Benjamin%20 Netanyahu, accessed September 15, 2011.

48. Shaul Mishal and Avraham Sela, *The Palestinian Hamas: Vision, Violence, and Coexistence* (New York: Columbia University Press, 2006), 21.

49. Dreyfuss, *Devil's Game*, 197.

50. Gerges, *America and Political Islam*, 52.

51. Kepel, *Jihad*, 9.

52. See chapter 9 of Gerges, *America and Political Islam*.

53. Kepel, *Jihad*, 10.

54. Samih Farsoun, "Roots of the American Antiterrorism Crusade," in Elaine Hagopian, ed., *Civil Rights in Peril* (Chicago: Haymarket Books and Pluto Press, 2004), 137.

55. Gerges, *America and Political Islam*, 52.

56. Lewis, "Roots of Muslim Rage."

57. Judith Miller, "The Challenge of Radical Islam," *Foreign Affairs*, Spring 1993, available at http://www.foreignaffairs.com/articles/48755/judith-miller/the-challenge-of-radical -islam, accessed April 10, 2012.

58. See Gerges, *America and Political Islam*, 20–28.

59. Quoted in ibid., 80.

60. Ibid., 91.

5. The Separation of Mosque and State

1. Willard Oxtoby and Alan Segal, *A Concise Introduction to World Religions* (Oxford: Oxford University Press, 2007), 200.

2. Lewis, "Muslim Rage."

3. Ibid.

4. Bernard Lewis, *What Went Wrong? The Clash between Islam and Modernity in the Middle East* (New York: Harper Perennial, 2003). Quoted in Mamdani, *Good Muslim*, 23.

5. Samuel Huntington, *The Clash of Civilizations and the Remaking of World Order* (New York: Simon and Schuster, 1997), 217.

6. Olivier Roy, *The Failure of Political Islam* (Cambridge, MA: Harvard University Press, 1996), 13–14.

7.   Ali, *Clash of Fundamentalisms*, 29.

8.   Goldschmidt and Davidson, *Concise History*, see chapter 3.

9.   Some scholars argue that during the reign of the first four descendants of Muhammad, the "righteously guided" caliphs, religious and political power were synonymous. Yet Ayoob suggests that even during this era it was politics that drove religious war. See Mohammad Ayoob, *The Many Faces of Political Islam: Religion and Politics in the Muslim World* (Ann Arbor: University of Michigan Press, 2008).

10. Roy, *Failure of Political Islam*, 14.

11. Ayoob, *Many Faces*, 5.

12. Ibid., 11.

13. Goldschmidt and Davidson, *Concise History*, 108–9.

14. Roy, *Failure of Political Islam*, 29.

15. Ayoob, *Many Faces*, 11.

16. Goldschmidt and Davidson, *Concise History*, 114.

17. Ayoob, *Many Faces*, 5.

18. Ibid., 13.

19. Ibid.

20. Esposito, *Islamic Threat*, 52.

21. Goldschmidt and Davidson, *Concise History*, 173–74.

22. Ibid., 173–74.

23. Ibid., 228.

24. Rodinson, *Arabs*, 97.

25. Esposito, *Islamic Threat*, 49.

26. Roy, *Failure of Political Islam*, 33.

27. Ibid. See also Joel Beinin and Joe Stork, "On the Modernity, Historical Specificity, and International Context of Political Islam," in *Political Islam: Essays from Middle East Report* (Berkeley: University of California Press, 1997), 5–6.

28. Roy, *Failure of Political Islam*, 33. Salafist thought has been influential in various Sunni Islamist circles. The connections with Wahhabism are close, particularly since both traditions draw on the teachings of a fourteenth-century *ulama* named Ibn Taymiyya (see Kepel, *Jihad,* 219–20). Today, the Wahhabis prefer to be called Salafis: see Fawaz Gerges, *Journey of the Jihadist: Inside Muslim Militancy* (Orlando, FL: Harcourt, 2006), 106. As an aside, let us note that not all Wahhabis are radicals. While Saudi Arabia is a Wahhabi nation, only a small subset of Saudis are jihadi extremists. The Wahhabi-Salafi jihadis based in the tribal areas of Pakistan offer a literal and even stricter interpretation of Wahhabi-Salafi doctrine.

29. Kepel, *Jihad,* 34.

30. Ibid.

31. Dreyfuss, *Devil's Game*, 20. While there are many connections between the various Islamist forces that Dreyfus points out well, each of these currents also has its own history. In India, for instance, after the last Muslim ruler was deposed by the British in 1857, Muslims found themselves in the minority in a country dominated by Hindus. The Deobandi Islamic movement came into being shortly afterward, in 1867, as a response to this situation. It was founded as a means to provide Muslims in the Indian subcontinent with a set of rules to live by, in order to preserve Islam in a country where Muslims were a minority. Toward this end, the Deobandis trained a core of *ulama* to issue fatwas, or legal opinions, to make sure that Muslims in India conformed to their very rigorous and conservative interpretation of Islam (Kepel, *Jihad,* 223). In this, the Deobandis became very similar to the Wahhabis and in the later part of the

twentieth century established close ties with them in the context of US-sponsored activities in Pakistan (57–58).

32.   Rodinson, *Arabs*, 100–101. See also Laqueur, *Communism and Nationalism*, on popular discontent with feudal landowners and corrupt regimes in Lebanon. The Lebanese Communist Party was in power at this time (after 1954). No doubt it influenced the Baath party's shift leftward. Similarly, student struggles in Egypt in 1952–55 (which were Communist-led) and workers' strikes must have impacted Nasser (*Communism and Nationalism,* 54–57 on Egypt, 163 on Lebanon).

33.   John L. Esposito and John O. Voll, *Islam and Democracy* (New York: Oxford University Press, 1996), 5.

34.   Rodinson, *Arabs*, 111.

6. Political Islam: A Historical Analysis

1.   Ervand Abrahamian, *Khomeinism: Essays on the Islamic Republic* (Berkeley: University of California Press, 1993), 19.

2.   Nikki Keddie, ed., *Religion and Politics in Iran: Shi'ism from Quietism to Revolution* (New Haven, CT: Yale University Press, 1984). See also Kepel, *Jihad*, 39–42.

3.   Abrahamian, *Khomeinism,* 24–26. See also Nikki Keddie, *Roots and Results of Revolution* (New Haven, CT: Yale University Press, 2003), 193.

4.   Ayoob, *Many Faces*, 4–5.

5.   Khaled Hroub, *Hamas: A Beginner's Guide* (Ann Arbor, MI: Pluto, 2006), 15.

6.   Ibid., 13.

7.   Sa'id al Ghazali, "Islamic Movement versus National Liberation," *Journal of Palestine Studies* 17, no. 2 (Winter 1988): 177.

8.   Tareq Ismael, *The Arab Left* (Syracuse, NY: Syracuse University Press, 1976), 79.

9.   Ibid., 89.

10.   Ibid., 79.

11.   Rodinson, *Arabs*, 115.

12.   Kepel, *Jihad*, 82.

13.   Dreyfuss, *Devil's Game,* 153.

14.   Phil Marshall, "The Children of Stalinism," *International Socialism Journal* 68 (1995): 118–19.

15.   See Laqueur, *Communism and Nationalism*, for a discussion of these struggles.

16.   Tareq Ismael, *The Communist Movement in the Arab World* (New York: Routledge, 2005).

17.   Ibid., 21.

18.   Ibid., 19–20.

19.   Ibid., 55.

20.   Marshall, "Children of Stalinism," 122.

21.   Ibid., 120.

22.   Paul Lubeck, "Antinomies of Islamic Movements under Globalization," Center for Global, International, and Regional Studies Working Paper Series, 1999. Available at www2.ucsc.edu/globalinterns/wp/wp99-1.PDF, accessed October 12, 2011.

23.   Kepel, *Jihad*, 66.

24.   Roy, *Failure of Political Islam*, 49.

25.   Ibid., 50.

26.   Ibid.

27.   Chris Harman, "The Prophet and the Proletariat," *International Socialism Journal* 64

(Autumn 1994): 8–10. Available at www.marxists.de/religion/harman/index.htm, accessed October 12, 2011.

28.   Ibid., 9–10.

29.   Kepel, *Jihad*, 6.

30.   Dreyfuss, *Devil's Game*, 161–62.

31.   Hroub, *Hamas*, 69, 125.

32.   Roy, *Failure of Political Islam*, 41–42.

33.   Cihan Tu, et al., "Nato's Islamists," *New Left Review* 44 (March–April 2007): available at http://www.newleftreview.org/?view=2657, accessed April 9, 2012.

34.   Harman, "Prophet," 23–24.

35.   Khaled Hroub, *Hamas: Political Thought and Practice* (Washington, DC: Institute for Palestine Studies, 2000), 44.

36.   See also Deepa Kumar, "Behind the Myths about Hamas," *International Socialist Review* 64 (March–April 2009).

37.   Patrick Cockburn, *Muqtada: Muqtada al-Sadr, the Shia Revival, and the Struggle for Iraq* (New York: Simon and Schuster, 2008).

38.   Anand Gopal, "Who Are the Taliban?," lecture at the Socialism 2010 Conference, Chicago, June 17, 2010.

39.   Miles Amoore, "Pakistan Puppet Masters Guide the Taliban Killers," *Times of London*, June 13, 2010.

40.   Jonathan Schanzer, "Palestinian Uprisings Compared," *Middle East Quarterly*, Summer 2002, 27–37. Available at www.meforum.org/206/palestinian-uprisings-compared, accessed October 12, 2011.

41.   Ibid., 114–16.

7. The Foreign Policy Establishment and the "Islamic Threat"

1.   Project for the New American Century, *Rebuilding America's Defenses: Strategy, Forces and Resources for a New Century* (Washington, DC: Project for the New American Century, 2000), 9, available at http://www.newamericancentury.org/publicationsreports.htm, accessed April 4, 2012.

2.   Ibid, 83.

3.   Gary Dorien, *Imperial Designs: Neoconservatives and the New Pax Americana* (New York: Routledge, 2004).

4.   Ibid., 7.

5.   Stewart Patrick and Shepard Forman, *Multilateralism and US Foreign Policy: Ambivalent Engagement* (Boulder, CO: Lynne Rienner, 2002), 7.

6.   Ibid.

7.   Danny Cooper, *Neoconservatism and American Foreign Policy: A Critical Analysis* (New York: Routledge, 2011), 14 (both quotes).

8.   Dorien, *Imperial Designs*, 21.

9.   Quoted in ibid., 11.

10.   Ibid., 13.

11.   Charles Krauthammer, "The Unipolar Moment," *Foreign Affairs*, 1990.

12.   Dorien, *Imperial Designs*, 39.

13.   Ibid., 40.

14.   Ibid.

15.   Maria Ryan, *Neoconservatism and the New American Century* (New York: Palgrave Macmillan, 2010), 22.

16. Ibid., 14.

17. Quoted in Gerges, *America and Political Islam*, 24.

18. Max Boot, "What the Heck Is a 'Neocon'?" *Wall Street Journal*, December 30, 2002.

19. Seymour, *Liberal Defence*, 160.

20. Ibid., 159–60.

21. Dorien, *Imperial Designs*, 196.

22. Robert Kaplan, *Arabists: The Romance of an American Elite* (New York: Free Press, 1995).

23. Stephen Sniegoski, *The Transparent Cabal: The Neoconservative Agenda, War in the Middle East, and the National Interest of Israel* (Norfolk, VA: Enigma Editions, 2008), 84.

24. Quoted in ibid., 26.

25. Quoted in Ryan, *Neoconservatism*, 34.

26. Dorien, *Imperial Designs*, 197.

27. Sniegoski, *Transparent Cabal*, 52.

28. Noam Chomsky, *Fateful Triangle: The United States, Israel and the Palestinians* (Cambridge, MA: South End, 1999), 455.

29. Sniegoski, *Transparent Cabal*, 5.

30. Benjamin Netanyahu, ed., *International Terrorism: Challenge and Response* (New Brunswick, NJ: Transaction Books, 1981).

31. Ibid., 3.

32. Ibid., 6.

33. All quotes taken from ibid., 5.

34. Ibid., 6.

35. Robert Moss, "The Terrorist State," in Netanyahu, ed., *International Terrorism,* 128.

36. Mordecai Abir, "The Arab World, Oil and Terrorism," in Netanyahu, ed., *International Terrorism*, 135–41.

37. Benjamin Netanyahu, ed., *Terrorism: How the West Can Win* (New York: Farrar, Strauss and Giroux, 1986), 12.

38. Ibid., 11.

39. Bernard Lewis, "Islamic Terrorism?," in Netanyahu, ed., *International Terrorism,* 66.

40. Ibid., 67.

41. Elie Kedourie, "Political Terrorism in the Muslim World," in Netanyahu, ed., *International Terrorism*, 70.

42. Ibid., 72.

43. Ibid., 76.

44. Quoted in Halliday, *Islam and the Myth of Confrontation*, 190–91.

45. Dreyfuss, *Devil's Game*, 197.

46. Halliday, *Islam and the Myth of Confrontation*, 190.

47. Ryan, *Neoconservatism*, 57.

48. Ibid.

49. Seymour, *Liberal Defence*, 23.

50. Jean Bricmont, *Humanitarian Imperialism: Using Human Rights to Sell Wars* (New York: Monthly Review Press, 2006), 20.

51. Stephen M. Walt, "What Intervention in Libya Tells Us about the Neocon-Liberal Alliance," *Foreign Policy*, March 21, 2001, available at http://walt.foreignpolicy.com/posts/2011/03/21/what_intervention_in_libya_tells_us_about_the_neocon_liberal_alliance, accessed April 4, 2012.

52. Ibid.

53. Quoted in Noam Chomsky, *The New Military Humanism* (Monroe, ME: Common Courage, 1999), 14.

54. Jean-Marc Coicaud, *Beyond the National Interest: The Failure of UN Peacekeeping and Multilateralism in an Era of U.S. Primacy* (Washington, DC: United States Institute of Peace Press, 2007), 119.

55. Ibid., 117.

56. Chomsky, *New Military Humanism*, 14.

57. See Sheehi, *Islamophobia*.

58. Quoted in Dreyfuss, *Devil's Game*, 85.

59. Lee Wengraf, "Operation Restore Hope, 1992–1994," *International Socialist Review* 77 (May–June 2011).

60. Madeleine Albright, interview by Leslie Stahl, *60 Minutes*, CBS, May 12, 1996, clip available at http://www.youtube.com/watch?v=FbIX1CP9qr4, accessed April 4, 2012.

61. Phyllis Bennis, *Challenging Empire: How People, Governments, and the UN Defy US Power* (Northampton, MA: Olive Branch, 2006).

62. Quoted in Ryan, *Neoconservatism*, 78.

63. Ibid., 79.

64. Ibid., 142.

65. Patrick and Forman, *Multilateralism*, 23.

66. Quoted in Richard A. Clarke, *Against All Enemies: Inside America's War on Terror* (New York: Free Press, 2004), 32.

67. United States Department of Defense, *National Security Strategy,* 2010 USNSS 2 (Washington, DC: United States Department of Defense, 2010), available at www .whitehouse.gov/sites/default/files/rss_viewer/national_security_strategy.pdf, accessed April 4, 2012.

68. Quoted in Jessica Tuchman Matthews, "September 11, One Year Later: A World of Change," Carnegie Endowment for International Peace policy brief, August 2002, available at http://carnegieendowment.org/2002/08/18/september-11-one-year -later-world-of-change/ekx.

69. Sheehi, *Islamophobia*, 44.

70. Ibid., 78.

71. Quoted in ibid.

72. Cooper, *Neoconservatism,* 92.

73. Sheehi, *Islamophobia*, 56.

74. United States Army, *Counterinsurgency* (Washington, DC: United States Department of Defense, 2006), available at http://www.fas.org/irp/doddir/army/fm3-24.pdf, accessed April 4, 2012.

75. James Udris, Michael Udris, and James Der Derian, *Human Terrain*, DVD, UDRIS Film and OXYOPIA Productions (Oley, PA: Bullfrog Films, 2010).

76. Leadership Group on U.S.–Muslim Engagement, "Changing Course: A New Direction for U.S. Relations with the Muslim World" (Washington, DC: U.S.–Muslim Engagement Project, 2009), available at http://www.usmuslimengagement.org/storage/ usme/documents/Changing_Course_Second_Printing.pdf, accessed April 4, 2012.

77. Barack Obama, "A New Beginning," speech delivered in Cairo, Egypt, June 4, 2009, video and transcripts available at http://www.whitehouse.gov/blog/NewBeginning/ transcripts, accessed April 4, 2012.

78. Joseph S. Nye Sr., "Get Smart: Combining Hard and Soft Power," *Foreign Affairs*, July 2009.

79. Quoted in Ryan Lizza, "The Consequentialist," *New Yorker*, May 2, 2011.

80. United States Department of Defense, *National Security Strategy*, 3.

81. Ty Cobb, "The Defense Strategic Guidance: What's New, What Is the Focus, Is It

Realistic?," *Harvard Law School National Security Journal*, January 8, 2012, available at http://harvardnsj.org/2012/01/the-defense-strategic-guidance-whats-new-what-is -the-focus-is-it-realistic/, accessed April 4, 2012.

82. United States Department of Defense, *Sustaining U.S. Global Leadership: Priorities for 21st Century Defense* (Washington, DC: United States Department of Defense, 2012), available at http://www.defense.gov/news/Defense_Strategic_Guidance.pdf, accessed April 4, 2012.

83. Ibid., 1.

84. Ibid., 2.

85. Ibid., 2.

86. Ibid., preface.

87. Ibid., 6.

8. Legalizing Racism: Muslims and the Attack on Civil Liberties

1. Moustafa Bayoumi, *How Does It Feel to Be a Problem?* (New York: Penguin, 2008), 3.

2. Stephen Downs, *Victims of America's Dirty Wars: Tactics and Reasons from COINTELPRO to the War on Terror* (Albany, NY: Project Salam, 2012), 71, available at http://project-salam.org/downloads/Victims_of_Americas_Dirty_Wars.pdf.

3. Stephan Salisbury, *Mohamed's Ghosts: An American Story of Love and Fear in the Homeland* (New York: Nation Books, 2010), 23.

4. Associated Press, "Documents Show NYPD Infiltrated Liberal Groups," *New York Times*, March 23, 2012, available at http://www.nytimes.com/aponline/2012/03/ 23/us/ap-us-nypd-intelligence.html?_r=1, accessed April 4, 2012.

5. Rick Perlstein, "How FBI Entrapment Is Inventing 'Terrorists'—and Letting Bad Guys Off the Hook," *Rolling Stone*, May 15, 2012, available at http://www.rollingstone .com/politics/blog/national-affairs/how-fbi-entrapment-is-inventing-terrorists-and -letting-bad-guys-off-the-hook-20120515, accessed May 22, 2012.

6. Salisbury, *Mohamed's Ghosts*, 128.

7. Elaine Hagopian, "Minority Rights in a Nation-State: The Nixon Administration's Campaign against Arab Americans," *Journal of Palestine Studies* 5, no. 1/2 (Autumn 1975): 97–114, quote on pp. 100–101.

8. Hagopian, *Civil Rights in Peril*, 11.

9. Ibid., 18–19.

10. John F. Sugg, "Steven Emerson's Crusade," *Extra!*, January–February 1999, available at http://www.fair.org/index.php?page=1443, accessed April 4, 2012.

11. Ian F. Haney Lopez, "The Social Construction of Race," in Julie Rivkin and Michael Ryan, eds., *Literary Theory: An Anthology*, 2nd ed. (Oxford: Blackwell, 2004), 964–74.

12. Hagopian, *Civil Rights in Peril*, 31.

13. Cited in ibid., 39.

14. Ibid., 44.

15. Salisbury, *Mohamed's Ghosts*, 125.

16. Ibid., 36.

17. Ibid., 37.

18. Ibid., 11.

19. Faiza Patel, *Rethinking Radicalization* (New York: NYU School of Law, 2011), 20.

20. Center for Human Rights and Global Justice, *Targeted and Entrapped: Manufacturing the "Homegrown Threat" in the United States* (New York: NYU School of Law, 2011),

10–11, available at www.chrgj.org/projects/docs/targetedandentrapped.pdf, accessed April 4, 2012.

21. Associated Press, "Highlights of AP's Probe into NYPD Intelligence Operations," last updated March 23, 2012, available at http://www.ap.org/media-center/nypd/investigation, accessed April 4, 2012.

22. New York Police Department, "The Demographics Unit," PowerPoint presentation, published by Associated Press, available at http://wid.ap.org/documents/nypd-demo.pdf, accessed March 29, 2012.

23. Quoted in David B. Caruso, "NYC Mayor, Yale Leader Spar over Muslim Spying," *USA Today*, February 22, 2012, available at http://www.usatoday.com/USCP/PNI/Nation/World/2012-02-22-BCUSNYPD-IntelligenceUniversities4th-Ld_ST_U.htm, accessed April 4, 2012.

24. Alex Kane, "Newark Mayor and Yale President Slam NYPD Spying Program," *Mondoweiss*, February 24, 2012, available at http://mondoweiss.net/2012/02/newark-mayor-and-yale-university-head-slam-nypd-spying-program.html, accessed April 4, 2012.

25. Jeanne Theoharis, "Guantánamo at Home," *Nation*, April 2, 2009, available at http://www.thenation.com/article/guant%C3%A1namo-home, accessed April 4, 2012.

26. Center for Human Rights and Global Justice, Asian American Legal Defense and Education Fund, *Under the Radar: Muslims Deported, Detained, and Denied on Unsubstantiated Terrorism Allegations* (New York: NYU School of Law, 2011), available at http://chrgj.org/projects/docs/undertheradar.pdf, accessed April 4, 2012.

27. Ibid., 2.

28. Ibid., 4.

29. Ibid., 4–5.

30. Alia Malek, ed., *Patriot Acts: Narratives of Post-9/11 Injustice* (San Francisco: McSweeney's, 2011), 23.

31. Bayoumi, *How Does It Feel*, 26.

32. Downs, *Victims of America's Dirty Wars*, 17.

33. Project Salam is analyzing about 750 cases, of which it has found 150 to be cases of preemptive persecution. See the database of cases at projectsalam.org.

34. Michael Ratner, interview by Nicole Colson, "A New Stage in the War on Dissent," *Socialist Worker*, October 19, 2010, available at http://socialistworker.org/2010/10/19/new-stage-in-the-war-on-dissent, accessed April 4, 2012.

35. Downs, *Victims of America's Dirty Wars*, 22.

36. Ibid., 14.

37. Quoted in Jeanne Theoharis, "My Student, the 'Terrorist,'" *Chronicle of Higher Education*, April 3, 2011, available at http://chronicle.com/article/My-Student-the-Terrorist/126937/, accessed April 4, 2012.

38. Ibid.

39. Downs, *Victims of America's Dirty Wars*, 28.

40. Center for Human Rights and Global Justice, *Targeted and Entrapped*, 2.

41. Ibid.

42. Ted Conover, "The Pathetic Newburgh Four," *Slate*, November 23, 2010, available at http://www.slate.com/articles/news_and_politics/jurisprudence/2010/11/the_pathetic_newburgh_four.html, accessed April 4, 2012.

43. Ibid.

44. James Donaghy, "We're Lost without *Lost* and Can No Longer Count on *24*," *Guardian* (UK), May 21, 2010, available at http://www.guardian.co.uk/tv-and-radio/2010/may/22/television-lost, accessed April 4, 2012.

45. Downs, *Victims of America's Dirty Wars*, 17.

46. Charles Kurzman, *Muslim-American Terrorism in the Decade since 9/11* (Chapel Hill, NC: Triangle Center on Terrorism and Homeland Security, 2012), available at http://sanford.duke.edu/centers/tcths/documents/Kurzman_Muslim-American_Terrorism _in_the_Decade_Since_9_11.pdf, accessed April 4, 2012.

47. Ibid.

48. Charles Kurzman, David Schanzer, and Ebrahim Moosa, "Muslim American Terrorism since 9/11: Why So Rare?," *Muslim World* 101:464–83. doi: 10.1111/j.1478 -1913.2011.01388.x, available at http://sanford.duke.edu/centers/tcths/documents/ Kurzman_Schanzer_Moosa_Muslim_American_Terrorism.pdf, accessed April 4, 2012.

49. Ibid., 471.

50. Ibid., 475.

51. United States Department of State, *Country Reports on Terrorism 2010* (Washington, DC: US State Department, 2010), available at http://www.state.gov/s/ct/rls/crt/ 2009/index.htm, accessed April 4, 2012.

52. United States Department of State, "Terrorism Deaths, Injuries, Kidnappings of Private U.S. Citizens, 2010," in *Country Reports on Terrorism 2011* (Washington, DC: US State Department, 2011), available at http://www.state.gov/j/ct/rls/crt/2010/170267.htm, accessed April 4, 2012.

53. Zaid Jilani, "Chart: Only 15 Americans Died from Terrorism Last Year—Fewer Than from Dog Bites or Lightning Strikes," *Think Progress*, August 25, 2011, available at http://thinkprogress.org/security/2011/08/25/304113/chart-only-15-americans-died-from -terrorism-last-year-less-than-from-dog-bites-or-lightning-strikes/, accessed April 4, 2012.

54. Susan Heavey, "Study Links 45,000 U.S. Deaths to Lack of Insurance," Reuters, September 17, 2009, available at http://www.reuters.com/article/2009/09/17/us-usa-healthcare -deaths-idUSTRE58G6W520090917, accessed April 4, 2012.

55. Hagopian, *Civil Rights in Peril*, 38.

56. Patel, *Rethinking Radicalization*, 1.

57. Mitchell D. Silber and Arvin Bhatt, *Radicalization in the West: The Homegrown Threat* (New York: NYPD Intelligence Division, 2007), 5, available at http://www.nypdshield.org/ public/SiteFiles/documents/NYPD_Report-Radicalization_in_the_West.pdf, accessed April 4, 2012.

58. Quoted in Patel, *Rethinking Radicalization*, 15.

59. United States Department of Homeland Security, *Rightwing Extremism: Current Economic and Political Climate Fueling Resurgence in Radicalization and Recruitment* (Washington, DC: United States Department of Homeland Security, 2009), available at http://www .fas.org/irp/eprint/rightwing.pdf, accessed April 4, 2012.

60. Downs, *Victims of America's Dirty Wars*, 39.

61. Center for Human Rights and Global Justice, *Targeted and Entrapped*, 16.

62. Patel, *Rethinking Radicalization*, 3.

63. Ibid., 8.

64. United States Department of Defense, *Protecting the Force: Lessons from Fort Hood* (Washington, DC: United States Department of Defense, 2010), available at http://www .defense.gov/pubs/pdfs/DOD-ProtectingTheForce-Web_Security_HR_13jan10.pdf, quoted in Patel, *Rethinking Radicalization*, 9.

65. Clark McCauley and Sophia Moskalenko, "Individual and Group Mechanisms of Radicalization," in Laurie Fenstermacher et al., eds., *Protecting the Homeland from International and Domestic Terrorism Threats* (College Park, MD: National Consortium for the Study

of Terrorism and Responses to Terrorism, 2010), available at http://www.start.umd.edu/start/publications/U_Counter_Terrorism_White_Paper_Final_January_2010.pdf, quoted in Patel, *Rethinking Radicalization*, 9.

66.   Ibid., 13.

67.   Arun Kundnani, "The FBI's 'Good' Muslims," *Nation*, September 19, 2011, available at http://www.agenceglobal.com/article.asp?id=2629, accessed April 4, 2012.

68.   Ibid.

9. Green Scare: The Making of the Domestic Muslim Enemy

1.   CNN, "Woman in Pennsylvania," *American Morning*, March 10, 2010, accessed March 25, 2010 through Campus Westlaw Research.

2.   SourceWatch, "Taking the Fight to the Terrorists," *SourceWatch*, August 11, 2008, available at http://www.sourcewatch.org/index.php?title=Taking_the_fight_to_the_terrorists, accessed January 20, 2012.

3.   Quoted in Gerry J. Gillmore, "Bush: West Point Grads Answer History's Call to Duty," American Forces Press Service, June 1, 2002, available at http://www.defense.gov/news/newsarticle.aspx?id=43798, accessed January 20, 2012.

4.   Kurzman, Schanzer, and Moosa, "Muslim American Terrorism since 9/11."

5.   Ibid., 466.

6.   Arun Kundnani, "Islamism and the Roots of Liberal Rage," *Race and Class* 50, 2 (2008): 40–68.

7.   Deepa Kumar, "Jihad Jane: Constructing the New Muslim Enemy," *Fifth Estate Online*, April 2010, available at http://www.fifth-estate-online.co.uk/comment/Jihad_Jane_Deepa_Kumar.pdf, accessed January 20, 2012.

8.   Anthony DiMaggio, "Fort Hood Fallout: Cultural Racism and Deteriorating Public Discourse on Islam," *Znet,* December 3, 2009, available at http://www.zcommunications.org/fort-hood-fallout-cultural-racism-and-deteriorating-public-discourse-on-islam-by-anthony-dimaggio, accessed January 20, 2012.

9.   Jerry Markon, "Pakistan Arrests Five Virginia Men at House with Jihadist Ties," *Washington Post,* December 10, 2009.

10.   Tunku Varadarajan, "Going Muslim," *Forbes*, November 2009.

11.   Barack Obama, "Remarks by the President in Address to the Nation on the Way Forward in Afghanistan and Pakistan," speech delivered in West Point, New York, December 1, 2009, transcript available at http://www.whitehouse.gov/the-press-office/remarks-president-address-nation-way-forward-afghanistan-and-pakistan, accessed April 5, 2012.

12.   Gregory F. Treverton, "Terrorists Will Strike America Again," *Los Angeles Times*, January 19, 2010, available at http://articles.latimes.com/2010/jan/19/opinion/la-oe-treverton19-2010jan19, accessed April 10, 2012.

13.   United States Department of State, *Country Reports on Terrorism 2008* (Washington, DC: United States Department of State, 2008), 298–99, available at http://www.state.gov/documents/organization/122599.pdf,

14.   United States Department of Labor, "Fatal Occupational Injuries by Industry and Event or Exposure," Bureau of Labor Statistics, available at http://www.bls.gov/iif/oshwc/cfoi/cftb0241.pdf, accessed January 20, 2012.

15.   National Highway Safety Administration, "Fatality Analysis Reporting System (FARS) Data Tables," NCSA Data Resource Website, available at http://www-fars.nhtsa

.dot.gov/Main/index.aspx, accessed January 20, 2012.

16. United States Departmentof State, *Country Reports on Terrorism 2008*.

17. Rick "Ozzie" Nelson and Ben Bodurian, "A Growing Terrorist Threat?," Center for Strategic and International Studies, March 2010, available at http://csis.org/files/publication/100304_Nelson_GrowingTerroristThreat_Web.pdf, accessed January 20, 2012.

18. Quoted in Ralph Blumenthal and Sharaf Mowjood, "Muslim Prayers and Renewal near Ground Zero," *New York Times*, December 9, 2009.

19. Justin Elliot, "How the 'Ground Zero Mosque' Fear Mongering Began," *Salon*, August 16, 2010, available at http://www.salon.com/2010/08/16/ground_zero_mosque_origins/, accessed January 20, 2012.

20. Laura Ingraham, interview with Daisy Khan, Fox News, December 21, 2009, available at http://www.youtube.com/watch?v=q7WbTv_gsx4, accessed December 1, 2010. Fox News filed copyright infringement notifications against sites that posted the video (see http://www.aolnews.com/2010/08/17/laura-ingrahams-change-of-heart-on-the-ground-zero-mosque/ for an example), and it no longer appears on the Fox News website.

21. Elliot, "How the 'Ground Zero Mosque' Fear Mongering Began."

22. Pamela Geller, "Monster Mosque Pushes Ahead," *Atlas Shrugs*, May 6, 2010, available at http://atlasshrugs2000.typepad.com/atlas_shrugs/2010/05/monster-mosque-pushes-ahead-in-shadow-of-world-trade-center-islamic-death-and-destruction.html, accessed January 20, 2012.

23. Chris McGreal, "The US Blogger on a Mission to Halt 'Islamic Takeover,'" *Guardian*, August 20, 2010, available at http://www.guardian.co.uk/world/2010/aug/20/rightwing-blogs-islam-america, accessed January 20, 2012.

24. Pamela Geller and Eliza Saxon, "Indomitable Israel," *Israel National News*, May 11, 2008, available at http://www.israelnationalnews.com/Articles/Article.aspx/7968, accessed January 20, 2012.

25. Julie Shapiro, "Politicians Rally against Tea Party Bashing of World Trade Center Mosque," *DNAinfo*, May 20, 2010, available at http://dnainfo.com/20100520/manhattan/politicians-rally-against-tea-party-bashing-of-world-trade-center-mosque, accessed January 20, 2012.

26. Quoted in Oliver Willis, "Mark Williams Calls Allah a 'Monkey God': Is He Still Welcome on CNN's Air?," *Media Matters for America*, May 18, 2010, available at http://mediamatters.org/blog/201005180064, accessed January 20, 2012.

27. Wajahat Ali, Eli Clifton, Matthew Duss, Lee Fang, Scott Keyes, and Faiz Shakir, *Fear Inc.: The Roots of the Islamophobia Network in America* (Washington, DC: Center for American Progress, 2011), 22, available at http://www.americanprogress.org/issues/2011/08/pdf/islamophobia.pdf, accessed January 20, 2012.

28. Quoted in ibid., 30.

29. Quoted in Edward Wyatt, "Three Republicans Criticize Obama's Endorsement of Mosque," *New York Times*, August 14, 2010, available at http://www.nytimes.com/2010/08/15/us/politics/15reaction.html, accessed April 5, 2012.

30. Quoted in Ali et al., *Fear Inc.,* 44.

31. Newt Gingrich, *Fox & Friends*, Fox News, August 16, 2010, available at http://mediamatters.org/mmtv/201008160005, accessed April 5, 2012.

32. Abraham Foxman, "The Mosque at Ground Zero," *Huffington Post*, August 2, 2010, available at http://www.huffingtonpost.com/abraham-h-foxman/the-mosque-at-ground-zero_b_668020.html, accessed January 20, 2012.

33. Quoted in Elliot, "How the 'Ground Zero Mosque' Fear Mongering Began."

34. Adam Lisberg, "Mayor Bloomberg Stands Up for Mosque," *Daily Politics*, August 3, 2010, available at http://www.nydailynews.com/blogs/dailypolitics/2010/08/bloomberg -stands-up-for-mosque.html, accessed January 20, 2012.

35. David W. Dunlap, "When an Arab Enclave Thrived Downtown," *New York Times*, August 24, 2010, available at http://www.nytimes.com/2010/08/25/nyregion/25quar-ter.html, accessed April 5, 2012.

36. Bobby Ghosh, "Islamophobia: Does America Have a Muslim Problem?," *Time*, August 30, 2010, available at http://www.time.com/time/magazine/article/0,9171,2011936 ,00.html, accessed April 5, 2012.

37. Aryn Baker, "Afghan Women and the Return of the Taliban," *Time*, August 9, 2010, available at http://www.time.com/time/magazine/article/0,9171,2007407,00.html, accessed April 5, 2012.

38. Rasmussen Reports, "20% Favor Mosque Near Ground Zero, 54% Oppose," *Rasmussen Reports*, July 22, 2010, available at http://www.rasmussenreports.com/public_content/ politics/general_politics/july_2010/20_favor_mosque_near_ground_zero_54_oppose, accessed January 20, 2012. See also Jordan Fabian, "Public Strongly Opposes Ground Zero Mosque," *The Hill*, November 8, 2010, available at http://thehill.com/blogs/blog -briefing-room/news/113747-poll-public-strongly-opposes-ground-zero-mosque-, accessed January 20, 2012.

39. Brian Montopoli, "Nancy Pelosi Questions Funding of NYC Mosque Criticism," *CBS News Political Hotsheet*, August 18, 2010, available at http://www.cbsnews.com/ 8301-503544_162-20014003-503544.html, accessed January 20, 2012.

40. Chris Cillizza, "Democrats Divided over Proposed New York City Mosque," *Washington Post*, August 17, 2010, available at http://www.washingtonpost.com/wp-dyn/ content/article/2010/08/16/AR2010081605425.html, accessed April 5, 2012.

41. Ibid.

42. Glenn Greenwald, "Howard Dean: 'Mosque' Should Move," *Salon*, August 18, 2010, available at http://www.salon.com/2010/08/18/dean_19/, accessed January 20, 2012.

43. Associated Press, "Obama Clarifies Statement in Mosque Debate," *NBC New York*, August 17, 2010, available at http://www.nbcnewyork.com/news/local-beat/Obama -Backs-Mosque-Near-Ground-Zero-100665264.html, accessed January 20, 2012.

44. Quoted in David Jackson, "Obama: Quran Burning Is 'Stunt' that Threatens Troops," *USA Today*, September 9, 2010, available at http://content.usatoday.com/communities/ theoval/post/2010/09/obama-quran-burning-is-stunt-that-threatens-troops/1, accessed January 20, 2012.

45. Max Blumenthal, "The Great Islamophobic Crusade," *Tom Dispatch*, December 19, 2010, available at http://maxblumenthal.com/2010/12/the-great-islamophobic-crusade/, accessed January 20, 2012.

46. Joel Beinin, "The New American McCarthyism: Policing Thought about the Middle East," *Race and Class* 46, no. 1 (2004): 101–15.

47. Ibid., 109.

48. Ibid., 110. Beinin quotes this assertion, and it was also cited on the media watchdog website *SourceWatch* (see http://www.sourcewatch.org/index.php?title=Daniel_Pipes). While the phrase has been taken down from the *Campus Watch* website, the site still links to articles that quote it; a campus-watch.org site search for the phrase "Middle East studies in the United States has become the preserve of Middle East Arabs" returned 123 articles on April 5, 2012.

49. Jeff Jacoby, "The Boston Mosque's Saudi Connection," *Boston Globe*, January 10, 2007,

available at http://www.boston.com/news/globe/editorial_opinion/oped/articles/ 2007/01/10/the_boston_mosques_saudi_connection/?page=full, accessed April 5, 2012.

50. Blumenthal, "Great Islamophobic Crusade."

51. Pamela Geller, "NYC Public School Madrassa a Failure," *Atlas Shrugs*, March 8, 2011, available at http://atlasshrugs2000.typepad.com/atlas_shrugs/khalil_gibran_international _academy/, accessed January 20, 2012.

52. Daniel Pipes, "A Madrassa Grows in Brooklyn," *New York Sun*, April 24, 2007, available at www.nysun.com/foreign/madrassa-grows-in-brooklyn/53060/, accessed April 5, 2012.

53. Chuck Bennet and Jana Winter, "City Principal Is 'Revolting,'" *New York Post*, August 6, 2007, available at http://www.nypost.com/p/news/regional/item_UerzwvF7 fcSQY8YOP1ln4K, accessed April 5, 2012.

10. Islamophobia and the New McCarthyism

1. Ali et al., *Fear Inc.*, 1.

2. Andrea Elliot, "The Man behind the Anti-Shariah Movement," *New York Times*, July 30, 2011, available at http://www.nytimes.com/2011/07/31/us/31shariah.html, accessed April 5, 2012.

3. Bob Smietana, "Anti-Muslim Crusaders Make Millions Selling Fear," *Tennessean*, October 24, 2010, available at http://www.tennessean.com/article/20101024/ NEWS01/10240374/Anti-Muslim-crusaders-make-millions-spreading-fear, accessed January 25, 2012.

4. Ali et al., *Fear Inc.*

5. Beinin, "New American McCarthyism," 103.

6. See the AVOT website: http://www.claremont.org/projects/projectid.35/project _detail.asp, accessed January 25, 2012.

7. William Kristol and Robert Kagan, "Toward a Neo-Reaganite Foreign Policy," *Foreign Affairs*, July 1, 1996, available at http://www.foreignaffairs.com/articles/52239/william -kristol-and-robert-kagan/toward-a-neo-reaganite-foreign-policy, accessed April 5, 2012.

8. Maria Ryan, *Neoconservatism and the New American Century* (New York: Palgrave Macmillan, 2010), 79.

9. Ibid.

10. Cooper, *Neoconservatism*, 12.

11. Ibid.

12. Dorien, *Imperial Designs*, 2.

13. Elliot, "Man behind the Anti-Shariah Movement."

14. In his *New York Times* column, Friedman focuses blame on internal conditions such as autocratic governments and population explosion, among other factors, as a way to explain the harsh economic conditions in the Arab world. US imperialism and its economic arms, the IMF and World Bank, are of course left blameless. See Thomas Friedman, "Green Shoots in Palestine," *New York Times*, August 4, 2009, available at http:// www.nytimes.com/2009/08/05/opinion/05friedman.html, accessed April 5, 2012.

15. Emma Brockes, "Ayaan Hirsi Ali: 'Why Are Muslims So Hypersensitive?'" *Guardian* (UK), May 7, 2010, available at www.guardian.co.uk/world/2010/may/08/ayaan-hirsi -ali-interview, accessed April 5, 2012.

16. Quoted in Sheehi, *Islamophobia*, 103.

17. Ali et al., *Fear Inc.*, 3.

18. Quoted in ibid., 51.

19. Debbie Schlussel, "HAMASGOP: Chris Christie Calls Opponents of Hamas 'Crazies,'" *Debbie Schlussel Blog*, July 29, 2011, available at http://www.debbieschlussel.com/40455/hamasgop-chris-christie-calls-opponents-of-hamas-crazies/, accessed January 25, 2012.

20. Cited in Ali et al., *Fear Inc.*, 41.

21. Ibid., 37.

22. Ibid., 39.

23. David Horowitz, "Muslim Liars: How the Muslim Students Association Deceives the Naïve," *Front Page*, April 27, 2011, available at http://frontpagemag.com/2011/04/27/muslim-liars-how-the-muslim-students-association-deceives-the-naive-2/, accessed January 25, 2012.

24. See the list of interviewees at *The Third Jihad*'s website, http://www.thethirdjihad.com/about_new.php, accessed April 5, 2012.

25. Ali et al., *Fear Inc.*, 14.

26. Blumenthal, "Great Islamophobic Crusade."

27. Nicole Naurath, "Most Muslim Americans See No Justification for Violence," Abu Dhabi Gallup Center, August 2, 2011, available at http://www.gallup.com/poll/148763/muslim-americans-no-justification-violence.aspx, accessed January 25, 2012.

28. Samih Farsoun, "Roots of the American Antiterrorism Crusade," in Hagopian, ed., *Civil Rights in Peril*, 150–52.

29. Elaine Hagopian, "The Interlocking of Right-Wing Politics and US Middle East Policy: Solidifying Arab/Muslim Demonization," in Hagopian, ed., *Civil Rights in Peril*, 194.

30. Quoted in Farsoun, "Roots," 152.

31. Quoted in Ali et al., *Fear Inc.,* 75.

32. Ibid., see chapter 3.

33. Ibid., 64.

34. Quoted in ibid., 66.

35. Quoted in ibid., 58.

36. Thom Cincotta, *Manufacturing the Muslim Menace: Private Firms, Public Servants, and the Threat to Rights and Security* (Somerville, MA: Political Research Associates, 2011), available at http://www.publiceye.org/liberty/training/Muslim_Menace_Complete.pdf, accessed January 25, 2012.

37. Ibid., 15.

38. Quoted in ibid., 31.

39. Ibid., 31.

40. Quoted in Ali et al., *Fear Inc.*, 57.

41. Ibid.

42. Cincotta, *Manufacturing the Muslim Menace,* 23.

43. Spencer Ackerman, "FBI's '101 Guide' Depicted Muslims as 7th-Century Simpletons," *Wired*, July 27, 2011, available at http://www.wired.com/dangerroom/2011/07/fbi-islam-101-guide/, accessed January 25, 2012.

44. Spencer Ackerman, "Obama Orders Government to Clean up Terror Training," *Wired*, November 29, 2011, available at http://www.wired.com/dangerroom/2011/11/obama-islamophobia-review/, accessed May 22, 2012.

45. Anderson Cooper, interview with Walid Shoebat, *Anderson Cooper 360*, CNN, July 13, 2011, available at http://www.youtube.com/watch?v=pJN00dBhZVk, accessed January 25, 2012.

46. Will Youmans, "The New Cold Warriors," in Hagopian, ed., *Civil Rights in Peril*, 111.

47. Ibid., 112.

48. WND, "Congressman: Muslims 'Enemy amongst Us,'" *WND*, February 13, 2004,

available at http://www.wnd.com/2004/02/23257/, accessed January 25, 2012.

49. Quoted in Ali et al., *Fear Inc.*, 86.

50. Ibid., 41.

51. Hamid Dabashi, *Brown Skin, White Masks* (London: Pluto, 2011), 72–73.

52. Ibid., 35.

53. Sheehi, *Islamophobia*, 97.

54. Dabashi, *Brown Skin*, 14.

55. Ibid., 76.

56. Ibid., 35–36.

57. Kundnani, "Islamism."

58. Ibid., 42.

59. Seymour, *Liberal Defence*, 241–42.

60. Ibid., 12.

61. Ibid.

62. Kundnani, "Islamism," 44.

63. Youmans, "New Cold Warriors," 119.

64. Noah Schachtman and Spencer Ackerman, "U.S. Military Taught Officers: Use 'Hiroshima' Tactics for 'Total War' on Islam," *Wired*, May 10, 2012, available at, http://www.wired.com/dangerroom/2012/05/total-war-islam/all/1, accessed May 22, 2012.

65. Ibid.

66. William J. Boykin et al., *Shariah: The Threat to America* (Washington, DC: Center for Security Policy, 2010).

67. Suzan Clarke and Rich McHugh, "President Obama Says Terry Jones' Plan to Burn Korans Is 'a Destructive Act,'" *ABC Good Morning America*, September 9, 2010, available at http://abcnews.go.com/GMA/president-obama-terry-jones-koran-burning-plan-destructive/story?id=11589122#.TxBi8oH4WSo, accessed January 25, 2012.

68. Joe Cenker, "Gainesville's Victory over Bigotry," *Socialist Worker*, September 17, 2010, available at http://socialistworker.org/2010/09/17/gainesville-victory-over-bigotry, accessed January 25, 2012.

Conclusion: Fighting Islamophobia

1. Council on American-Islamic Relations, "American Muslims and the 2008 Elections," November 7, 2008, available at http://www.cair.com/Portals/0/pdf/Post_2008_Election_American_Muslim_Poll.pdf, accessed January 22, 2012.

2. Dabashi, *Brown Skin, White Masks*, 121.

3. Hillary Clinton, interview by Kirit Radia, al-Arabiya network, March 2, 2009, partial transcript available at http://abcnews.go.com/blogs/politics/2011/01/secretary-clinton-in-2009-i-really-consider-president-and-mrs-mubarak-to-be-friends-of-my-family/, accessed April 6, 2012.

4. Amanda Simon, "President Obama Signs Indefinite Detention into Law," ACLU website, December 1, 2011, available at http://www.aclu.org/blog/national-security/president-obama-signs-indefinite-detention-law, accessed January 22, 2012.

5. Barack Obama, "Empowering Local Partners to Prevent Violent Extremism in the United States," August 2011, available at http://www.whitehouse.gov/sites/default/files/empowering_local_partners.pdf, accessed January 22, 2012.

6. Greg Miller, "US Officials Believe al-Qaeda on the Brink of Collapse," *Washington Post*, July 26, 2011, available at http://www.washingtonpost.com/world/national-security

/al-qaeda-could-collapse-us-officials-say/2011/07/21/gIQAFu2pbI_story.html, accessed April 6, 2012.

7.   John Mueller, "The Truth about al-Qaeda," *Foreign Affairs*, August 2, 2011, available at http://www.foreignaffairs.com/articles/68012/john-mueller/the-truth-about-al-qaeda ?oth-internal-magazine-the_truth_about_al_qaeda-110111, accessed April 6, 2012.

8.   Obama, "Empowering Local Partners," 1.

9.   Abdul Malik Mujahid, interview by Eric Ruder, "The United States of Islamophobia," *Socialist Worker*, January 19, 2010, available at http://socialistworker.org/2012/01/19/ united-states-of-islamophobia, accessed April 6, 2012.

10.   "NYPD Spied on Muslim Anti-Terror Partners," *CBS News*, October 6, 2011, available at http://www.cbsnews.com/stories/2011/10/06/national/main20116496.shtml, accessed January 22, 2012.

11.   Associated Press, "White House Helps Pay for NYPD Muslim Surveillance," *USA Today*, February 27, 2012, available at http://www.usatoday.com/news/nation/ story/2012-02-27/white-house-muslim-NYPD/53267060/1, accessed April 6, 2012.

12.   Quoted in Ashley Lopez, "Muslim Activists Say that Democratic Party Is Taking their Vote for Granted," *Florida Independent*, March 21, 2012, available at http:// floridaindependent.com/73346/muslim-activists-say-democratic-party-is-taking -their-vote-for-granted, accessed April 6, 2012.

13.   Andrew Stern, "Most American Muslims Are Satisfied Obama Backers," Reuters, August 30, 2011, available at http://in.reuters.com/article/2011/08/30/idINIndia -59043020110830, accessed April 6, 2012.

14.   Chris Hawley, "Muslims Upset by NYPD to Boycott Mayor's Breakfast," Associated Press, December 29, 2011, available at http://www.ap.org/pages/about/whatsnew/ wn_122911a.html, accessed January 22, 2012.

15.   Mujahid, "United States of Islamophobia."

Index

24 (television show), 152
60 Minutes, 126

Abbasid caliphate, 49, 50, 83–84
Abduh, Muhammad, 88
Abortion, 46
Abrahamian, Ervand, 94
Abrams, Elliott, 125
Abshire, David, 125
Abu Dhabi, 25
Abu Ghraib, 33, 145
ACT! for America, 183
"Afghan Arabs," 73, 104
Afghani, Jamal al-Din al-, 88–89
Afghanistan
    political Islam in, 64, 134
    Soviet war in, 104, 109
    training camps in, 153
    US relations with, 70–74
    US war in, 56, 78, 108–9, 128–29, 154,
        163
    women in, 45
Af-Pak strategy, 133–35, 160, 163, 194
Agents provocateurs, 140, 143, 147, 150–52
Ahmed, Leila, 47
Ajami, Fouad, 125, 129, 186, 187
Al-Andalus, 11, 12–13, 14, 16, 23, 24, 165
Albright, Madeleine, 125, 126, 131, 133
Algeria
    colonization by France, 25

Communist Party in, 100
mujahedeen from, 73
national liberation movements in, 37,
    57, 200
neoliberalism in, 102
political Islam in, 76, 104
secular nationalism in, 90, 97–98
Ali, Ayaan Hirsi, 178, 186, 187–88
Ali, Caliph, 83, 121
Ali, Mehmet, 87
Ali, Tariq, 83
Almontaser, Debbie, 171–72
Al-Qaeda, 64, 96, 102, 189
    formation of, 73
    as terrorist organization, 77, 149–50,
        164, 195–96
    US strategy against, 134
    US support for, 72
Al-Qaeda in the Arabian Peninsula
    (AQAP), 96
Al-Shabaab, 96, 160
Amal, 96
American Civil Liberties Union, 195
American Enterprise Institute (AEI), 118,
    187
American exceptionalism, 114–15
American Israel Public Affairs Committee
    (AIPAC), 123, 170
American Jewish Committee (AJC), 118,
    169–70
American Oriental Society, 34–35

Americans for Victory Over Terrorism (AVOT), 177–79
Amis, Martin, 188
Amnesty International, 192
Anchorage Charitable Fund, 181
Anthony, Andrew, 188
Anti-Defamation League, 167, 169–70, 172, 182
Anti-Imperialist League, 36
Antiterrorism and Effective Death Penalty Act (AEDPA), 141–42
Antiwar movements, 56, 139, 143, 149, 198–200
Arab Americans
    approval of Obama, 197–98
    history of, 168
    ideological attacks on, 178
    professors, 170–71
    public perception of, 182
    repression of, 130, 139–58
    stereotypes of, 41
    violence against, 79–80
Arab socialism, 90, 97–98
Arab Socialist Ba'ath Party, 98, 100–101, 189
Arab Spring, 58–59, 105, 194–95
Arab stereotypes, 74–75, 79–80, 129–30, 139, 142, 147
Arab Women Active in the Arts and Media (AWAAM), 172
Arabic language, 12–13, 27
Arafat, Yasser, 118–19
Area studies, 35–36, 38–39, 65, 170–71
Aristotle, 47, 51
Armitage, Richard, 125, 131
Aswan Dam, 36
Ataturk, Mustafa Kemal, 87
Atheism, 66, 126
Austria, 25
Awakening Councils, 108
Awlaki, Anwar al-, 195
Ayoob, Mohammed, 84, 85
Azzam, Sheik, 72–73

Ba'athism. see Arab Socialist Ba'ath Party
Babar, Junaid, 149–50
Bachmann, Michele, 186
Bah, Adama, 146
Bah, Mamadou, 146
Bahrain, 194–95, 199

Balance-of-forces realism, 114
Balfour, Arthur James, 55
Balibar, Etienne, 30
Banna, Hassan al-, 66, 88–89
Barlas, Asma, 47
Bauer, Jack, 152
Bayoumi, Moustafa, 146–47
Beck, Glenn, 16
Becker Foundation, 181–82
Begin, Menachem, 120
Beinin, Joel, 170
"Benevolent supremacy," 37–38
Bennett, William, 177
Bennis, Phyllis, 127
Ben-Yehuda, Hemdah, 75
Berman, Howard, 132
Berman, Paul, 126, 188–89
Berrie Foundation, 181–82
Bhutto, Benazir, 74
Bhutto, Zulfikar Ali, 98
Bible, 9, 34
Biden, Joseph, 133
Bin Laden, Osama, 72, 132–33, 134
Black Hawk Down, 126
Black Power movement, 143
Bloomberg, Michael, 152, 165–67, 172, 198
Blumenthal, Max, 169, 171, 182
Booker, Corey, 144
Boot, Max, 117, 118
Bosnia, 73, 77
Boston, 171
Boykin, William, 190
Bradley Foundation, 181
Breivik, Anders Behring, 175, 178–79, 196
Brennan Center for Justice, 157
Bricmont, Jean, 123–24
Bridgman, Frederick, 34
Britain
    colonization of Egypt, 25, 44, 55, 97
    colonization of Palestine, 109
    colonization of Sudan, 25
    intervention in Jordan, 110
    oil interests in Iran, 70
    political Islam in, 76, 157
    role in Iraq wars, 127
    role in Six-Day War, 36
Brookings Institute, 125
Brzezinski, Zbigniew, 71–72, 125
Burqa. see Veil

Bush, George H. W., 120, 133
  foreign policy, 76–77, 116, 124, 126
  on Islam, 79
  surveillance of Arab Americans, 141
Bush, George W.
  on Afghan women, 45
  and Arab Americans, 131–32, 142, 148
  Bush Doctrine, 128–31
  failures of, 114
  foreign policy of, 113
  justifications for Iraq war, 56, 159
  and neoconservatives, 170
  talks with Taliban, 79
  use of religion, 188
Bush, Laura, 45
Bush Doctrine, 128–31
Byzantine Empire, 14, 18, 24, 47, 53

CAMERA, 182
Campus Watch, 170, 178
Capitalism
  and crisis, 104–5
  and democracy, 87
  influence on secularism, 86
  opposition to, 110–11, 200
  and political Islam, 102–3
  rise of, 21
  and US imperialism, 76–77
Carter, Jimmy, 71, 72, 125, 141
Catholic Church. see Roman Catholic
    Church
Caute, David, 176
Center for American Progress, 175
Center for Constitutional Rights, 148
Center for Human Rights and Global
    Justice, 145, 150
Center for Security Policy (CSP), 179–80,
    190
Center for Strategic and International
    Studies (CSIS), 125, 164, 194
Center for Strategic Policy (CSP), 115, 119
Central Intelligence Agency (CIA), 109–10,
    132, 181, 196
  aid to Afghan mujahedeen, 71–74, 77
  covert operations by, 58
  and domestic terrorism investigations, 144
  relationship with Muslim
      Brotherhood, 66
  role in Iran, 70

role in overthrowing governents, 37–38
role in systemic racism, 189–90
ties to Islamophobic network, 185
Centre for Counterintelligence and Security
    Studies (CI CENTRE), 184–85
Chase Manhattan Bank, 69
Chavez, Linda, 118
Cheney, Dick, 116, 130
Chernick, Aubrey, 167, 182
Chernick, Joyce, 182
Chile, 72
China, 128–29, 130, 134, 135
Chomsky, Noam, 119, 125
Christian Broadcasting Network, 185
Christianity
  Christian Right, 176, 182–83
  clashes with state, 85
  concept of God, 15
  fundamentalism of, 93
  and justification of colonialism, 29
  under Muslim rule, 11, 53, 165
  Orthodox, 18
  separation of religion and politics, 82
  support for Zionism, 182–83
  violence and, 141–42, 156
  and women, 46
Christians United for Israel, 183
Christie, Chris, 180
Christopher, Warren, 125
Cincotta, Thom, 184
Citibank, 69
Civil rights movement, 139
Clarke, Richard, 128
"Clash of civilizations" theory, 33, 39, 78,
    82, 130, 164
Clinton, Bill
  connections with Mubarak, 194
  foreign policy, 76–80, 126, 127
  liberal imperialism of, 79, 124
  and Oslo Accords, 118–19
  and terrorism, 141
  terrorism policy, 78, 80
Clinton, Hillary, 133
Cohen, Nick, 188
Cohn-Bendit, Daniel, 126
Coicaud, Jean-Marc, 125
COINTELPRO, 143
Colbert, Stephen, 168
Cold War, 36–39, 40, 124, 191

Afghanistan as proxy for, 71–74
anticommunism during, 139, 160, 179
Communist Parties during, 100
neocons and, 115
and US Middle East objectives, 63–76
US support for political Islam during, 60
use of fear, 154
Colonialism
"enlightened," 26–29, 44
opposition to, 64, 95
racism and, 29–33
rise of, 21
as threat to Muslim identity, 88
use of Orientalism scholarship in, 29
Columbia University, 170–71
Commentary, 115, 118
Communists
influence in Muslim-majority countries, 67, 100–101
Islamist opposition to, 68
and McCarthyism, 139–40
opposition to, 65
and opposition to "open door," 37
parties in Middle East, 90
role in Arab secular movements, 57
as threat to US in Middle East, 65
US policy toward, 64
Confrontationism, 78
Congo, 72
Conover, Ted, 151–52
Conservative Alliance, 46
Constantinople, 18
Convivencia, 12
Cooper, Anderson, 185
Cooper, Danny, 114–15, 130, 177
Córdoba, Spain, 12, 165
Cordoba House. *see* Park51 community center
Coulter, Ann, 52
Council on American-Islamic Relations (CAIR), 171–72, 180–81, 184, 193, 198
Council on Foreign Relations (CFR), 64, 125–26
Counterinsurgency, 130–31, 196
Cromer, Lord, 44, 49, 56
Crusades, 13–17, 82
rhetoric of, 26
treatment of Jews, 53
violence of, 53–54

Dabashi, Hamid, 186, 187–88, 194
Daniel, Norman, 11, 15, 22
Darwish, Nonie, 183–84
David Project, 170–71, 178
Davidson, Lawrence, 87, 190
Dean, Howard, 169
Defense Planning Guidance reports, 116, 134
Democracy
bourgeois democratic tasks, 87
and "clash of civilizations," 33
as justification for imperialism, 55–59, 129–30
as justification for Iraq war, 56
movements for, 99, 107–8
Democratic Party, 124, 133, 168, 169, 186, 190, 193–97
Denmark, 52, 161
Deobandi Islam, 74
Department of Homeland Security (DHS), 140, 156–57, 181, 184, 193
Department of Justice (DOJ), 140, 141, 154
Desis Rising Up and Moving (DRUM), 198
Despotism, 20, 34, 55–59, 129–30
Donors Capital Fund, 181
Dorien, Gary, 115, 117–18, 177
Downs, Steve, 143, 147, 152–53, 156
Dreyfuss, Robert, 69
Dulles, John Foster, 37, 57

Egypt
1973 war with Israel, 68
and Arab Spring, 58, 105, 199–200
colonization by Britain, 25, 44
colonization by France, 26–29
colonization by Greece, 47
Communist Party in, 100
effect on US oil supply, 66
labor movement in, 97
middle class in, 103
modernization in, 86–87
Muslim Brotherhood in, 69
national liberation movements in, 56, 57
neoliberalism in, 102
political Islam in, 99, 104
role in Afghanistan, 72–73
secular nationalism in, 89, 97
and Six-Day War, 36–37, 67
as tool of US, 67–68

women in, 47–48
Eisenhower, Dwight D., 57, 65, 66
Eisenhower Doctrine, 65
Elliott, Justin, 166
Ellison, Keith, 169
Emerson, Steve, 142, 175, 179–80, 186
English Defense League, 166
Enlightenment, 22, 30–31, 132
Esposito, John, 14, 90
Eze, Emmanuel Chukwudi, 22

Fairbrook Foundation, 181–82
Faisal, King, 68
Fallujah, Iraq, 108
Falwell, Jerry, 183
Farahi, Foad, 145–46
Farouk, King, 97
Federal Aviation Administration (FAA), 141
Federal Bureau of Investigation (FBI)
    and Arab Americans, 142, 145–46,
        152–53, 197
    raids on antiwar activists, 149
    role in systemic racism, 190
    terrorism list, 141
    trainings, 165, 185
    use of provocateurs, 140, 143, 150–52
    use of radicalization theories, 157, 181
Feminist Majority, 45
First Amendment, 168
Forbes magazine, 52
Foreign Affairs, 39, 64, 78, 115–16, 125,
    127, 132–33
Former Muslims United, 183–84
Fort Hood, 52, 161–65, 195
Fox News, 118, 166, 167, 171, 184, 185, 186
France, 25, 26–29, 36, 45
Frank, Anne, 74
Free Officers movement, 97
Freedom Center, 181
French, Bill, 175
Friedman, Milton, 69
Friedman, Thomas, 178
Front Islamique du Salut (FIS), 76, 102, 104
Fukuyama, Francis, 118

Gabriel, Brigitte, 183, 186
Gaddafi, Muammar, 68, 133
Gaffney, Frank, 115, 119, 167, 175, 176–77,
    178, 179–80, 190
Gainesville, Florida, 169, 192, 199
Gates, Bob, 133
Gaubatz, David, 180
Gaza Strip, 75, 95, 172, 183
Geller, Pamela, 166, 171–72, 175, 179, 186
Gerges, Fawaz, 71, 73, 78
German Americans, 139
Gérôme, Jean-Léon, 34
Ghazali, al-, 85
Gibb, H. A. R., 35–36
Gingrich, Newt, 167, 186
Giuliani, Rudy, 167, 181
Glazer, Nathan, 114
Goldman Sachs, 69
Goldschmidt, Arthur, 87
Gorbachev, Mikhael, 115
Goss, Porter, 185
Graham, Franklin, 183
Greece, 25, 47, 199
Greene, Jeff, 168–69
Ground Zero mosque. *see* Park51
    community center
Grunebaum, Gustave von, 35, 43–44
Guandolo, John, 190
Guantánamo Bay, 145, 161
Guatemala, 72
Guiliani, Rudolph, 50
Gulf Cooperation Council, 134–35

Haass, Richard, 125, 133
Habsburg Empire, 19
Hagee, John, 183
Hagopian, Elaine, 141, 182
Halliday, Fred, 122
Hamas, 72, 75–76, 99, 103, 104, 107–8,
    122, 148, 172, 180
Haney Lopez, Ian F., 142
Harman, Chris, 102, 105
Harrington, Michael, 114
Hasan, Nidal Malik, 161–65
Hashami, Hacene, 102
Hashmi, Fahad, 149
Hassan, Major Nidal, 52
Hayden, Michael, 185
Hazaras, 108
Headley, David Coleman, 161–63
Hekmatyar, Gulbuddin, 72, 102
Hezb-e-Islami, 72

Hezbollah, 75–76, 96, 103, 106, 121, 172
Hijab. *see* Veil
Hinduism, 43, 83
Hindutva, 93
Hitchens, Christopher, 126, 188–89
Holbrooke, Richard, 125
Holy Land Foundation, 148
Holy Warriors, 64
Horowitz, David, 170–71, 178, 180–81,
    184, 189
Hroub, Khaled, 95, 107
Hudson Institute, 118, 182
Human Terrain System, 131
Huntington, Samuel, 33, 39, 40, 78,
    81–82, 129
Hussain, Shahed, 151
Hussein, Caliph, 83
Hussein, Saddam, 126, 128, 188

Iberian peninsula. *see* Al-Andalus
Ibn Rawandi, 51
Ibn Rushd, 13, 51
Ibn Sina, 13, 50–51
Ignatieff, Michael, 126, 189
Immigrants
    Arabs in New York, 168
    detention of, 145–47, 193, 195
    ICE treatment of, 142–43
    Japanese internment camps, 139
Immigration and Customs Enforcement
    (ICS/formerly INS), 142
Imperialism
    "benevolent supremacy" model of, 37
    conservative vs. liberal, 59, 124
    as enemy of Nasserism, 98
    and liberalism, 123–35, 188–89
    neocon vs. balance-of-forces realism, 114
    under Obama, 131–35
    opposition to, 36, 110–11, 139
    relationship with Orientalism, 33
    rise of, 21, 25–26
    of United States, 33–40, 106–11
India
    Hindu extremism in, 93
    Muslims in, 43
    political Islam in, 89
    as rival to US, 128
    secular nationalism in, 89, 200
    US relations with, 134

Indochina, 37
Indonesia
    and President Obama, 163
    secular nationalism in, 90, 97–98
    US support for dictatorship, 72
Indyk, Martin, 79, 123
Informants, 144, 150–52, 195, 197
Ingraham, Laura, 166
International Conferences on Terrorism,
    120–23, 141
International Counter-Terrorism Officers
    Association, 184–85
International Monetary Fund (IMF), 101–2,
    106
International Socialist Organization, 192
Inter-Services Intelligence (ISI). *see* Pakistan
Intifada, 75, 76, 95, 172
Investigative Project on Terrorism, 179–80
Iran
    Communist Party in, 100
    hostage crisis, 64, 141
    Israeli relations with, 121
    middle class in, 103
    modernization in, 87
    political Islam in, 96
    as regional strongman, 67
    revolution, 64, 70–71, 94
    role of Mossadegh, 66
    as "terrorist state," 121–22
    US relations with, 50, 70–71, 109, 129,
        134, 135
    US sanctions on, 77
    women in, 46, 187
Iran-Contra, 71
Iran-Iraq war, 71
Iraq
    1991 US war in, 76, 141
    2003 US war in, 56, 108, 120, 128–31,
        188
    Communist Party in, 100–101
    drawing of borders, 26
    national liberation movements in, 57
    political Islam in, 96, 103, 105
    relationship with Jordan, 119
    sanctions on, 126
    as threat to US, 116
Islam
    concept of God, 15
    conversion of Christians to, 16

as inherently terrorist, 81, 113
Napoleon's understanding of, 27
origins of, 10–11
revivalism, 88–90
separation of religion and politics, 67, 81–91
tolerant views of, 16–17
US rhetoric about, 79, 163–64
as violent, 15, 144, 162–64, 168
Islam strategy, 65, 67
Islamic Associations, 99
Islamic Centers. *see* Mujamma'
Islamic Dawa Party, 96
Islamic financial system, 69, 102
Islamic fundamentalism. *see* Political Islam
Islamic Jihad, 96
Islamic Republican Party, 96
Islamic Society of Boston, 171
Islamic Society of North America, 184
Islamic Supreme Council of Iraq (ISCI), 96
Islamism. *see* Political Islam
Islamization, 71, 103, 166, 175, 179–80
Israel
    1973 war with Egypt, 68
    2006 invasion of Lebanon, 106
    formation of, 90
    Jewish fundamentalism in, 93
    neocon support for, 117–23, 176
    and Obama, 194
    occupation of Palestine, 94–95, 103
    as regional strongman, 67
    relations with Arabs, 74–76
    role in Afghanistan, 72
    role in Six-Day War, 36, 67
    Soviet support for, 100
    and terrorism, 141

Jackson, Henry "Scoop," 120
Jamaat-e-Islami, 89
Japan, 116
Japanese Americans, 139
Jerusalem, 17, 54, 119, 120–21
Jewish Defense League (JDL), 141
Jewish Institute for National Security
    Affairs (JINSA), 118, 123
Jews
    Biblical origins of, 11
    fundamentalism of, 83, 93
    liberal antiracist, 171

under Muslim rule, 11, 165
nationalism and, 74
and neoconservatism, 117–23
as nonthreatening to Church, 15
stereotypes of, 139
treatment during Crusades, 53
Jihad, 73, 89, 95, 151–52, 155, 164, 180–81, 184
Jihad Jane. *see* LaRose, Colleen
Jihad Watch, 179, 181
Johnson, Lyndon B., 65, 114
Jonathan Institute, 75, 120, 178
Jones, Terry, 169, 183, 191–92
Jordan
    Communist Party in, 100
    Muslim Brotherhood in, 69, 89
    relationship with Israel, 119
    uprising in, 110
Joya, Malalai, 45
Justice and Development Party (Turkey), 104
Jyllands-Posten, 52

Kagan, Robert, 118, 127, 177
Kashani, Ayatollah Abolgassem, 70
Kashmir, 73, 77
Kedourie, Elie, 121
Kelly, Raymond, 149, 152, 181, 198
Kennedy, John F., 37, 65, 133
Kenya, 77–78
Khadija, 47
Khalil Gibran International Academy, 171–72
Khalilzad, Zalmay, 116, 118, 125
Khan, Daisy, 131, 166
Khobar bombing, 77
Khomeini, Ayatollah, 64, 70–71, 76, 94, 109–10, 121, 122
King, Peter, 186, 196
Kipling, Rudyard, 28, 32, 123
Kirkpatrick, Jeane, 79, 114, 118, 121
Kissinger, Henry, 65, 125
Koran, 9, 10, 184
    burning of, 169, 183, 191–92
    Napoleon's understanding of, 27
    nonviolence in, 53
    as political text, 88–89
    questioning of by Muslims, 51
    textual analysis of by Orientalists, 30–31

translation of, 13
and women, 31, 46–47
Kramer, Martin, 170, 178
Krauthammer, Charles, 115–17, 118, 121
Kristol, Bill, 115, 118, 127, 177
Kristol, Irving, 114, 115, 118
Ku Klux Klan, 169
Kundnani, Arun, 188–89
Kurds, 101
Kuwait, 69

Lake, Anthony, 79, 124–25
Laqueur, Walter, 67
LaRose, Colleen, 159, 161, 162
Lashkar-e-Taiba, 96, 161
Lawrence of Arabia, 74
League of Arab States, 89
Lebanon
    1958 US intervention in, 57–58, 110
    1982 Israeli invasion, 119
    2006 Israeli invasion, 106
    Christians in, 166, 183
    Communist Party in, 100
    drawing of borders, 26
    Muslim Brotherhood in, 89
    national liberation movements in, 57
    political Islam in, 96, 103, 105, 106–7
    relationship with Iran, 121
    relationship with Israel, 119
    Shi'a Islam in, 43
Lens, Sidney, 36, 37
Lerner, Daniel, 38
Levi, Edward H., 143
Levin, Richard, 144
Lévy, Bernard-Henri, 188
Lewis, Bernard, 33, 36, 40, 58–59, 78,
    81–82, 85, 121, 129–30, 135, 170, 187
Libby, Scooter, 116
Liberalism
    and humanitarian imperialism, 123–35,
        188–89
    and Islamophobia, 41, 132–33, 160, 196
    liberal antiwar groups, 140
    and sexism, 48
    view of US as humanitarian force, 59
Libya
    and Arab Spring, 58
    under Gaddafi, 68
    national liberation movements in, 57

US immigrants from, 158
US intervention in, 133, 135, 195
Lieberman, Joe, 181
Likud, 117, 118, 119, 120, 122, 135
Little, Douglas, 65
Lockman, Zachary, 20, 30
London, 81, 149–50
Luce, Henry, 37, 127
Lugar, Dick, 132
Luther, Martin, 19
Luttwak, Edward, 194

Madrid bombings, 81
Maghred, 43
Maimonides, 13
Makiya, Kanan, 186, 187
Malek, Alia, 146
Malik, Muhammad, 197
Manji, Irshad, 178, 186, 187–88
Manuel II Paleologus, 51
Marshall, Phil, 101
Mashreq, 43
Massad, Joseph, 170–71, 172
Mawdudi, Mawlana, 88–89
McAlister, Melani, 37
McCain, John, 41, 193
McCarthy, Andrew, 178, 190
McCarthyism, 139, 160, 161–62, 176, 195
McGovern, George, 114–15
McVeigh, Timothy, 9, 40, 80, 141–42
McWilliams, Alicia, 151
Men's League for Opposing Women's
    Suffrage, 44
Middle class
    and political Islam, 102–4
    political role, 105
    role in modernization, 86–87
Middle East Forum (MEF), 118, 122,
    179–80
Middle East Media Research Institute
    (MEMRI), 118
Miller, Judith, 78
Minority Report, 147–48
Mishal, Shaul, 75
Modernization
    in Muslim-majority countries, 86–88
    vs. Orientalist theory, 39
    theory, 38–39
    and US policy in Middle East, 64–68

Mohammad, Sohail, 180
Montesquieu, 20, 55
Morocco, 57
Mossadegh, Mohammed
   John Foster Dulles on, 57
   opposition to, 66, 110
   toppled by CIA, 58, 70
   US attempt to influence, 65
Moynihan, Daniel Patrick, 114, 118, 121
Mu'awiyah, 83
Mubarak, Hosni, 105–6, 194
Mueller, John, 196
Muhammad
   attacks on legitimacy of, 15–16, 42
   cartoon controversy, 52
   Enlightenment scholarship on, 22
   life of, 10–11, 47
   political legacy of, 81, 83, 85, 121
   in Salafism, 88
Mujahedeen, 70–74, 102, 104
Mujahid, Abdul Malik, 197, 199
Mujamma,' 75, 122
Mumbai bombings, 161
Muravchik, Joshua, 118, 123
Murdoch, Rupert, 171, 185
Murfreesboro, Tennessee, 183, 199
Murray, Nancy, 143
Muslim American Society, 180–81
Muslim Brotherhood
   alleged front groups, 171, 181
   banning by Nasser, 90
   in Egypt, 89, 103, 109
   funding by Islamic banks, 69
   future of, 105–6
   in Jordan, 69, 89, 110
   offshoots of, 96
   in Palestine, 75, 94–95
   relationship with US, 66
   and Sadat, 68
Muslim Peace Coalition, 198
Muslim Peace Council, 197
Muslim Student Association, 180–81
Muslims. see also Women
   differentiation from Arabs, 43
   as "enemy," 9, 13–17
   former, 176, 178, 183–84
   racism against, 80, 193
   world population of, 42–43
Mu'talizites, 51

Nafisi, Azar, 186, 187–88
Napoleon, 26–29, 131
Nasr, Vali, 131
Nasser, Gamal Abdel, 36–37, 57, 103
   and Arab socialism, 90, 97–99
   communist opposition to, 100
   defeat in Six-Day War, 67
   US attempt to influence, 65
   US reaction against, 63
   use of Muslim Brotherhood against, 66
National Counterterrorism Center
   (NCTC), 140, 157
National Defense Authorization Act, 195
National Liberation Front (FLN), Algeria,
   98, 100
National liberation movements, 36–37,
   200. see also Secular nationalism
   and capitalism, 86
   colonial attitudes toward, 55–59
   support by US when convenient, 57
National Security Entry-Exit Registration
   System (NSEERS), 142
Nationalism
   and opposition to "open door," 37
   rise of, 17
Neoconservatives, 113–36, 178–79
   and Breivik attacks, 175, 178–79
   and Christian Right, 182–83
   and foreign policy, 128–31
   identification of Islamism as threat, 78–
   79
   and Islamophobic network, 176–82
   origins of, 114–23
Neoliberalism
   Chicago school, 69
   economic effects, 98, 101–2, 110–11
   and US imperialism, 77
Netanyahu, Benjamin, 75, 119, 120–21
Netanyahu, Benzion, 120
Netanyahu, Jonathan, 120
Netherlands, 52, 166, 187
New Left, 117, 126, 139, 143
New York City
   and Occupy Wall Street, 198–200
   and Park51 controversy, 52–53, 165–68
   repression of Muslims in, 140, 144,
   146–47, 149–50
New York Police Department (NYPD)
   surveillance program, 140, 144, 149,

197, 198
  use of radicalization theories, 155, 157,
    181
New York University (NYU), 145, 151, 157
Newburgh Four, 151–52
Nicaragua, 71
Nixon, Richard, 67, 141
Nixon Doctrine, 67
North Atlantic Treaty Organization
  (NATO), 125, 127, 133–35
North Korea, 116, 143
Northern Alliance, 109
Norway, 175, 178–79, 196
Norwegian Labor Party, 178–79
Not Without My Daughter, 70
Novak, Michael, 114
Nuclear weapons, 50, 134–35, 190, 191, 197
Nunn, Sam, 125
Nye, Joseph, 125, 128, 132–33

Obama, Barack
  and Bin Laden assassination, 79
  as liberal imperialist, 131–35, 160, 161
  perception of as Muslim, 41, 169, 178
  reaction to Koran-burning threat, 169,
    191–92
  use of fear, 163
  and War on Terror, 114, 179, 193–97
Occupy Wall Street, 140, 198–200
Oil
  and Afghanistan, 74
  Carter administration policies, 72
  in Iran, 70
  secular nationalism as threat to, 66
  and US Middle East objectives, 64, 77,
    116–17, 129
  and US-Saudi relations, 63, 69
Oklahoma City bombing, 80, 141–42
Olbermann, Keith, 168
Olympics (Munich 1972), 141
Omnibus Counterterrorism Act, 40, 80
Operation Ajax, 70
Operation Boulder, 141
Operation Restore Hope, 126
Organization of the Islamic Conference, 69
Orientalism, 25–40
  conflation of religion and politics, 85
  construction of Orient in, 28
  development by Napoleon, 19, 26–29
  as enabler of colonialism, 26–29
  influence on US Middle East policy,
    65, 66
  vs. modernization theory, 39
  and monolithic view of Islam, 42, 164
  myths about Islam and politics, 81–83,
    122
  and neoconservatives, 125
  revival of after 9/11, 124, 129–30
  and terrorism, 121
  in US press, 63
Oslo Accords, 118–19, 122
Osman, 18
Ottoman Empire
  advance into Europe, 23
  contradictory views of, 18–21
  decline of, 23–24, 25
  Mark Twain on, 34
  modernization in, 86–87
  role of religion in, 84

Pajamas Media, 167
Pakistan
  immigrants in US, 140
  middle class in, 103
  Muslim Brotherhood in, 69
  political Islam in, 71, 76, 89, 96, 134,
    161
  role in Afghanistan, 72–74, 77, 109
  secular nationalism in, 97–98
  Sunni Islam in, 43
  training camps in, 153
  US attacks on, 133, 163, 194
Pal, Amitabh, 53
Palestine
  colonization of, 26, 109
  drawing of borders, 26
  Hamas government of, 148
  leftist support for, 117
  Muslim anger about, 97
  Muslim Brotherhood in, 89, 94–95
  oppression of by Israel, 90, 194
  and Oslo Accords, 118–19
  political Islam in, 68, 76, 105, 107–8
  racism toward, 74–75, 182–83
  terrorism and, 49–50, 141
Palestine Liberation Organization (PLO),
  76, 99, 121, 141
Palin, Sarah, 167

Panetta, Leon, 132
Park51 community center, 52–53, 131,
    160, 165–68, 172, 175, 198
Pashtuns, 74, 108–9
Patai, Raphael, 33, 185
Patriot Act. *see* USA PATRIOT Act
Pearl Harbor, 113, 139, 167
Pelosi, Nancy, 168
Perle, Richard, 115, 118, 123, 176–77
Peter the Venerable, 13, 15
Petraeus, David, 130–31, 133
Phares, Walid, 184, 186
Pipes, Daniel, 78, 117, 122, 123, 167, 170,
    172, 176, 179–80, 184, 185–86, 189
Pipes, Richard, 79, 115, 117, 120
Podhoretz, Norman, 114, 115, 117, 118,
    120, 177, 189
Point Four Program, 65
Political Islam
    in Afghanistan, 71–74
    contradictions of, 104–6
    definition of, 94
    economic basis, 101–4
    history of, 93–109
    and Iranian revolution, 70–71
    opposition to secularism, 122
    in post-Cold War era, 76–80
    as threat to Israel, 74–76
    US relationship with during Cold War, 64
    US support for, 60, 70–74
    use of religion, 46
Political Research Associates, 184
Pope Benedict XVI, 48, 51–52
Pope Urban II, 14
Powell, Colin, 125
Preemptive war, 116, 128–31
    and preemptive prosecution, 147, 148–50
Price Waterhouse, 69
Project for the New American Century
    (PNAC), 113, 177
Propaganda
    of Catholic Church, 13, 23
    of Islamophobes, 170, 178–80, 185–86
    of US during Cold War, 66
Protestant-Catholic conflict, 19

Qajar dynasty, 86–87
Qassam, Izz ad-Din al-, 109
Qatar, 58

Qutb, Sayyid, 103

Rabin, Yitzhak, 121
Racial profiling, 141, 143–44, 198
Racism
    and Christian Right, 182–83
    cultural, 162–63
    and Enlightenment, 22
    of Islamophobes, 142, 176, 189–92
    and legal apparatus, 143–44
    and myth of Muslim irrationality, 50–52
    and Park51 controversy, 166–67
    scientific justifications for, 29–33
    of Truman administration, 65
    and Zionism, 74–75, 122
Radicalization theories, 144, 155–57, 181,
    196–97
Ramadan, Said, 66
Rambo III, 70
Rand Corporation, 141, 163
Ratner, Michael, 148
Ratzinger, Joseph. *see* Pope Benedict XVI
Rauf, Feisal Abdul, 131, 165–68
Reagan, Ronald
    and neoconservatives, 115
    neo-Reaganism, 127, 133
    policy toward Afghanistan, 70–74
    policy toward Iran, 70–71
    and terrorism, 141
Reconquista, 13–17, 23, 26
Reed, Ralph, 183
Refah, 77
Reformation, 19
Reid, Harry, 168
Renaissance, 19, 86, 132
Renan, Ernest, 35, 48
Republican Party, 124, 168, 182, 190
Rice, Condoleezza, 129
Richard the Lionheart, 54
Rida, Rashid, 88
Ridge, Tom, 181
Riverdale Jewish Center, 151
Riyadh bombing, 77
Rodinson, Maxime, 17, 19, 21, 22, 30, 31,
    47, 98–99
Rogers, Everett, 38
Roman Catholic Church, 14–18
    attempts to unite Europe, 23
    and Habsburg Empire, 19

history of persecuting scientists, 51–52
as political actor, 82
and reason, 48
Romanticism, 21–23, 24
Roosevelt, Franklin Delano, 63, 179
Roosevelt, Theodore, 56
Rosenwald Family Fund, 181
Rostow, Walt, 65
Rushie, Salman, 76
Russia, 25, 116, 128, 130. *see also* Soviet Union (USSR)
Rwanda, 126
Ryan, Maria, 123, 127

Sacy, Silvestre de, 29, 30
Sadat, Anwar, 68, 99
Sadr, Muqtada al-, 96, 108
Sadrism, 96, 103
Said, Edward, 27, 28–29, 43–44
Saladin, 17, 54
Salafism, 88, 155
Salisbury, Stephan, 139
Sandinistas, 71
Saracens, 11, 23
Sassanid dynasty, 11, 53
Satanic Verses, 76
Saud, King, 63, 65, 68–69
Saudi Arabia
    ancient, 10, 43, 47
    Christians in, 166
    effect on US oil supply, 66
    political Islam in, 96
    promotion of Islamism by, 68–69
    as regional strongman, 67
    repressive monarchy of, 57, 194
    response to Arab Spring, 58
    role in Afghanistan, 72–73
    secular nationalism in, 97
    special relationship with US, 63
Scaife Foundation, 181
Schlussel, Debbie, 180
School of Living Oriental Languages, 26
Schultz, Debbie Wasserman, 197
Science
    development in Muslim cultures, 50–51
    and modernization theory, 38
    and racism, 29–33
    stereotypes of Muslims and, 48–50
Scowcroft, Brent, 125

Secular nationalism
    Communist Parties and, 100–101
    dominance in postwar period, 90
    in Egypt, 89
    failure of, 96–100, 110–11
    in India, 89
    influence in Muslim-majority countries, 67, 86–88
    in Iran, 57
    US policy toward, 64, 65
Security Solutions International, 185
Sela, Avraham, 75
Seljuq Turks. *see* Turks
September 11, 2001 (9/11), 9, 81
    and attacks on US Muslims, 139–58
    Islamophobia since, 41
    and myth of violent Muslims, 52
    as turning point for US policy, 113, 128–31, 135–36, 160
    and War on Terror, 76, 163
Serbia, 127
Sex and the City 2, 25
Seymour, Richard, 117, 123, 189
Shah Reza Pahlavi, 60, 70–71, 94, 121
Sharia law, 84, 87, 89, 94, 96, 160, 167, 175, 179, 184
Shata, Reda, 197
Sheehi, Stephen, 129
Shi'a Islam, 42–43, 83, 94–96, 101, 122
Shoebat, Walid, 183–84, 185, 186
Shultz, George, 121
Six-Day War, 36–37, 67, 74, 98–99
Slavery, 29
Smith Act, 179
Sniegoski, Stephen, 120
Socialists. *see also* Arab socialism; Communists
    democratic socialists in US, 114
    fighting racism, 192
    and McCarthyism, 140
    role in Arab secular movements, 57, 97–98
socialism, 200
Society of Americans for National Existence, 179
Somali Americans, 160, 161, 178
Somalia, 187
    political Islam in, 96, 134, 160
    training camps in, 153
    US intervention in, 126, 133, 194
South Africa, 119, 166

Soviet Union (USSR). *see also* Russia
    Afghanistan war, 70–74
    collapse of, 76, 177
    and Iran, 121
    Islamist opposition to, 68
    neocons and, 115
    as pole of attraction, 65
    role in Six-Day War, 36–37
    support for Israel, 100
    support for Nasser, 98
    US policy toward, 64
Soyster, Edward, 190
Spain, 11, 12–13, 199
Special administrative measures (SAMs),
    149–50
Spencer, Robert, 175, 179, 181, 182, 184,
    185
Stahl, Lesley, 126
Stand Up Florida, 192
State capitalism, 98, 101–2
Stern, Jessica, 131
Stewart, Jon, 168
Stop Islamization of America (SIOA), 166,
    175, 179–80
Stop the Madrassa, 171–72
Students for a Democratic Society, 192
Students for Justice in Palestine, 192
Sudan, 25, 76, 78, 89
Suez Canal, 36–37, 97
Sufi Islam, 43
Sukarno, 98
Sultan, Wafa, 183–84
Sunni Islam, 42–43, 83, 94–96
Surveillance, 134, 144, 197
Syria
    Communist Party in, 100
    drawing of borders, 26
    national liberation movements in, 57
    relationship with Israel, 119
    US intervention in, 195
    US relations with, 129

Tajiks, 108
Talbott, Strobe, 125
Taliban, 46, 96, 161
    formation of, 73–74
    politics of, 108–9
    relations with Clinton administration, 77
    relations with G. W. Bush administration,

79
    and women, 45
Tanzania, 77–78
Tea Party, 167, 183
Terrorism
    as basis for foreign policy, 113, 116–17
    by Christians, 121, 141–42
    conferences on, 120–23
    identification with political Islam, 71
    by Jews, 121, 141
    as logical offshoot of Islam, 81
    media experts on, 185
    as new world threat, 75–76
    portrayal as irrational, 49–50
    as spectacle, 140, 152–55
    training camps, 153
    against US, 77–78, 163–64
    by white supremacists, 156
Textual analysis, 30–31, 85
Theoharis, Jeanne, 145, 149–50
Torture, 144–45
Transjordan, 26
Treverton, Gregory, 163
Triangle Center on Terrorism and
    Homeland Security, 153
Troutbeck, John, 46, 65
Truman, Harry, 65
Tunisia
    and Arab Spring, 58, 105, 199–200
    colonization by France, 25
    national liberation movements in, 57
Turabi, Hassan al-, 76
Turkey
    middle class in, 103
    modernization in, 87
    Muslim Brotherhood in, 69
    political Islam in, 104
    secular nationalism in, 97
    as tool of US, 67
    US relations with, 77
Turks, 14, 18–21, 43, 84
Twain, Mark, 34, 36
Twitter, 59

Ulama, 84–85, 86–87, 88, 95
Umayyad dynasty, 11, 50, 83–84
United National Antiwar Coalition, 198
United Nations, 116, 125, 126, 127
United States Institute of Peace, 170

Uris, Leon, 74
USA PATRIOT Act, 80, 142
USS Cole, 77
USS Quincy, 63
Uzbeks, 108

Valentino, Rudolph, 34
Varadarajan, Tunku, 162–63
Vatikiotis, Panyotidis, 121
Veil
    in Afghanistan, 72
    in Europe, 45, 160
    and Obama campaign, 194
Venerable Bede, 11
Venezuela, 130
Vietnam War, 39, 72, 114–15, 139
Violence
    association with Islam, 15, 52–55, 142,
        144, 162–64, 168
    of Christians, 121
    of Jews, 121, 141
    of white supremacists, 156
Voll, John, 90
Volney, Comte de, 27
Voltaire, 22, 188

Wahhabi Islam, 43, 68–69, 171, 181
Walt, Stephen, 124
War on Terror, 59, 64, 113, 114, 129, 146
    branding of, 170
    and legal apparatus, 140, 152–53
    parallels with anticommunism, 154,
        176, 189–93
    propaganda, 177
    use of name, 164–65
Warraq, Ibn, 183, 186
Washington Institute for Near East Policy
    (WINEP), 118, 123, 182
Wattenberg, Ben, 118, 120
Weber, Max, 38
Weiner, Anthony, 171
Weiner, Tim, 72
West, Allen, 186
Wilders, Geert, 166
Williams, David, 151–52
Williams, Mark, 167
Wilson, Woodrow, 32
Wolfowitz, Paul, 115, 116, 118, 123, 129,

    187
Women
    in Afghanistan, 45, 72, 74, 124, 168
    in Egypt, 99
    in Islam vs. Christianity, 16
    and the Koran, 31
    and myth of sexism in Islam, 44–48
    in Palestine, 107
    struggle for liberation, 48
Woodward, Bob, 130
Woolsey, James, 118, 123, 181, 190
World Bank, 106
World Muslim League, 69
World Trade Center, 1993 bombing of,
    77, 79, 142. see also September 11,
    2001 (9/11)
World Trade Organization (WTO), 106
World War I, 25, 139
World War II, 26, 35, 36, 123
Wurmser, Meyrav, 118

Yale University, 144
Yemen
    political Islam in, 134
    secular nationalism in, 97
    US intervention in, 133, 194
Yemeni Americans, 172
Yerushalmi, David, 175, 179–80, 186, 190

Zakaria, Fareed, 129, 170, 178
Zawahiri, Ayman al-, 73, 102
Zazi, Najibullah, 161–65
Zia ul-Haq, Mohammad, 71
Zinni, Anthony, 132
Zionism
    as anti-Muslim, 74–75, 141
    and Islamophobic network, 176–82
    justifications for, 55
    and neoconservatives, 117–23, 166–67
    opposition to, 94–95, 106–7
    US funding for, 181–82

About Haymarket Books

Haymarket Books is a nonprofit, progressive book distributor and publisher, a project of the Center for Economic Research and Social Change. We believe that activists need to take ideas, history, and politics into the many struggles for social justice today. Learning the lessons of past victories, as well as defeats, can arm a new generation of fighters for a better world. As Karl Marx said, "The philosophers have merely interpreted the world; the point, however, is to change it."

We take inspiration and courage from our namesakes, the Haymarket Martyrs, who gave their lives fighting for a better world. Their 1886 struggle for the eight-hour day reminds workers around the world that ordinary people can organize and struggle for their own liberation.

For more information and to shop our complete catalog of titles, visit us online at www.haymarketbooks.org.

Also from Haymarket Books

Civil Rights in Peril
The Targeting of Arabs and Muslims, Elaine C. Hagopian

American Insurgents
A Brief History of American Anti-Imperialism, Richard Seymour

Boycott, Divestment, Sanctions
The Global Struggle for Palestinian Rights, Omar Barghouti

The Democrats
A Critical History (updated edition), Lance Selfa

Field Notes on Democracy
Listening to Grasshoppers, Arundhati Roy

The Meek and the Militant
Religion and Power across the World, Paul N. Siegel

About the Author

Deepa Kumar is an associate professor of media studies and Middle East studies at Rutgers University. She is the author of *Outside the Box: Corporate Media, Globalization and the UPS Strike*. She has offered her analysis of Islamophobia to numerous outlets around the world including the BBC, *USA Today*, *Philadelphia Inquirer*, Mexico's *Proseco*, China International Radio, Gulf News from Dubai, and Al Arabiya.